WITHDRAWN

JIHĀD AND SHAHĀDAT

Struggle and Martyrdom in Islam

JIHĀD AND SHAHĀDAT
Struggle and Martyrdom in Islam

Ayatullāh Mahmūd Ṭaleqāni
Ayatullah Murtaḍa Muṭahhari
Dr. Ali Shari'ati

Edited by: Mehdi Abedi
Gary Legenhausen

The Institute for Research and Islamic Studies
(IRIS)

In Memoriam
Isma'il Rajā al-Farūqi (1920-1986)

For information contact: The Institute for Research and Islamic Studies
                        P.O. Box 35844   Houston, Texas 77235 U.S.A.
                        Tel: (713) 721-1980

First published 1986
Printed in the United States of America

Library of Congress Cataloging-in-Publication Data

Taliqani, Mahmud.
  Jihad and shahadat.

  Bibliography: p.
  Includes index.
    1. Jihad. 2. Martyrdom (Islam) 3. Shi'ah--Doctrines.
I. Mutahhari, Murtaza. II. Shari'ati, Ali. III. Abedi, Mehdi.
IV. Legenhausen, Gary. V. Title.
BP182.T33 1986   296'.72   86-82500
ISBN 0-932625-03-7
ISBN-0-932625-00-2 (pbk.)

Cover design by Husayn Ava

Contents

TRANSLITERATION

Letter	Transliteration
ء	'
ب ث ت	b
	t
	th
ج ح خ د	j
	ḥ
	kh
	d
	dh
ر ز س ش	r
	z
	s
	sh
ص ض ط ظ ع غ ف	ṣ
	ḍ
	ṭ
	ẓ
	'
	gh
	f
ق ك ل م ن ه و ى ة	q
	k
	l
	m
	n
	h
	w
	y-i
	t

Short Vowels

ــَ	a
ــُ	u
ــِ	i

Long Vowels

ـَا	ā
ـُو	ū
ـِي	ī

Dipthongs

ــَوْ	aw
ــَىْ	ay
ــِيّ	iyy
ــُوّ	uww

Persian Letters

پ	P
چ	ch
ژ	zh
گ	g
و	V

Persian Short Vowels

ــِ	e

Persian Diphthongs

ــَوْ	ow
ــَىْ	ey

A NOTE FROM THE INSTITUTE

Two years ago, in the midst of the events which have shaken the Middle East, including the Islamic revolution of Iran and the efforts for reform which have influenced the entire Muslim world, the idea of this volume was conceived. Our intention was threefold. First we wished to design a volume which would aid those who sought an understanding of the philosophy behind the sacrifices borne by the Muslims who have given up their lives for their ideals. Second, we wanted to answer some of the questions raised by those who attacked Islam as a religion of violence and irrationality. Those who have made such claims rarely have made even a cursory investigation of the roots of the problems existing in the Muslim world today, or to explore the reasons behind the actions of the Muslim martyrs. Instead, they have theorized that a central component of Islamic culture is the glorification of violence. Third, we wanted to examine the distinction made in Islamic doctrine between defensive and offensive war.

Although this book does not answer all the questions associated with the problems mentioned above, it may be considered as an attempt to delineate some of the main issues of the Islamic doctrine of *jihād* and *shahādat*.

The task of editing this volume was accepted by our colleagues Gary Legenhausen and Mehdi Abedi, to whom we hereby express our gratitude for their work of translating, editing, and extensively annotating the volume, and for their valuable introduction to the work. Without them the dream of compiling this volume would never have been realized. We are also grateful to the many others who have contributed to the completion of this volume: members of the IRIS editorial board, especially Majid Yazdi, who read the text, footnotes and introduction, and who offered valuable suggestions for their improvement. We especially thank Prof. Michael Fischer of Rice University, who read the introduction and offered his valuable criticism and suggestions. We would also like to express our appreciation to the president, Thomas Deveraux, and board of directors of FIL, Inc., the parent organization of IRIS, which provided us with financial support for the publication of this volume.

Finally, a few words should be mentioned about the contributions of the authors of this volume. Under no circumstances should discussions with a critical tone be considered as an insult to any faith, or to any sect of Islam. We are confident that none of the authors have had any intention to belittle any faith. Critical views expressed in this volume are included solely as aids to understanding. The members of IRIS believe that only by the free expression of various viewpoints can one hope to progress towards the truth.

May God accept our endeavors.

Mehdi Noorbakhsh
Director, IRIS
October 17, 1986

Foreword

Faith is essentially an active commitment to an ideal, to a socio-religious order, or to a person or group of people who embody this ideal. In this broad sense, faith differs from belief in that its ideal becomes an ultimate goal for its adherents everywhere. The realization of this goal in Islam means the radical transformation of human society under God, into a social order governed by God's law. This quest for the establishment of the 'kingdom of God' on earth, or the realization of the true *islām*, the submission of all the affairs of human life and society to God, demands willingness to struggle (to perform *jihād*) and to sacrifice everything, even life itself. This goal is at once ideal and practical, unattainable in this imperfect world, yet demanding to be fulfilled in the life of each individual and in every sphere of human society. In its ideal dimensions, this goal represents the primordial and eternal *islām* to God of all things. In is practical dimensions, it represents social justice and equality, freedom and fulfillment and true righteousness and obedience to the will of God.

It is this goal which has motivated Muslim society throughout its long history to struggle in the way of God for good against evil, for justice against oppression, and for the service of God alone and the rejection of all idols. This struggle, with all its human imperfections, its successes and failures, has characterized Islamic history from the time when the Prophet of Islam was commanded by God to leave the solitude of the cave of Ḥirā' and to proclaim God's will to humankind, to our own time when this struggle has caught the attention of the world. When the struggle in the way of God was turned into a struggle for power and wealth, pious men and women rose up to struggle and die for the original ideal and its message. It is only in the context of this struggle throughout Muslim history that any Islamic movement can be studied, assessed and judged.

Although the term revolution is a relatively new term in the social and intellectual history of Muslim society, revolutionary movements are as old as the Muslim *'ummah* itself. It was people like 'Alī and his close associates, men like Abū Dharr al-Ghifārī, 'Ammār ibn Yāsir, and others, who from the start raised the banner of opposition to the aristocracy of the Quraysh. 'Ali, in particular, and his martyred son, Ḥusayn, provided the model and motivation for this revolutionary Islam. Thus from the movements of the penitents (*al-tawwābūn*) to the Islamic revolution in Iran, the brief and tragic reign of 'Ali and his personal life-style provided the model of a just society and its hero. Above all, however, it was the battle-cry of Hysayn, the martyr of Karbalā' against the oppression of a corrupt rule that continues to resound in the world of Islam, providing both the ethos of revolution as well as its tenacious hope in the face of continued frustration and failure.

'Ali, the son-in-law and cousin fo the Prophet, was also the first Imam or the Shi'i community. He alone was regarded as the legitimate 'commander of the faithful' (*amīr al-mu'minīn*), but whose right was, according to the Shi'i community, usurped by others. This spiritual and temporal prerogative of the rightly guided Imam, moreover, was to continue in 'Ali's decadents, or more correctly expressed, in the descendants of the Prophet through 'Ali, until the end of time. But alas, Muslims proved themselves unworthy of this Divine gift of grace, the grace of *imāmah*, or Divinely guided leadership of the *ummah* of Islam. By thus rejecting the theocratic rule of the Imams, Muslims have, according to Shi'i belief, condemned themselves to perpetual division, injustice and error. This long history of imperfection and injustice will only be rectified at the end of time by the hidden Imam, the *mahdī*, the one whom God shall raise with the sword to vindicate his forbears, the Imams, and their followers, (Shi'ah), and establish God's rule on earth. It is, therefore, both the ethos of sorrow and suffering and the hope for a noble order (*dawlah karīmah*) which provide the foundation and background of Shi'i theology, piety and Weltanshauung. It is with this background in mind that the essays, or rather sermons, contained in this volume must be read.

The editors' introduction provides a useful guide to Islamic views of *jihād* and *shahādat* (struggle and martyrdom) and a good background to the Iranian Islamic revolution. This is important because the three authors presented in this volume represent three important types of people responsible for the ideology and leadership of the revolution. As the introduction provides an adequate biographical sketch of the authors, I need only emphasize briefly the role and ideological orientation of each author.

Ayatūllah Maḥmūd Ṭāleqanī was a noted Shi'i *mujtahid*. Perhaps because of his own social background, he championed the cause of the poor and oppressed. This brought him into contact with leftist elements of the Iranian intelligentsia with whom he shared the prison cells of the Shah's authorities. This experience left an indellible mark on his socio-religious thought, as will be seen by the short oration in this volume.

Ayatullāh Muṭahharī was more of a traditional *mujtahid* and scholar. His works in theology, philosophy and jurisprudence are traditional and scholastic. Nevertheless, his social concerns and the role he played in the leadership of the revolution brought him into prominence. Mutahhari, moreover, must be counted among the martyrs of the revolution.

While both Taleqani and Mutahhari were traditional mullas, different though they were in thought and intellectual orientation, 'Alī Sharī'atī was neither a mulla nor an official leftist leader. He was trained in the intellectual tradition of western Europe. He nonetheless grew up in the religious city of Mashhad, and in the family of a traditional mulla. Thus he combined traditional Shi'i piety and learning with the humanistic tradition of the West. While the mullas directed and lead the revolution, he presented the challenge of martyrdom in a way which fixed the imagination and enthusiasm of he young intellectuals of Iran, many of whom have remained loyal servants of the revolution. It may be said without exaggeration that Dr. 'Ali Shari'ati, in his lectures and debates, prepared the ground for the "tenth night of the (new) dawn" of the revolution.

It must be observed that while *jihād* is an obligation dictated by the need for defense of life, faith, land and personal property for Sunni jurists, it is one of the fundamental obligations (farā'iḍ) in the Shi'i legal school. It is with this important point in view that the present work should be read. The significance of this point will be amply demonstrated by the materials here presented. Hence, there is no need to dwell on it further in this discussion. It may, however, be useful before concluding these general remarks to discuss briefly some of the issues and problems which each of the three authors present.

It must be observed that the essays presented in this volume are transcriptions of recorded speeches or sermons which the authors delivered from the pulpit for special occasions, or to students of traditional religious schools. It must be further observed that both the pulpits and the traditional schools were important weapons against the regime of the Shah.

After presenting the traditional views of *jihād*, Talegani stresses the necessity of *jihād* against a tyrannical ruler. This is one of the distinctive points of the Shi'i understanding of this concept. For Taleqani, however, true *jihād* is the struggle in defense, and for the liberation of the masses. He argues further that in Islam, which here means Shi'i Islam, there is no government or ruler, since the Imam is absent. Rather the masses themselves, under the guidance of a *mujtahid*, must run their own affairs.

While Taleqani's sermon is a fiery oration aimed at creating a confrontation with government authorities, Mutahhari's lectures on *jihād* and *shahādat* are scholastic discursive talks delivered to students. Both authors argue that *jihād* must be waged essentially in self-defense, broadly understood. It is this law of *jihād* in defense of one's life, faith, property and the integrity of the Muslim'*ummah* which, according to both authors, makes Islam a religion meant for human society in contradistinction to some Christian sects which demand the total absence of violence under all circumstances. Mutahhari, moreover, interprets defense broadly to include resistance to oppression not only in one's society, but against oppression anywhere. Thus defense here means defense of humanity, defense of the oppressed (*mustaḍ'afīn*) of the earth.

Muttahhari argues, on the basis of the Qur'anic dictum: "There is no compulsion in religion," (2:256), that while wars aimed solely at the spread of Islam by force are not allowed, oppression must be resisted whether it is in a Muslim or non-Muslim society. To fight oppression in Muslim society is an obligation (*farīḍah*). In a non-Muslim society oppression must be fought in order to help the weak and to prepare the ground for the spread of Islam by peaceful means.

It must be clear from the discussion thus far that Mutahhari accepted a just war theory. The Qur'anic dictum, "There is no compulsion in religion," has created a legal problem for Muslim jurists of all schools. Thus, while Mutahhari insists on the strict application of this dictum, he limits religion to freedom of thought, or the freedom to choose between Islam and ones own faith, provided that this does not violate the principle of *tawḥīd*, or Divine Oneness. He argues, unconvincingly, in our view, that since belief in the One God (*tawḥīd*) is the 'straight path' of human progress, then it must be defended and propagated even by violent means if necessary.

Mutahhari's lecture on martyrdom is, in contrast with his other lectures, an emotional an poetic oration. Although he begins with the legal aspects of martyrdom, his main concern is the role of a *shahīd* in society. A *shahīd*, he argues, is one who, by his courage and death, infuses new blood into an otherwise anaemic society.

It has already been observed that 'Ali Shari'ati played a crucial role as a herald of the revolution. The first lecture of his included in this volume was delivered eight years before the revolution. The occasion was the death of ten people at the hands of the authorities, two of whom were Shari'ati's students. It is also significant that the lecture was delivered on the ninth day of Muharram, that is, during the annual commemoration of the martyrdom of Imam Ḥusayn.

Shari'ati combined the methodology of Western research and analysis with the rhetorical gift of an educated Iranian mulla. For him, the two highest principles of Islam are freedom and equality. In defense of these two principles, *jihād* stands below martyrdom. True martyrdom, however, is not to fight and die in battle, but to die knowing that the only choices one has are either death or surrender. He thus defines *shahādat* as follows: "*Shahādat*, in summary, in our culture, contrary to other schools where it is considered to be an accident, an involvement, a death imposed upon a hero, a tragedy, is a grade, a level, a rank. It is not a means but it is a goal itself. It is originality. It is a completion. It is a lift. It itself is mid-way to the highest peak of humanity, and it is a culture . . . *Shahādat* is an invitation to all generations in all ages, if you cannot kill your oppressor, then die." For Shari'ati, the problems of the Muslim community were not only corruption and the movement away from the piety of earlier generations, but an even greater danger was present when piety itself became devoid of political content. This danger was not only posed by corrupt rulers in their palaces, but also by recluses and ascetics in the corners of mosques and religious schools. The danger stemmed not only from the wealth of society and its carelessness, but also from its turning away from active Islam to the study of philosophy, jurisprudence and theosophy, and above all, defeatist sufism.

Shari'ati was an intellectual, free from the constraints of the traditional learning of the 'ulama. He could thus question the traditional views of *jihād* and martyrdom and insist that *shahādat* is a challenge to today's Muslim society. The challenge is this: the martyrs, Husayn and his friends and relatives are alive, but we are dead. Their message resounds in all the spheres of our social life, but we are deaf. When Husayn called for people to defend him and his family in the last moments of his life, he was calling not for mourners to weep for him after his death, but for followers who must in every age rise up and die with him. In this sense then, *shahādat* becomes the foundation and framework of revolution. Revolution, according to Shari'ati, has two faces, that of blood and that of a message. Likewise, Shari'ati distinguishes two kinds of death, black death which is the death of the cowards of history, and red death, the death of martyrs. The red face of revolution was shown by Husayn and his fellow martyrs. The message of this martyrdom was carried by his sister Zaynab into the courts and palaces of all oppressive rulers and their corrupt governors. Those who choose neither of the two faces of martyrdom and revolution are in every age followers of Yazīd, whether they fast and pray or not. Husayn went to his martyrdom, Shari'ati argues, with his pilgrimage rites half finished, in order to show that every pilgrimage without him in all subsequent ages is a circumambulation of the Ka'bah of the idols, the Ka'bah before Islam.

The present volume is intended for the interested intelligent reader. The material it presents, however, can help scholars, media specialists, and interested Muslim and non-Muslim readers to understand one of the most epoch-making phenomena in contemporary history, the Iranian Islamic revolution. The uniqueness of this phenomenon lies in the fact that it is the only revolution in modern times based not on Marxist or capitalist ideologies, but on a homegrown religious, and significantly Islamic, ideology. It is hoped that this volume will help Western, and more particularly, American readers, to understand the ideals, dreams and motivations of sincere

men and women in Iran, Lebanon and elsewhere who have chosen
the red face of revolution, not in order to die as heroes, but to defend
their lives and the lives of their children, to defend their faith and the
integrity of their history and culture.

Mahmoud Ayoub
September, 1986

*Mahmud Ayoub is professor of Islamic Studies and Comparative Religion in Center
for Religious Studies at University of Toronto. Among his Publications are: **The
Qur'an and its Interpreters** (SUNY Press), **Redemptive Suffering in Islam: Study of
the Devotional aspect of Ashura in Twelver Shi'ism** (Mouton Publisher). Some of his
translations are: **The Revealer, The Messenger and the Message, Muhammad the
Prophet and Fatima the Radiant, Beacons of Ligft** and also numbers of articles.*

1.

Introduction

The topics of *jihād* and *shahādat*, struggle and martyrdom in Islam, are widely misunderstood in the West, although, due to the prominence of the Islamic world in contemporary international politics, they have aroused considerable interest, and perhaps fear. G. H. Jansen, in his recent book, *Militant Islam*, writes that "the image of the Muslim armies converting as they advanced has sunk so deeply into the Western mind that no amount of repetition of the truth is likely to dislodge it."[1] Although there may be some reason to accept such a pessimistic appraisal regarding overall perceptions in the West, it is hoped that this volume will provide insight to those who are genuinely interested in an unbiased understanding of contemporary Islamic political though on the issues of jihad and shahadat. The living realities of international events are another matter. Scholarly treatises on the philosophy of martyrdom can never substitute for empathy. A Shi'ite religious leader from Lebanon has remarked, "If the Americans try to understand us, try to feel the tragedy, or understand the causes that created the tragedy, then they would understand martyrdom."[2]

Each of the authors whose thoughts are presented in this volume helped to set the stage for the Islamic revolution in Iran. They were popular lecturers who attracted especially large followings among the youth because they preached Islam as a vibrant ideology with obvious relevance for contemporary world and national political life. No topics are more important in the development of this contemporary Islamic ideology than those of jihad and shahadat. Thus, the writings translated here are essential for an understanding of contemporary Shi'ite political thought, and for an understanding of the ideological developments which made possible the Islamic revolution in Iran. But these works have a worth beyond what we may learn from them about Iran, or Shi'ism or Islam. The questions raised in this volume about martyrdom, about struggle against oppression and the role of religion in this struggle, are questions which must be raised by all people. Unless the writings in this volume are read as an attempt to answer the human questions of how one should live in an unjust world, and what is worth dying for, the development of Islamic ideology in Iran will also remain a mystery.

In order to understand the pieces in this book, some background discussion of the notion of jihad and shahadat will be helpful. It will also be useful to learn something of the lives of the three authors of this collection. These two tasks occupy the two sections which constitute the remainder of this introduction.

I

The subjects of the pieces assembled in this volume are jihad and shahadat. The Arabic word *jihād* means struggle, exertion, or expenditure of effort. Often it has military connotations, but it would be incorrect to translate it as *holy war* or *crusade*, since even as applied to fighting, the senses of these words do not coincide with that of *jihād*. The root letters of *jihād* are *J H D,* from which are formed a number of related words. The verb *jahada* means to struggle or strive. In the Qur'an, this verb, and the verbal noun, *jihād,* are frequently followed by the phrase, *fī sabīl Allāh* (in the path of God, or in the way of God). Believers are encouraged to strive with their possessions and their selves for God's cause. One who so strives is a *mujāhid.* An important related term which is not used in the Qur'an is *ijtihād* which refers to the struggle of a scholar to determine the correct ruling on a point of religious law, the shari'ah. One who has the ability to make independent assessments of points of law is called a *mujtahid.* Like the word *struggle, jihād* can be used with reference to fighting; however, not only do simple strivings to please God fall within the extension of *jihād,* but the Qur'an has a number of terms which are used specifically for military endeavors and for fighting.

Shahādat means martyrdom. Like *martyr,* the root of *shahādat* signifies witnessing,[3] and although this etymological point is hidden in English by the fact that *martyr* and *witness* do not share the same root, in Arabic the connection is obvious. The root letters of shahadat, *SH H D* are used to form the verb for witnessing or giving testimony, *shahida*. A Muslim affirms his or her acceptance of Islam by uttering the testimony of faith, the shahadat, that there is no god but God, and that Muhammad is God's messenger. One described as a *shahīd* (pl. shuhada) can be a witness or a martyr, depending on the context in which the term is used. In the Qur'an *shahida* and its cognates are never used for univocal reference to martyrdom. The sense of martyrdom is, however, clearly present in the following *ayah*:[4]

> If you have received a blow, the (disbelieving) people have received a blow the like thereof. These are (only) the vicissitudes which We cause to follow one another for mankind, to the end that God may know those who believe and may choose *shuhadā* from among you; and God does not love the unjust. (3:140).

We are also told that the shuhada are in the company of those upon whom God has bestowed his grace, and that they shall be rewarded.[5] The Qur'an also enjoins us: "And say not of those who are slain in the way of God: 'They are dead.' Nay they are living, though you perceive not."[6] Here martyrdom is discussed, though not by name, and the martyrs are promised a great reward.[7]

In order to gain a full understanding of jihad and shahadat we need to investigate these concepts not only as they occur in the Qur'an, but in pre-Islamic traditions as well. The Qur'an acknowledges that Islam is rooted in the Abrahamic tradition, and especially with respect to the code of war, the teachings of the Torah invite comparison with Muslim law. In chapter twenty of Deuteronomy some elements of a code of war are given:

> 10. When thou comest nigh unto a city to fight against it, then proclaim peace unto it. 11. And it shall be, if it shall be, that all the people that is found therein shall be tributaries unto thee, and they shall serve thee. 12. And if it will make no peace with thee, but will make war against thee, then thou shalt besiege it: 13. And when the Lord thy God hath delivered it unto thine hands, thou shalt

smite every male thereof with the edge of the sword: 14. But the women, and the little ones, and the cattle, and all that is in the city, even all the spoil thereof, shalt thou take unto thyself; and thou shalt eat the spoil of thine enemies, which the Lord thy God hath given thee. 15. Thus shalt thou do unto all the cities which are very far off from thee, which are not of the cities of these nations. 16. But of the cities of these people, which the Lord thy God doth give thee for an inheritance, thou shalt save alive nothing that breatheth: 17. But thou shalt utterly destroy them; namely, the Hittites, the Canaanites, and the Perizzites, the Hivites, and the Jebusites; as the Lord thy God hath commanded thee: 18. That they teach you not to do after all their abominations, which they have done unto their gods; so should ye sin against the Lord your God. 19. When thou shalt besiege a city a long time, in making war against it to take it, thou shalt not destroy the trees thereof by forcing the axe against them: for thou mayest eat of them, and thou shalt not cut down (for the tree of the field is man's life) to employ them in the siege: 20. Only the trees which thou knowest that they be not trees for meat, thou shalt destroy and cut them down; and thou shalt build bulwarks against the city that maketh war with thee, until it be subdued.

Here the first six verses (10-15) refer to the conduct of war outside the land of Isreal. Nations outside of Isreal may become tributaries of Isreal, or face military engagement. The nations within Isreal are to be destroyed in order to purify that land of defiling practices. These verses have been the subject of much debate among Jewish (and non-Jewish) commentators, but even without a full comparative study of Jewish *halakhah* and Islamic *fiqh*, there are important similarities between the law of the Torah as stated above, and the doctrine of jihad. Both require a call to arbitration before engaging in warfare. With the exception of certain enemies, (e.g. the Caananites in Jewish law and the polytheists in Islamic law) if the enemy is willing to submit, to become tributaries of the Jewish state, or to pay the poll tax to the Islamic state, no violence is to be done. If one does lay siege to a city, fruit trees are to be spared by both Jewish and Muslim warriors. Captured women, children and animals are not be slaughtered.[8]

This biblical code contains in an embroyonic form, the two essential elements of a just war doctrine. It places conditions on the initiation of combat (which medieval Christian scholars discussed under the rubric *'jus ad bellum'*, and conditions on the behavior of the combatants (*jus in bello*). Prior to the initiation of armed conflict, the call of peace must be given. The Jewish law as elaborated in the *Mishnah* requires that wars to enlarge the boundaries of the Holy Land can only be fought if permitted by the Sanhedrin, the assembly. In case of invasion, on the other hand, all are obligated to fight, 'even the bridegroom and the bride', and the declaration of war by the Sanhedrin is not necessary. As for the conduct of warfare, we have the restriction of the destruction of fruit trees upon which the society depended for its nourishment, and restrictions concerning violence to be done to women and children.

While the Mosaic code is not a source for Muslim law, the law revealed to Muhammad is described in the Qur'an in terms of the tradition of the law brought by Moses (and by Jesus). "It was We who revealed the Torah; therein was guidance and light." (5:47). ("And in their footsteps We sent Jesus the son of Mary, confirming the Torah." (5:49)).

There are two reasons for keeping the Jewish rules of war in mind when considering the doctrine of jihad. First, the Jewish and Muslim laws are in the same tradition. Second, the Jewish law provides a point of contact between Islamic and Western thinking about war. Through this point of contact we might come to appreciate the doctrine of jihad as a counterpart to the Western notion of just war theory.

As already remarked, the Mosaic law contains the ingredients of a just war theory: restrictions on the initiation of combat, and rules for the proper conduct of warfare. However, some recent writers have contrasted the idea of just war as this was developed in medieval Christendom with the idea of a holy war to be found in the Old Testament. The Christian concept of just war built upon the notions of war found in the Bible and on Roman law. Christian scripture, however, is sketchy at best on the topic of war, and so Christians who took up the topic of war were faced with the question, "When, if ever, is it justifiable for a Christian to engage in war?" R. H. Bainton describes three Christian responses to this question: pacifism, just war theory, and the crusade.

> The crusade differed from the just war primarily in its intensely religious quality. The just war, to be sure, was not devoid of religion, and to disregard its conditions would be to incur the displeasure of the gods, but it was fought for mundane objectives, albeit with a religious sanction, whereas the crusade was God's war. As such it could scarcely have originated in antiquity save among the Jews.[9]

Bainton's distinction between the just war and the crusade has been criticized by LeRoy Walters who has shown that the historic crusades were conceived by their participants as just wars, and defended with the same sorts of arguments.[10] In Bainton's work, as in much other writing on war in the West, there is an assumption that religious war is more prone to barbarity and excess than wars fought for non-religious purposes under secular authorities; in Bainton's words, "War is more humane when God is left out of it."[11] James Turner Johnson has shown how, in Western civilization, "the ideological value base for just war ideas had shifted from the religious— the church's notion of 'divine law'— to a secular concept of 'natural law.'"[12] The fact that a process of secularization accompanied the development of ideas concerning the restraint of war in the West does not justify the claim that crusades are unrestrained *because* they are religious!

If Bainton's distinction between crusade and just war is accepted we are sure to fail to understand jihad. For given this dichotomy, jihad will surely be considered a type of crusade, for several reasons. First, the crusading idea has its origins in the Old Testament, according to Bainton, and we have already pointed out similarities between the Torah and the Muslim law in this regard. Second, the jihad is fought for religious reasons, as is the crusade. Third, the jihad is initiated under religious authority, as is the crusade. Superficially then, it seems that the jihad is simply the Muslim version of the

Christian crusade. The historical fact that the wars fought in the Middle Ages were called *crusades* by Christians, and were considered to be instances of jihad by Muslims further bolsters this misconception.

In order to see that the identification of the crusade with the jihad is mistaken, it is necessary to briefly review the Christian origins of the just war idea in Augustine.[13] Augustine's preoccupation was with the question of whether it was ever just for a Christian to engage in war. So he was more concerned with the issues of *jus ad bellum* than in issues of *jus in bello*. In the Old Testament wars, Augustine saw that the question of whether the combat was justified was moot because God had ordained those wars. For justification of wars without express divine sanction, Augustine turned to Roman law, which he considered to express the divine will indirectly because it was based on reason. However, without the explicit command of God, doubts must always remain as to whether a war really is justified. In the presence of such doubts, caution must be taken in the conduct of war, and so issues of *jus in bello* are introduced. Holy wars are then seen as absolute wars, while wars justified by natural reason must be fought with restraint.

In the Muslim (and Jewish) view, the fact that certain wars are divinely sanctioned by no means implies that they are to be fought without restraint. Indeed, the fact that a war is fought for God is all the more reason to scrupulously obey all the rules regarding the proper conduct of war. Although the wars described in the Torah may appear relatively unrestrained when compared to the stylized forms of combat between Christians which took place in some instances in the middle ages, the appropriate contrast to the wars of the prophets is not medieval warfare, but the kind of war which was fought by non-Jews during the period of the Jewish prophets. It is only in this context that the significance of restraints on war in Mosaic law becomes clear.

Two more points of caution must be broached which indicate the difference between the jihad and the crusade; these concern religious purposes for war and religious authority for war. In the Christian tradition, to speak of a war fought for religious purposes is to speak of a war of conversion or a war against heresy. Johnson describes the great advance toward international law and against holy war made by Francisco de Vitoria who argued that difference in religion is not a cause of just war.[14] However, at least some Muslim scholars (like Mutahhari, in this volume) have cited the Qur'an and incidents in the life of Muhammad in order to argue that jihad is never to be fought merely because of religious difference. Unfortunately, Muslims have not always interpreted the law in this way. Most notably, Ibn Khaldun (1332-1406 C.E.) bluntly states that one of the purposes of jihad is conversion: "In the Muslim community, the holy war is a religious duty, because of the universalism of the Muslim mission and (the obligation to) convert everybody to Islam either by persuasion or by force."[15] Some medieval authors described the purpose of jihad as to "void the earth of unbelievers." Despite such lapses, which persist to this day, many Muslim authors, even in medieval times, viewed the purpose of jihad not as a fight for the sake of conversion, but, at its most aggressive, as a struggle to expand the territory governed by the shari'ah.[16] It is not mere difference in belief which underlies jihad, but the belief that the divine law is more just than any man made law.

The superiority of the shari'ah to human law was believed by Muslims to be universally evident. That the law of the Muslims is less oppressive than other law was confirmed in Muslim eyes by the fact that the Jews and Monophysite Christians of Syria preferred Muslim rule to that of the Byzantine Empire.[17] Reason and faith were not seen in opposition, as often happened in Christianity, and the dictates of religion were expected to be in harmony with (enlightened) self-interest. Like Francisco de Vitoria, the Muslims sought to justify their wars by appeal to universal standards. But unlike de Vitoria, they did not feel that this required a denial of the religious justification of jihad.

Several Muslim writers have seen in the doctrine of jihad a foreshadowing of modern international law. This view is rejected by Rudolf Peters, who argues that since the laws pertaining to jihad apply only to Muslims, such laws are not truly international in scope.[18] From the Muslim point of view however, it is an essential feature of the shari'ah that it does have universal scope. If the shari'ah is in accord with natural reason, it should be acceptable to all peoples. Furthermore, Muslim law makes provisions for the limited autonomy of at least some non-Muslim communities within the framework of a wider Islamic jurisdiction. Laws pertaining to jihad specify the rights and responsibilities of the *dhimmi* as well as those of the Muslim. Thus, contrary to Peters, the Muslim code of jihad applies not only to Muslims, but to all people, although in fact it may be that only *dhimmīs* and Muslims accept this code. The fact that Islamic law is not universally accepted does not detract from its international status any more than the fact that the codes established by the League of Nations were disregarded by Hitler undermines their international character.

The distinction between crusade and just war based on whether the war is fought for religious purposes or for just political purposes does not apply to jihad because in Islam religious and just political purposes are not distinguished. On this point Peters is clear:

> It may well be questioned whether the term 'Holy War' is an adequate translation of the concept jihad. By 'Holy War' is commonly understood a war which is conducted exclusively or almost exclusively for religious reasons. Islamic law, however, does not distinguish between state and religion.[19]

Like the conflation of religious aims and just political aims, the conflation of religion and state in Islam makes the distinction between crusade and just war inappropriate. The authority under which jihad is waged is at once both religious and political. Historically, the unification of religious and political authority has more often than not remained an unrealized ideal. Exactly when the ideal has been realized, and what to do when it is not, are two central points of controversy within the Islamic world. However, the ideal of a unified Islamic state in which religious and political authority are combined, has never been totally abandoned. All Muslim political theory must accomodate this ideal within the limitations of historical reality.[20]

In short, it is an error to classify the doctrine of jihad as a doctrine of crusade or holy war as opposed to just war. The diversity of Muslim views on issues of war and peace is no less extensive than those of Christians. There have been Muslim as well as Christians who have seen war as an instrument for the propagation of faith. On the other hand, like Origen, who considered the Old Testament an allegory of the New and that the Old Testament wars must be understood by Christians in a purely spiritual sense, so too, the Ikhwan al-Safa felt that the military exploits of the Prophet of Islam had an exclusively spiritual significance for their contemporary co-religionist.[21] The dichotomy between crusade and just wars does not aid an understanding of the diversity of Christian or Muslim views, not to mention that this division is inadequate even for an understanding of war as it is discussed in the Torah. Much of what has been argued above with respect to jihad could be defended in regard to the Mosaic code of war. This is not to say that just war theory is useless for an understanding of jihad. Many of the same moral consideratins which have gone into Christian just war thinking have been taken up by Muslim jurisprudents in their discussions of jihad. In what follows the key moral considerations of just war theory are used as a framework through which to view the doctrine of jihad. The interpretation of this doctrine is not something upon which all Muslims are in agreement, and as the discussion proceeds we will attempt to elucidate the main points of contention.

Jus ad Bellum

A. Just cause

We have already mentioned that there was some controversy among Muslims as to what constitutes a just cause for engaging in jihad. Defense of territory is generally considered to be sufficient cause for engaging in jihad. Traditionally, jihad was understood to be justified for three reasons: to repel invasion or its threat, to punish those who had violated treaties, and to guarantee freedom for the propagation of Islam. Fighting is also permitted against rebels, but there is some disagreement as to whether this sort of military action should be considered jihad.

The issue of whether jihad may be waged solely because of difference in religion has been mentioned above. Most scholars agree that difference in religion alone is never a sufficient justification of jihad. However, there are ambiguities here. One such ambiguity concerns the interpretation of the Qur'anic passages: "*Fitnah* is more heinous than slaying," (2:217); and "Fight them, till there is no *fitnah* and the religion is God's," (2:193; 8:39). There is some disagreement over the meaning of *fitnah*. From the root *FTN* come the verb, *fatana,* and the noun *fitnah*. *Fatana* is used in the Qur'an for tempting, trying, persecuting and afflicting. Accordingly, most Muslim scholars take *fitnah* to mean persecution, in the ayat cited, while according to *Lane's Lexicon* it means unbelief. The great commentators on the Qur'an, Mujahid ibn Jabr (d. 104/722) and al Tabari (d. 310/923) defined *fitnah* as disbelief. In the commentary of ibn Kathir (d. 774/1373) *fitnah* is interpreted as idolatry or polytheism.[22] Even the recent Shi'ite philosopher and commentator on the Qur'an, Allahmah Tabataba'i, defines *fitnah* as "ascribing a partner to Allah and worshipping idols."[23] Given such an interpretation of *fitnah* the passages from the Qur'an cited above seem to justify jihad on grounds of belief alone. There is, however, good reason to take issue with this conclusion. Ibn Rushd (Averoes) (1126-1198 C.E.) claims that although jurists agree that all polytheists should be fought in accordance with ayah (8:39), the Ethiopians and the Turks are to be left in peace, according to the great Sunni jurisprudent, Malik, on the strength of the reported saying of the Prophet, "Leave the Ethiopians in peace as long as they leave you in peace." This seems to indicate that it is not merely their disbelief, but the hostility of the unbelievers toward the Islamic state which justifies jihad. The Shi'ite jurisprudent Al-Muhaqqiq al-Hilli (d. 676/1278) also qualifies the command to fight the unbelievers with the condition that they be hostile.[24] Ibn Rushd testifies to the fact that the issue of whether it is their hostility or their disbelief which justifies the killing of an enemy was a controversial issue among jurisprudents even is his day.

> Basically, however, the source of their controversy is to be found in their divergent views concerning the motive why the enemy may be slain. Those who think that this is because they are unbelieving do not make exceptions for any polytheist. Others, who are of the opinion that this motive consists in their capacity for fighting, in view of the prohibition to slay female unbelievers, do make an exception for those who are unable to fight or who are not as a rule inclined to fight, such as peasants and serfs.[25]

Tabataba'i, immediately after explaining *fitnah* as polytheism, claims that because hostility should only be directed against the oppressors, those who cease in their disbelief should not be fought. These remarks are fairly typical. Disbelief is generally seen as coextensive with oppression. This is the reverse side of the Islamic vision of the inseparability of religion and politics. On the one hand just political aims and Islamic aims are identified, on the other hand, the political activity of the disbelievers is identified with injustice. While polytheism and oppression may have been coextensive in Arabia at the time of the Prophet, this does not seem to warrant the general identification of the two which seems to be taken for granted by many Muslim writers. However, the fact that the jurists and commentators on the Qur'an often fail to distinguish disbelief and political injustice does not mean that they sanction jihad merely on grounds of difference in belief. The very possibility of mere difference of belief is not recognized.

Many modern Muslim thinkers, on the other hand, do distinguish disbelief from persecution or injustice, and hold that disbelief alone is by no means a sufficient condition for waging war. The famous Egyptian jurist, Mahmud Shaltut (1893-1963), argues taht the Qur'anic verses which command fighting against the unbelievers do not say that the unbelievers should be fought because of their unbelief, but rather that reference to unbelievers is factually descriptive of those who had assailed the Muslim mission.[26] The piece by Mutahhari on jihad in this volume also distinguishes persecution from disbelief. Mutahhari considers oppression or persecution to be an additional requirement to disbelief for the justification of jihad. Nevertheless, he also claims that polytheism itself is a form of oppression. Thus, while Mutahhari goes to great length to argue that oppression is an additional requirement to disbelief for the justification of jihad, even if this requirement is not alway explicitly stated in the Qur'an, this requirement is not really additional if it is a logical consequence of disbelief.

Among other recent Muslim authors, opinions regarding the justification of jihad range from those of the Indian modernists, who argued that combat against British imperialism could not be considered a jihad, to the view of the contemporary Ayatullah Ahmad Jannati, who defends aggressive war against the unbelievers "so that they may abandon their false beliefs and incline towards Islam."[27]

Many modern Muslim authors have attempted to defend Islam against Western charges that Islam is a violent religion by claiming that jihad is only justified for purposes of defense. For example, the Pakistani thinker, Muhammad Asad, argues that jihad is purely defensive and that Islam forbids aggression.[28] Muhammad Shaltut has already been mentioned as holding this position. Likewise the Egyptian modernists Muhammad Abduh and Rashid Rida have interpreted those verses of the Qur'an which had been seen as unconditional commands to fight the unbelievers as conditional commands to fight those who had broken pledges, or had otherwise initiated aggression against the Muslim community.[29] The Indian modernists such as Ahmad Khan and Cheragh Ali are notorious in the Islamic world for their attempt to justify complacency under British rule by claiming that there could be no jihad against the British, since even defensive jihad is restricted to defense against those who would deny the Muslims freedom of worship. Although few would agree with the extreme view of the Indian modernists, the view that only defensive war is permitted in Islam remains a fairly common one among Muslim apologists. However, the notion that jihad is restricted to defensive warfare is by no means the invention of modernism. Majid Khadduri argues that beginning with Ibn Taymiyyah (d. 728/1328), an important line of Muslim thought interpreted jihad as exclusively defensive.[30]

Most Muslim authors of the colonial period took a more militant stance against European imperialism than did the Indians. Most notably, Jamal al-Din Asadabadi (al-Afghani) (1839-1897) and later the Muslim Brothers *(Ikhwān al-Muslimīn)* of Egypt called for jihad against British imperialism. Hasan Al-Banna claimed that since Muslim lands had been invaded, it was incumbent upon all able Muslims to repel the invader. Since the domination of Egypt had been accomplished already by the time of Hasan's writings, the situation was not exactly one of defense against an invasion. The invasion was over. So, Hasan appealed to reports of sayings of Muhammad *(ḥadīth)*, to the Qur'an, and to medieval legists, in order to defend the position that jihad is justified against all non-Muslims, Christians as well as pagans, whether they fight against the Muslims or not.[31] Sayyid Qutb, the chief spokesman of the Egyptian Muslim Brothers after 1954, explicitly attacks those Muslim thinkers who would limit jihad to defense. He enunciates the traditional position that jihad is not for the sake of conversion, but to make the shari'ah the law of the land, and thereby to abolish oppressive political systems.[32] While the position Sayyid Qutb defends is no different than that found in many medieval authors, the language he uses reflects an awareness of the appeal of struggles for national liberation. *Jihad* may be justified not only for defense of the Islamic state, but for attack against any oppressor.

The language of national liberation as used by Marxists is explicitly taken up by the influential founder of Pakistan's *Jama'at Islami*, Abul a'la Maududi. In an important address delivered in 1939, Maududi argues that the offensive-defensive distinction makes no sense as applied in thinking about jihad. The offensive-defensive distinction is primarily applicable to the actions of sovereign states with respect to one another. But for Maududi, jihad is primarily conceived of as revolution:

> Islam is a revolutionary ideology and programme which
> seeks to alter the social order of the whole world and
> rebuild it in conformity with its own tenets and ideals.
> 'Muslim' is the title of that International Revolutionary
> Party organized by Islam to carry into effect its revolu-
> tionary programme. And 'Jihad' refers to that revolu-
> tionary struggle and utmost exertion which the Islamic
> Party brings into play to achieve this objective.[33]

Among medieval thinkers we saw some disagreement as to whether jihad should be waged by the Muslim state against all unbelievers, or only against hostile unbelievers. We may expect that among twentieth century Muslims there will be disagreements over whether revolutionary activity should be taken up against all governments which are not instituted to uphold the shari'ah, or only against those governments which are oppressive. If conformity to the shari'ah is the sole criterion for determining whether the laws of a nation are just or not, no difference will be perceived between these alternatives. This is the position of Sayyid Qutb and of Maududi. Islam is hailed as the opponent of oppression, where oppression is seen as that which is not in conformity with Islam. Both Maududi and Sayyid Qutb explicity condemn forcible conversion, but they have no tolerance for any government which does not enforce the shari'ah.

What then, constitutes a just cause for the initiation of jihad? There is no one answer upon which all Muslims are in agreement. We may, however, list the most widely accepted answers to this question.

1. Defense
2. Revolution against tyranny
3. Establishment of the shari'ah.

The traditional justification of guaranteeing freedom of the propagation of Islam may be covered by (2) or (3) above. The punishment of treaty violators may be added as a fourth justification; however, this condition has been given hardly any attention in modern times.

The question of defense is enormously complicated. There is no agreement as to what constitutes defensive war. In the face of criticism from the West, many Muslim modernists claimed that defense was the only justification of jihad, and that all of the wars fought in the early days of Islam were defensive. These claims have come under attack both from Orientalists and Muslims. In response, the notion of 'defense' has been elaborated by some to include types of warfare which might not ordinarily be viewed as falling under this category. For example, Muhammad Hamidullah defines defensive war in such a way as to include the following:

(a) punitive war against the enemies of Islam
(b) sympathetic war in support of the struggle of oppressed Muslims in foreign lands
(c) punitive war against rebels within an Islamic state
(d) idealistic war fought in order to command the good and prevent the commission of evil.[34]

The problem here is that (d) could be interpreted in such a way as to include combat which could hardly be considered defensive as this is commonly understood.

While Shi'ite and Sunni authors are largely in agreement with respect to the issue of the conditions under which jihad is justified, there are some important differences. According to orthodox twelver Shi'ism, the twelfth Imam went into hiding over a thousand years ago; he is still living and one day will lead the true believers in the establishment of peace and justice on earth. Some Shi'ite scholars hold that only defensive war is permissible in the absence of the Imam, and that aggressive jihad will be waged upon his return. There are disagreements as to what constitutes defense. Many take a wide view of defense, not much different from Hamidullah's, cited above. However, there are difficulties with this. If defense is understood to encompass anything which would provide an ethical justification of war, it is a mistake to claim that the twelfth Imam will lead a non-defensive war, for this would mean that the Imam would lead an unjust war, which is unthinkable. If, on the other hand, defense is understood narrowly, to include only the defense of Muslim territories, it must be allowed that there are some wars which for moral reasons should be waged, but which are prohibited in the absence of the Imam (e.g. revolutionary struggle against a tyrant).

Many contemporary Shi'ite scholars avoid this difficulty by denying that there are types of jihad which may be led exclusively by an infallible Imam. In his speech included in this volume, Taleqani makes this point very clear. All the authors included in this volume agree that jihad is to be waged against injustice. Because of their historical circumstances, they are particularly concerned with injustice at the hands of a tyrant or colonial power. A fairly typical statement of this sort of view is voiced by Ibrahim Amini, a member of the Guardian Council of the Islamic Republic of Iran: "[T]he Quran has saddled Muslims with a heavy responsibility of fighting tyranny, corruption, exploitation, and colonialism, and defending the oppressed and the exploited."[35] For our authors, the issue of the limitation of warfare during the absence of the Imam is not considered to be very important; nevertheless, we shall have a closer look at this issue in the next section, when considering the nature of the right authority under which jihad may be waged.

B. Right authority

It is generally agreed that no jihad may be waged unless it is directed by the right authority. The question of what is the right authority has been one of the most divisive ones in Muslim history. The ideal has been for religious and political authority to be combined, as it was during the time of the Prophet of Islam. For

Sunnis, this political-religious authority was wielded by the first four caliphs after the Prophet, the *khulafā rāshidūn*, the rightly guided ones. For Shi'ites, this authority was intended for the Imams, but except for short periods during the lives of Ali and Hasan, political power was wrongly denied them.[36] Problems for both groups arose when political and religious authority were divided.

Among the Sunnis, during the Abbasid caliphate, although the caliph would exercise political power and would lead the jihad, the legitimacy of jihad and of all religious duties was to be determined by the ulama. According to the Maliki school, "The enemy may be combatted under any ruler, whether he is pious or immoral."[37] As the power of the caliphate declined, the ulama retained responsibility for issuing the legal decrees which would designate whether combat to be led by the head of state would be considered jihad.

Shi'ite attitudes toward authority after the occultation of the twelfth Imam in 260/874, is the subject of some dispute among scholars. Some have argued that since true authority must rest with the Imam, twelver Shi'ism makes the legitimacy of any other ruler precarious while enhancing the political power of the ulama.[38] However, during the reign of the Safavids (1502-1779), the shahs claimed to rule as representatives of the Hidden Imam, with the appelation "Shadow of God on Earth", and most of the ulama supported them in this claim. Furthermore, there have been strong elements within the ulama which insisted that neither the state nor the religious institution had any right to act on behalf of the Imam. The Akhbari school of Shi'ite jurisprudence, which was most influential in the seventeenth and early eighteenth centuries, is famous for this position.

On the other hand, the ulama did reserve for themselves the responsibility to act on behalf of the Imam in some regards, e.g., guardianship over orphans and admistration of mosques. Various ulama have taken different positions as to how far such authority should extend. Even at the height of Safavid power, the sanction of the ulama was sought for the waging of jihad against the Georgians by Shah Abbas (1587-1629). In times when state power was weaker, the claims of the ulama became more strident. During the Qajar period Shaykh Ja'far Kashif al-Ghita (d. 1127-28/1812-13) claimed that the duty to defend Islam through jihad falls upon the *mujtahids* during the occultation. The ruler retained political authority, but religious sanction was the prerogative of the ulama. It was held that the Imam had two kinds of authority, political and religious, symbolized by the sword and the pen. In the absense of the Imam, the ruler was entitled to act on behalf of the political authority of the Imam, while the ulama held the religious deputyship.

The ulama's claim to political authority reaches its culmination with the writings of Imam Khumayni and his supporters.[39] Among contemporary *mujtahids*, it is still a topic of some debate if there is any authority of the twelfth Imam which cannot be exercized in his absence. The most contentious aspect of this authority concerns jihad.

As mentioned above, there are a number of scholars who have held that in the absence of the Imam, only defensive jihad is permissible. Arjomand's discussion of the early development of this position is worth quoting at length:

> As for the jihad involving actual warfare, the obligation to undertake it became narrowly circumscribed in the time of the occultation. Al-Mufīd (d. 413/1022), following Kulayni, added the *dār al-īmān* (the realm of faith) to the traditional dichotomy of the *dar al Islam* (house/realm of Islam) and the *dār al-kufr* (realm of infidelity), and presented jihad as the (nonviolent) struggle to convert the realm of Islam to the realm of faith (i.e. Shi'ism), postponing the onslaught of the infidels. A generation later, al-Tusi (d. 460/1067) considered holy war in th absense of the Imam an error (*khaṭā*), and over two centuries later, the Muhaqqiq al-Hilli (d. 676/1277) similarly ruled that jihad was not obligatory unless the believer was summoned by the Imam. Except for a passage in which jihad was considered "commendable" (*mustaḥabb*) but not obligatory on the frontier in the absence of the Imam, the possibility of holy war during the occultation was not envisaged. Therefore, the Muhaqqiq in effect limited jihad to defensive war.[40]

Some Shi'ite writers even avoid using the term *jihād* for defensive war in the absence of the Imam and speak instead of "holy war of defense" (*harb difā'iyyah muqaddasah*). Such jurists restrict the term *jihād* to war initiated by the Muslims against unbelievers, the more precise technical term for which is "*jihād al-ibtidā-i*". More often, however, *jihād* is understood to include both offensive and defensive warfare. Sensitivity among the contemporary ulama on the issue of what constitutes jihad is reflected in the failure of leaders of the Islamic Republic to use the term *jihād* when reporting on the war with Iraq; instead they refer to "the Iraqi imposed war."[41]

An extreme example of what amounts to a provisional pacifism in the absence of the living Imam can be found in an introductory tract by the contemporary Shi'ite missionary Seyyid Saeed Akhtar Rizvi:

> [A]ccording to Ithna-'Ashari law, a war cannot be started unless specifically authorized by the Prophet or Imam himself, and that also to the limits prescribed by that Representative of Allah. After all, life is a creation of Allah and it should not be destroyed unless it has been authorized to do so by a Representative of Allah. Accordingly, the Holy-War is forbidden for the Shi'ah Ithna 'Ashari during the period when our Imam is hidden from us.[42]

Because the expectation of a Mahdi could take a quietistic form like that expressed by Rizvi, European colonialists in the Muslim world sometimes thought that Mahdism could be exploited as a force against jihad. In this they were sorely mistaken. Belief in the Mahdi can become activist in several ways. First, someone might appear who claims to be the Mahdi. Second, active struggle may be seen as required for the Mahdi's appearance. Ali Shari'ati has argued along these lines that the way must be prepared for the reappearance of the Imam. Third, and this is the dominent view among contemporary Shi'ite scholars, the responsibilities of the Imam may fall upon lesser souls during his absence.[43]

In reviewing the history of Shi'ite juridical opinion it is important to bear in mind that technically, legal precedent has no authority in religious law. Ayatullah Jannati points out: "A *mujtahid* of the days of Qajar rule may be expected to share few points of agreement with the faqih who has lived through the days of Islamic Revolution, about the issues of jihad. . ."[44] Indeed, Jannati argues that even in the absense of the Imam, Muslims have a natural right to "purify the earth of the pollution of polytheism" by means of aggressive jihad, although he also claims that this may be explained as being a part of defense![45]

In Ayatullah Khumayni's work on *Islamic Government* (from lectures delivered in 1970) the distinction between defensive and offensive jihad is not disclosed.[46] However, he does go to some length to argue that while the virtues of the Prophet and Imams are clearly superior to those of any *faqīh* (jurist), there is no function of government which is reserved for the living Imam.

> God has conferred upon government in the present age the same powers and authority that were held by the Most Noble Messenger and the Imams (peace be upon them) with respect to equipping and mobilizing armies. . .[47]
> . . . [By] means of jihad and enjoining the good and forbidding the evil, [the jurists] must expose and over-throw tyrannical rulers and rouse the people so that the universal movement of all alert Muslims can establish Islamic government in place of tyrannical regimes.[48]

In this volume, the piece by Taleqani seems to endorse a position similar to Khumayni's. Taleqani argues that previous jurists had restricted the authority for waging war to the infallible Imam, when what is really called for is simply the authority of a *just* ruler. The restrictions against congregational Friday prayer and jihad were intended to prevent the Shi'a from aiding and perpetuating unjust rule. Mutahhari does not take up the issue of authority, although he does claim that all legitimate forms of jihad may be considered defensive, in a broad sense which includes the "defense of humanity," in which case there is no restriction on the kind of jihad which may be waged in the absence of the hidden Imam, since even *jihād al-ibtida'ī* may be construed as fought in the defense of humanity.

Some of the more zealous supporters of Ayatullah Khumayni claim that he is actually in contact with the hidden Imam, and that the authority of his decisions derives from the fact that his orders are on behalf of the Imam. Ironically, this belief obviates the need for the point which Khumayni so carefully sought to support in his lectures on *Islamic Government*, namely, that the direct supervision of the Imam is not necessary for conducting the affairs of state.

The position of the contemporary ulama in Iran on this issue is outlined in a letter received from the *Islamic Propagation Organization* in Tehran:

There is no doubt that during the time of prophet Muhammad (S.A.W.) and the Immaculate Imam (A.S.) offensive Jihad existed already mentioned which led to the expansion of Islam. As for the period of the major occultation (absence) of Imam Mahdi (A.S.) the Twelfth Immaculate Imam, as the present time, if Muslims live in their own territory and infidels (kuffār) live in another territory, even if there is no attack and aggression upon Muslims by the Kuffār and even if there is no plunder, exploitation and colonialism, still the Muslims can invite the Kuffār - (the infidels) to accept Islam, and in case the infidels refuse to get converted to Islam, the Muslims can prepare themselves for war against the infidels.

According to our Fiqh, -(the Shi'a Fiqh), the above-mentioned case is considered to be valid during the presence of the Immaculate Imam-(Imam-e-Ma'soom) and the Islamic scholars (Fuqahā) consider offensive Jihad to be permissible during the presence of the Imma-culate Imam. yet, there are certain Islamic scholars-(certain Fuqahā) who hold that existence of a powerful Islamic government with sufficient force and power is enough for the Muslims to declare war on the defying infidels and if the Muslims are sure to win the war, then under such circumstances, too, offensive Jihad is per-missible.

According to the above view, any time such an ability exists for the Islamic government, offensive Jihad is per-missible, although the majority of the Fuqaha hold the former view.[49]

C. Right intention

As Ayatullah Taleqani points out, right intention (*niyyat*) is a fundamental condition for engaging in jihad. The importance of *niyyat*, in both Shi'a and Sunni schools, cannot be overemphasized. There are numerous *aḥādīth* to the effect that fighting for the sake of conquest, booty, or honor in the eyes of ones fellows will earn one no reward. If one is to engage in jihad one must have the intention of

doing so for the sole purpose of drawing nigh to God. In Shi'ite jurisprudence, this intention distinguishes acts of worship, *'ibādat*, from
other activities discussed in works on religious law.

The importance of having the correct intention during battle is
illustrated in a popular tale about Ali, which has been put into poetry
in Rumi's *Mathnavī.* During the battle of Khandaq (5/627), the
sixteen year old Ali engaged the leading Qurayshi warrior, Amr ibn
Abd Wudd. At one point during the conflict, Ali pinned his enemy to
the ground and was about to dispatch him when Amr spit in his face.
Ali then left Amr on the ground disabled. When he returned Amr
asked him why Ali had left. Ali replied that if he had killed Amr
immediately after being spat upon, the killing would have been to
appease his own anger, and so he had waited until he could kill Amr
for the cause of God. Ali then decapitated Amr, and brought the
head to the Prophet.[50]

D. Proportionality

In *jus ad bellum*, the condition of proportionality is the requirement that one should only engage in war provided that the good
obtained by means of war will outweigh the evil of warfare. Muslim
jurists agree that in itself, fighting is evil, *fasād*, which only becomes
legitimate and necessary by reason of the objective towards which it
is directed: to rid the world of a greater evil. This much is implied by
the Qur'anic dictum, *"fitnah* is worse than slaughter," (2:191; 2:217).
The use of the comparative implies that slaughter of itself is evil.
Unlike the conditions of just cause, right authority and right
intention, the condition of proportionality is not generally discussed
as such in works of Islamic jurisprudence. However, the issue of
proportionality is considered with respect to the conditions under
which peace treaties may be adopted. According to al-Muhaqqiq al-
Hilli, "If the general welfare requires it, it is permissible to make a
peace treaty."[51] Note, however, that according to al-Hilli, it is only
permissible, and not required that one act in accordance with the
general welfare, in this regard. Needless to say, according to al-Hilli,
only the Imam has the authority to conclude a peace treaty.

Traditional jurists also held that peace treaties were permissible in
case the Muslim forces were less than half those of their foes. It
became a matter of some controversy as to what kinds of conditions

could be accepted in such treaties. The early Hanafite theorist Shaybani (d. 189/804) held that the Muslims may even agree to pay tribute to their enemies if they judged that this would be better for them than continuing in a war in which they were afraid of destruction.[52]

E. Last resort

Jihād may only be initiated after the enemy has been offered the triple alternative: accept Islam, pay the poll tax, or fight. The second alternative was initially offered only to Jews and Christians, later Zoroastrians were also considered to be "people of the book." Jurists debated whether the invitation to Islam need be given to those who had previously been invited. Also the subject of some controversy was the question of whether groups other than those mentioned could be considered people of the book.

An interesting argument pertaining to the triple alternative is made by Hamidullah. He claims that in the Prophet's letter to Heraclius a fourth alternative was offered which required nothing more than that the Emporer allow his subjects freedom to accept Islam. Hamidullah further argues that since the *ḥadīth* to which traditional jurists appeal is one in which the Prophet tells the commander of a reconnaissance or punative mission to make the triple offer to any polytheists he encounters, the triple alternative was not intended as an imperative for opening new hostilities, but as a means by which peace was to be offered to those against whom the Muslim forces were already at war.[53]

F. Purpose to achieve peace

Even the most bellicose of Muslim theorists saw the aim of jihad as the establishment of peace. Fighting is never advocated for its own sake, but only an order to rid the world of *fitnah* by establishing a *pax Islamica* through the enforcement of the shari'ah.

Jus in Bello

A. Discrimination

In the earliest sources of jurisprudence, noncombatants are distinguished from warriors, and it is forbidden to harm them. In Maliki law, women and children are not to be killed, and the killing of monks and rabbis is to be avoided unless they have taken part in the fighting. Others are presumed to be combatants, with the exception of persons who have been given the promise of immunity, *amān*, which may be granted by any Muslim, male or female, of the age of reason. Hamidullah argues that noncombatants who assist an army, such as physicians, are also not to be killed.

The question is often raised in medieval texts as to what the Muslim forces are to do when the enemy shields itself behind Muslim children who have been taken captive. The jurists respond that it is permissible to shoot arrows at the enemy in such circumstances, but one should aim to avoid hitting the children. Also, although it is not permissible to kill noncombatants, if a Muslim soldier takes action necessary for the successful waging of jihad in which noncombatants are unintentionally killed, the soldier does not thereby do wrong; he is not required to pay blood money. In these two rulings a principle of double effect can be seen in operation.[54]

B. Proportionality

Proportionality in the *jus in bello* sense requires that the least amount of force be used which is necessary in order to obtain one's ends during combat. The opinion of al-Muhaqqiq al Hilli is fairly typical:

> It is permissible to fight the enemy by any means which will lead to victory, but it is reprehensible to cut down the trees, and throw fire, or cut off the water, unless it is necessary (for victory); and it is forbidden to throw poison. Some however say that this is only reprehensible.[55]

Muslim jurists generally agreed that war is to be waged in such a way as to utilize the least bloodshed and property damage as was necessary in order to achieve victory. This principle is explicitly emphasized by such modern writers as Hamidullah and Schleifer. Restrictions on mutilation of the victims of war provides another example of the prohibition against unnecessary violence in Islamic law. Mutahhari argues that if the destruction of property is the only means by which victory may be secured, it is permissible, but such activity may not be considered a proper part of the activity of jihad. Here again we find an implicit use of the principle of double effect.

From this brief survey of Muslim views on some issues concerning jihad, several points should be clear. There is no single doctrine of jihad which is universally accepted by Muslims. The Muslim understanding of what is required by the Qur'an and the practice of the Prophet regarding jihad has developed over time, and reflects the political and ideological environments in which Muslims have attempted to interpret shari'ah. On the other hand, this diversity of opinion does not imply that there is no content to Islamic law. There is no more (and no less) reason to accept relativism here, than with respect to moral law generally. The fact that there are Muslims who would sanction violent actions against civilians in the name of jihad by no means implies that such terror is condoned by Islam, anymore than the fact that some Christians give religious sanction to apartheid implies that apartheid accords with Christian principles. The laws of Islam pertaining to jihad form a doctrine of just war. The shari'ah restricts wars to combat against injustice (as judged by Islamic standards), and it requires that combat take as humane a form as is consistent with the achievement of its aims.

The writings in this volume pertaining to jihad are not records of jurisprudential decisions. Many of the topics mentioned above, such as the treatment of non-combatants and the treatment of prisoners, are not discussed by our authors. The primary issue with which Taleqani and Mutahhari are concerned is the just cause condition for jihad. Writing at a time when the issue of revolutionary struggle was prominent, these writers sought to explain how Islam does not neglect the right of a people to rebel against oppression. Underlying the discussion is an awareness of the leftist criticism that Islam is hidebound, and that only Marxism provides the ideological framework for struggles of national liberation. Our authors demonstrate the flexibility of Muslim thinking by invoking the doctrine of jihad in the face of the Pahlavi dictatorship.

The plasticity of Muslim thought is also evidenced in the elucidation of the concept of martyrdom by the authors included in this volume. The elevated status of the martyr is proclaimed in the Qur'an with the words: "Do not say of those who are slain in the way of God that they are dead; rather they are alive, but you do not perceive" (2:154). In Shi'ite belief, martyrdom takes on a special significance because of the magnificence of the martyrdom of the third Imam, a grandson of the Prophet, Husayn. A detailed accoaunt of the occasion of Husayn's martyrdom may be found in Shari'ati's *"Shahādat"*. This martyrdom has given rise to a voluminous tradition of elegies and poetry, read at mourning ceremonies whose origins can be traced to Zaynab, the sister of Husayn. With the gradual deterioration of Islamic institutions, the mourning cere- monies for Husayn lost much of their vitality, and by the modern era had become devoid of whatever political content they once had. Mourning for Husayn became an end in itself. Tears for Husayn would bring salvation; nothing else was sought. Over the course of the last fifty years, however, there has been a revitalization of the remembrance of the martyrdom of Husayn. This revival of the sharp sense of protest and agitation against injustice was initiated by the reflections of Sunni scholars on the martyrdom of Husayn. In 1936 the Egyptian Ibrahaim 'Abd al-Qādir Māzinī wrote that Husayn was an honest revolutionary, who recognized the odds against him, but was compelled by his sense of justice to fight against the Umayyad tyranny. Much the same sentiments are elaborated in Ali Shari'ati's *"Shahādat"*, delivered in 1972. During the thirty-six year period between the appearance of Mazini's work and the lecture of Dr. Shari'ati, numerous Sunni and Shi'ite scholars contributed to the reappraisal of the significance of the martyrdom of Husayn. By the time of the Islamic Revolution of Iran, the theme of Husayn's martyrdom had been developed in dramatic revolutionary propor- tions. No longer was Husayn merely to be cried over; he was to be emulated.[56]

As much as jihad may be viewed as a topic of *fiqh*, shahadat is not of much juridical interest. According to shari'ah, a shahid who is killed and dies on the battlefield is not to be washed and shrouded, as other corpses are; rather he is to be buried in his blood-stained clothes. The purity of death in the way of God as a shahid surpasses any which could be conferred by ritual purification. Even this bit of law points to the fact that shahadat is something which goes beyond the normal scope of the shari'ah. It is an issue for which under- standing can be gained only by looking into the most deeply spiritual and mythic dimensions of Islamic culture.

There are many fantastic reports concerning Muhammad's foreknowledge of Husayn's shahadat. Indeed, all of the prophets, according to some stories, were made aware of the fact that Husayn would become a shahid at Karbala. According to one such story, when Adam was looking for Eve he came upon the desert of Karbala, where he cut his foot on a rock. He asked God why he was made to suffer so. God replied that he wanted Adam's blood to flow on that land the way Husayn's blood would flow when he would be killed in his struggle against injustice and oppression. Adam then cursed Yazid, the murderer of Husayn.[57]

A grotesque report about the aftermath of Husayn's shahadat describes how the governor of Kufa had Husayn's head stuck on the end of a spear and sent to Yazid.

As the head was carried through the streets of Damascus it was heard to recite from the Qur'an: "Or do you think that the Companions of the Cave and the inscription were among Our wonderful signs." (18:9)[58] The reference to the companions of the cave pertains to the story of the seven sleepers of Ephesus. In the Qur'an it is related that these companions were persecuted Christians who put their faith in God, and were sheltered by him in a cave where they slept until Christians were no longer persecuted by the Roman state. Husayn's shahadat is an even greater example of courage in the face of persecution, and the words of his head draw attention to this.

In both of these stories it is emphasized not only that Husayn was killed, but that he was struggling against oppression. Without the deep reverence of such a struggle, the speech of Ayatullah Khumayni on the afternoon of Ashura, 1963, would be unthinkable. In that speech, Khumayni compares the children who died at Karbala with an eighteen year old theological student who had recently been killed by the Shah's troops. Husayn stands as a paradigm for dying in struggle against an oppressive regime. As such we find what appeared to be lacking in the jurisprudential discussions of jihad: explicit acknowledgement of the validity of revolutionary insurgency.

Hysayn was by no means the last of the shuhada. According to tradition, each of the twelve Shi'ite Imams (except for the twelfth) died the death of a shahid, usually by poisoning.

Another important shahid in Shi'ite history is Zayd ibn Ali ibn al-

Husayn. Zayd was the brother of Imam Muhammad al-Baqir (57/676-114/733). In 738 or 740, Zayd led an armed rebellion against the Umayyad caliph, al-Hisham (r. 724-743) to avenge the death of Husayn. He urged Imam Ja'far al-Sadiq (83/702-148/765) to take up the sword against the Umayyads, but Ja'far responded that the time was not ripe for such a move. Zayd insisted, and Ja'far is said to have told him that if he could not live well, he should die well. Zayd was killed during his revolt. The Umayyads displayed his crucified body for four years. Many of Zayd's supporters claimed that he was an Imam, and rejected the Imamate of Muhammad al-Baqir and of Ja'far, which led to the development of the Zaydi branch of Shi'ism, according to which the status of Imam can only be held by one who takes up the sword against unjust rulership. Despite the fact that his action led to sectarian difference, the twelver Shi'ites respecfully refer to him as "al-Zayd *al-Shahīd*".

Among the many other martyrs whose virtues are extolled in the Shi'ite tradition are Hujr ibn Adi (d. 50/670), the supporter of Ali who was executed for leading a rebellion against Mu'awiya in Kufa; Sa'id ibn Jubayr (d. 713 C.E.), an early exegete of the Qur'an; Shahid al-Awwal (d. 786/1384), a celebrated Imami scholar; and Shahid al-Thani (d. 966/1559), who wrote a commentary on the work of Shahid al-Awwal. It is told that on his deathbed, Muawiya was tormented by the image of Hujr, and likewise, Al-Hajjaj ibn Yusuf, the lieutenant of the Umayyad Caliph Abd al-Malik, who executed Ibn Jubayr, was also plagued by the image of the martyr in his dying moments.

With the exception of those who died fighting alongside the Prophet, the most famous of the martyrs of Islam were killed by other Muslims. Shi'i scholars were killed when their beliefs became known to certain Sunni jurists or to the caliph. The mystic tradition in Islam also has its share of shuhada, the most notable of whom are al-Halaj and Suhrawardi.

Mansūr al-Ḥallāj (858-922 C.E.) was charged with blasphemy and with claiming to have the authority to free the pious from the requirements of Islamic law. Al-Ḥallāj responded to the charge of blasphemy with the explanation that when he uttered the words, *"Ana al-Ḥaqq"* (*"I am the Truth"*), he had achieved a state of mystic union with God, and was speaking not for himself, but as the instrument of God. He was whipped, mutilated, crucified, decapitated, cremated, and his remains were scattered. It has been suggested that despite the official charges, his Isma'ili Shi'ite sympathies played the decisive role leading to his torture and execution.[59] Mansur had been imprisoned for nine years as a Qarmatian (Isma'ili) agent.

Yahya al-Shurawardi, the author of *Ḥikmat al-Ishrāq* (*The Wisdom of Illumination*) was killed in 1191 C.E. at the age of thirty-six or thirty-eight on suspicion of being in league with Isma'ilis to overthrow the Sunni government at Aleppo. He has been nicknamed *al-Maqtūl* (the murdered), and *al-shahīd*. His "Illuminationist" philosophy had a profound influence on subsequent Islamic philosophy, particularly as this was developed during the Safavid period in Iran. Like Ḥallāj, Suhrawardi provoked a violent reaction from those in power, not merely because of the unorthodoxy of his mysticism, but because of his Shi'ite (albeit Isma'ili) political sympathies.

The importance of the shuhada for Shi'ites has led to the development of a genre of literature called *Maqtal* (place of martyr-dom), in which the lives of the martyrs are related. In his *Husayn The Savior of Islam* (Baldwin: Tarikhe Tarsile Quran, 1981?), S.V. Amir Ahmed Ali has provided a typical book of Maqtal in the English language. A recent scholarly account of the lives of the martyrs is *Shuhāda al-Faḍīlah* (the Martyrs of Virtue) by Abd al-Husayn Amini. (Some of the important literature on martyrdom, with parti-cular emphasis on Karbala, is reviewed in the last pages of Hamid Enayat's *Modern Islamic Political Thought*. An important collection of addresses and essays in English on the martyrdom of Imam Husayn is provided in *Al-Serat* Vol. XII.)

The high regard in which the martyrs are held, and the pervasive consciousness of the phenomenon of shahadat in Shi'ite society cannot be sufficiently emphasized. The shuhada are heroes. Prior to the Islamic Revolution, any Iranian who was killed for his faith, even for faith in communism, was referred to by his sympathizers as a shahid. One of the most telling stories of the preoccupation with martyrdom since the Iraqi invasion of Iran is that of a woman of Tehran who sat in front of her house weeping. When asked why she was crying, she responded that all the other families on the block had sons who had become shuhada, but in her family, there was no shahid. The Muslim's longing for shahadat is too often portrayed in the West as a crazed desire for a shortcut to paradise. More important than this is the perceived need to emulate those who, in the struggle against injustice and persecution, have given their lives with courage and dignity.

The essays of this volume were written by three important ideologues of contemporary Shi'ite thought. Their work in providing the intellectual groundwork for the revolutionary activity which led to the formation of the Islamic Republic of Iran has been widely recognized.[60] Indeed, the writings collected here can only be fully appreciated in the light of some knowledge of the lives of our authors and of the pre-revolutionary Iranian situation.

Ayatullah Mahmud Taleqani was born in 1911 in the village of Gelird, northwest of Tehran.[61] His father was a religious scholar who provided for his own livelihood as a watchmaker. The elder Taleqani was also active in political and religious circles which were opposed to the Pahlavi dictatorship. He met regularly with other scholars and concerned Muslims in the house of the father of Mehdi Bazargan, and as a result came into frequent difficulties with governmental authorities. After the death of his father, Taleqani studied theology at Qum. He received certificates of *ijtihād* from several teachers and in 1938 moved to Tehran, where he taught at a seminary. He was arrested the following year for his opposition to the shah's religious policies. Taleqani blamed many of the problems faced by Iran on neglect of the Qur'an. The government found such teachings threatening, and so imprisoned Taleqani for six months, after which he was exiled from Tehran. This was the first of many imprisonments which kept him behind bars for a total of roughly fifteen years.

Just prior to the deposition of Reza Shah in 1941, Taleqani was able to begin teaching at the Hidayat Mosque in central Tehran, which became a center for Muslim opponents of the regime. Taleqani supported the government of Dr. Muhammad Musaddiq, and the movement to nationalize the oil industry. After the coup in 1953, which with CIA backing installed Muhammad Reza Pahlavi as shah, Taleqani was promptly arrested and sent to Zanjan, where he taught at a religious center. In 1955 he edited and commented on a political treatise of 1909 by Ayatullah Na'ini in which dictatorship is condemned. In it Taleqani argued that like the Constitutional Revolution, other democratic and socialist measures might be needed as steps against the idolatry of autocracy. Later, perhaps as late as the early sixties, he wrote *Islām va Malikiyat* (Islam and Ownership), [62] in which he criticizes both Marxism and capitalism, while affirming Islam's opposition to class exploitation. According to Islamic law, Taleqani argues, uncultivated lands should be relinquished by the landowners to peasants intending to reclaim them. In this way Taleqani saw that the implementation of Islamic law could be instrumental in a redistribution of wealth.

In 1956 the regime arrested Taleqani along with other leaders of the National Resistance Movement which numbered among its founding members the father of Ali Shari'ati, Muhammad Taqi Shari'ati, Mehdi Bazargan and Yadullah Sahabi. Taleqani was imprisoned for one year, after which he returned to the Hedayat Mosque where he taught the Qur'an and rallied anti-government sentiment. Internal divisiveness and police repression led to the demise of the National Resistance Movement. In 1961 Ayatullah Taleqani and his cohorts founded the Liberation Movement of Iran (*Nehzate Azādi-e-Iran*). This organization sought to promote Islamic *ideology* and to win support among students, intellectuals, and the ulama.

In January of 1963, Ayatullah Taleqani was arrested along with other members of the Liberation Movement. He was imprisoned for five months. On his release, he returned once again to Hedayat Mosque, and there, shortly before the June uprising of 1963, he delivered the speech translated below as *"Jihād"* and *"Shahādat."* On June 5, 1963, the 15th of Khordad, mass demonstrations were held in response to Ayatullah Khumayni's call for opposition to the regime. Thousands of demonstrators were massacred by the shah's troops. Taleqani issued a communique titled *"The Dictator Sheds Blood."* He was again arrested and publicly tried. During the trial he announced that the court did not have the competence to try him. He was sentenced to ten years in prison. Although he was released in 1965 due to public pressure and international outcry, he was in and out of prison until the victory of the Islamic Revolution. During his internments he was forced to witness the torture of the young foes of the shah whom he had inspired, and was himself brutally tortured.

Despite his frequent internment, Taleqani played a prominent role in the revolution. He was remarkable in his ability to forge a working unity among quite disparate groups. After the victory which came in February 1979, Ayatulla Taleqani was elected to the Assembly of Experts, which was responsible for framing the constitution of the Islamic Republic. He received more than two million votes in this election, almost one hundred percent of the Tehran electorate and more votes than were cast for any other candidate. The inclusion of a bill of rights in the constitution was won largely at the insistence of Ayatullah Taleqani.

On April 13, 1979 Taleqani's two sons and a daughter-in-law were arrested. On April 17 Taleqani announced from his village that he was retiring from politics, and warned against the prospects of dictatorship in the name of religion. There were large demonstrations both in favor of and against Taleqani. Finally, Taleqani met with Ayatullah Khumayni and announced his unwavering support for him and for the Islamic Republic. After Ayatullah Mutahhari's assassination, Khumayni appointed Taleqani as head of the Islamic Revolutionary Council, and in July he was appointed as Friday prayer leader for Tehran. On the Friday before he died, at Behest-e Zahra cemetery, Taleqani delivered his last sermon. He reminded the worshipers that the cause of God is the cause of the people, and he argued that the democratic principle of consultation, *shura*, is not a matter to be negotiated in the parliament, but is a requirement of Islam. He warned his countrymen to beware of despotism in religious garb. On September 10 he died of a heart attack. In his message of condolence to the people of Iran, Ayatullah Khumayni praised Ayatulla Taleqani as a Muslim of the status of Abu Dhar.[63]

Ali Shari'ati was born on November 23, 1933, probably in Mashhad. [64] His forefathers were important local religious scholars in Sabzavar.[65] His father, Muhammad Taqi Shari'ati, still living, is a well known religious scholar of national fame and an expert in Qur'anic exegesis.[66] Muhammad Taqi broke two family traditions: he permanently moved to the city of Mashhad at the age of twenty, and he did not wear the traditional garb of the ulama. Ali attended religious as well as political discussion groups organized by his father. Muhammad Taqi founded the Center for the Propagation of Islamic Truths around 1950. Ali and his father joined the Movement of God-Worshiping Socialists in the mid 1940's.

Ali graduated from the Teachers' Training College in Mashhad in 1953 and worked for four years in elementary schools in northern Khurasan. During this period he occupied himself with translation from Arabic into Persian of works with religious and political significance. He translated a long letter by Allamah Muhammad Husayn Kashif al-Ghita (d. 1954) addressed to Gerald Ivans Hopkins, then the vice-president of American Friends of the Middle East, in which Kashif al-Ghita had expressed the grievances of the Muslim world against the West.[67] In the mid-fifties Ali also produced a liberal translation of the Egyptian radical, Abdul Hamid Jawdat al-Sahhar's biography of Abu Dhar. In this book, Jawdat al-Sahhar had protrayed this companion of the Prophet of Islam as a Muslim socialist. Shari'ati subtitled this translation *The God-Worshipping Socialist*, an obvious reference to the underground organization of which he and his father were both members. This translation enjoyed great popularity and was reprinted several times.

During this stage of his career, Shari'ati also engaged in writing creative religious literature. Inspired by one of the most metaphoric ayah of the Qur'an (23:35)[68] and under the influence of Musaddiq's doctine of "Negative Equilibrium", he put forward his *The Median School of Thought*, according to which:

> [B]etween materialism and idealism, Islam has a method particular to itself which can be called 'realism'. The social and economic regime of Islam is practical socialism based on worship of God; it is the midpoint between the corrupt regime of capitalism and that of communism which is absolute common ownership. The political orientation of Islam is in the international arena - between the two antagonistic blocs of the East (under the leadership of the Soviet Union) and the West (under the leadership of America), is a mid-bloc unrelated to either side. it is a pure tree which is neither Eastern nor Western.[69]

In 1957 Ali, along with his father and other God-worshipping socialists, was arrested and subsequently imprisoned for eight months. After his release, he married the sister of a university student who had been recently slain by the police.[70] By this time Shari'ati had entered Mashhad University to study for a master's degree in foreign languages, specializing in Arabic and French. Upon the completion of his degree he won a state scholarship to study for a doctorate in Paris. The details of his studies in Paris are not very well known. He claims to have studied under the sociologist George Gurvitch for five years[71] and to have had the close companionship of the Orientalist Louis Massignon. He wrote his doctoral dissertation in Persian philology under the directorship of G. Lazard.[72]

While in Paris, Shari'ati became heavily involved in student politics, both Iranian and international. He edited *Irān-e Azād,* the organ of the Iranian Student Confederation. He also helped to establish a chapter of the Iranian Liberation Movement in Paris. He wrote as a critic of Iranian politics and supported armed struggle against the shah. He also supported the Algerian Revolution and served a short term in jail for his support of Patrice Lumumba. During this period he translated some works of Franz Fannon and Che Guevara's *Guerilla Warfare.*[73]

With his wife and two children he returned to Iran in 1964, whereupon he was arrested and imprisoned for six months on political charges. After his release, he began teaching as a high school instructor in a suburb of Mashhad. Meanwhile he sought a publisher for his translation of Massignon's *Salman Pak et Les Premices Spirituelle de l'Islam Iranien,*[74] and looked for a position at Tehran University. Both plans failed and he returned to Mashhad where between 1966 and 1970 he taught at Ferdowsi University. He became a popular lecturer at universities, mosques, and at the Husayniyah Irshad in Tehran.

A *ḥusayniyah* is a place where the martyrdom of Husayan is mourned. But the Husayniyah Irshad, founded by philanthropist Muhammad Humayun, was intended to be a modern institution of learning, somewhat of the style of a free university. The lectures Shari'ati gave there explored various facets of Islamic ideology and became extremely popular, although the view of Islam presented was not without its detractors among both the traditionalists who called him a heretic, and the Marxists who felt he was unscientific. The religiously conservative accused him of borrowing from Western schools of thought, particularly from existentialism and Marxism. This attitude is reflected by various commentators who describe Shari'ati's thoughts as Marxism dressed in Islamic terminology.[75]

Since Shari'ati advocated a radical ideology, he also had problems with the government. In 1973 the authorities closed the Husayniyah Irshad and Shari'ati went into hiding. After his aged father was arrested, Shari'ati gave himself up for the release of his father. Eighteen months later he was released and exiled to the village of Mazinan, where he continued to write and participate in semi-public gatherings. Finally, under the pressure of surveillance of the secret police, Shari'ati left Iran. Shari'ati was found dead in his London apartment on June 9, 1977. The British coroner ruled that he had died of a massive heart attack. Many of his followers believe that he was killed by SAVAK agents.

Ayatullah Murtada Mutahhari was born on February 2, 1920 in Fariman, a small town in the province of Khurasan. His father was a local *'ālim*. At the age of thirteen he went to Mashhad to begin his training in Arabic as a preliminary to the study of Islamic jurisprudence, *fiqh*. From the age of eighteen until he was thirty-three, Mutahhari was a resident of the Madrasah-e-Fayziyah in Qum, which later became famous as a center for revolutionary students of theology. Graduates or teachers at the Madrasah-e-Fayziyah include Ayatullah Muntazeri, Ayatullah Beheshti, Hojjat-al-Islam Rafsanjani, Hojjat-al-Islam Khamenehi, and others who have played a prominent role in the Islamic Revolution. Mutahhari studied *fiqh* under Grand Ayatullah Burūjirdī and from Ayatullah Khumayni, from whom he received the degree of *ijtihād*.

Mutahhari's interest in philosophy was kindled in the earliest years of his study. In an autobiographical sketch[76] he writes that from the age of thirteen he became preoccupied with philosophical questions about God. He viewed his study of Arabic, *fiqh*, and logic as a preparation for philosophical inquiry. Later when he went to Qum, he was impressed by Ayatullah Khumayni's knowledge of philosophy. Since he was too young to attend the advanced lectures of Islamic philosophy, Mutahhari went to Khumayni's sessions on ethics. Khumayni taught a blend of ethics and gnosticism which found an enthusiastic audience in the young Mutahhari, who became his devoted student for the next twelve years.

At the age of twenty-three Mutahhari began his formal instruction in philosophy, and at twenty-five he became acquainted with communist literature. He read everything he could find by Dr. Taqi Arani, an Iranian communist and spiritual forerunner to the Tudeh Party. Arani's exposition of Marxist theory, and that of George Politzer were formative in the development of Mutahhari's understanding of materialism and Marxist thought. At twenty-nine, he began to study Ibn Sina (Avicenna) with Allamah Muhammad Husayn Tabataba'i.[77] Mutahhari also regularly participated in private discussions with Tabataba'i, during which an Islamic rejoinder to Marxism was elaborated. Allamah Tabataba'i recalled his tutelage of Mutahhari in the following words:

> To be brief, thirty-two years ago I immigrated from Tabriz (because of its unfavorable conditions) to Qum, and started teaching philosophy. Besides me, Ayatullah Khumayni taught philosophy; particularly the *Asfār* of Mulla Sadra. Mr. Mutahhari was attending Ayatullah Khumayni's session. After a while he joined my classes and continued attending them for several years. His intelligence was extraordinary and no word of mine was wasted on him. He absorbed everything I taught him. He also possessed a high degree of piety, humanity and morality. I truly don't know how to put it; his presence in my sessions would overwhelm me to such an extent that I wanted to dance for joy. Some years later he got married and settled here (in Tehran). We started our discussions of *The Principles of Philosophy and the Method of Realism.* He was the only one I could trust with the task of completing this job in all respects. He wrote the footnotes on volumes one, two, three and five. Volume four has not yet been done.

Mutahhari was thirty-three when he married the daughter of a Khurasani *alim,* and three years later he began a tenure at the

University of Tehran's Faculty of Theology and Islamic Sciences which would last for twenty-two years. This period was one filled by political as well as philosophical activity. He was a frequent speaker at the Islamic Association of Doctors, where he encouraged links between the universities and the seminaries. He also organized the "Talk of the Month" lecture series in which Taleqani, Bazargan and others discussed the role of Islam in the contemporary world. Mutahhari, Beheshti, Taleqani, and Bazargan contributed papers to a discussion organized after the death of Ayatullah Burūjirdī in 1961 on the role of the *marja'taqlīd*.[78] and of the religious establishment generally.

The night following the uprising of the fifteenth of Khordad, in 1963, Ayatullah Mutahhari was arrested and imprisoned for forty-three days. In 1964 he began to serve as Ayatullah Khumayni's representative in the Society of Combatent Ulama. Mutahhari also served as Khomayni's agent in a variety of matters during the latter's exile.

In 1965 Mutahhari set up the managing board of the Husayniyah Irshad. He was joined on the board by Seyyed Hossein Nasr and Ali Shari'ati, among others. By the time the regime closed the institution in 1973, only Shari'ati remained of the original group on the governing board. Nasr left under the impression that the initial objectives were overstepped, and later Mutahhari complained that "Shari'ati brought pressure to bear on the political aspect. . ." of the Husayniyyah's activities.[79] Nasr and Mutahhari then accepted appointments to the board of the Imperial Academy of Philosophy.

Although Mutahhari and other ulama who were critical of the regime, such as Ayatullah Behesti and Hojjat-al-Islam Bahonar, accepted positions in institutions of the shah's government, they kept some contact with Khumayni during his exile. In January of 1978 Khumayni requested Mutahhari to form the Islamic Revolutionary Council. The IRC, whose other original members included Bazargan, Yazdi, Qotbzadeh, Beheshti, Bahonar, and Rafsanjani, later gained other members, including Taleqani and Bani-Sadr. Headed by Mutahhari, the IRC drafted a constitution. After the Shah was deposed, the IRC continued to play a focal role in organizing the revolutionary forces.

On May 1, 1979 Ayatullah Mutahhari attended an informal

meeting along with other officials of the IRC and other prominent supporters of the revolution. As he left the meeting, he was assassinated by members of *Furqan*. *Furqan* was a small radical group, whose membership never exceeded fifty, and which was founded in 1963 by a disenchanted seminary student who rejected the religious authority of the ulama, denied that Khumayni and the members of the ulama who supported him were worthy of leading an Islamic revolution, and used terrorism to fight against the newly formed government. Shortly before the martydom of Mutahhari, the group assassinated the Islamic Republic's first chief of staff, General Qarani. *Furqan* claimed to follow the teachings of the late Dr. Ali Shari'ati. During his eulogy for Mutahhari, Taleqani addressed the differences between the views of Mutahhari and Shari'ati with the claim that both men had the same vision, although their perspectives were different. Although Mutahhari had a traditional education and Shari'ati studied in Paris, both were committed to religious reform, to an activist understanding of the central precepts of Shi'ism, and to the elucidation of an authentically Islamic ideology. Indeed, all three of our authors were united in the pursuit of these goals.

The writings which are presented in this volume represent the avant garde of a long tradition of religious scholarship. All three of our authors were aware that this tradition faced two major sorts of challenges: the challenge of the West, and the challenge of Marxism. In order to meet these challenges new methods would have to be sought, and formulaic answers would have to be abandoned. The views of the jurisprudents as these had been traditionally handed down would no longer suffice, for what was sought was not simply the derivation of a legal ruling from accepted precepts, but a justification of these precepts themselves. When Taleqani discusses what the Qur'an has to say about war and martyrdom, he does so not merely to determine the teaching contained in the Qur'an, but to demonstrate the vitality of the Qur'an itself. When Shari'ati discusses themes familiar from Marxism and existentialism, he does so in such a way as to demonstrate that Islam is rich enough to provide the ideological framework in which Muslims might come to grips with such themes on their own cultural and religious terms.

The authors of this volume present a glimpse of a committment to justice which is at once both militant and pious. Such a commitment transcends sectarian divisions, for it is at the heart of Islam. It is expressed by the leader of the Egyptian Muslim Brotherhood, Hasan al-Banna, in the following words:

> [A]mong the descriptions of the Companions of Muhammad (May God bless and save him!) . . . occurs the following: "Monks by night and knights by day." You can just see one of them at night, standing erect in his oratory, clutching his beard, murmuring as the faultless murmur, weeping as the sorrowful weep, and saying: "O world, seduce some other than myself!" And when at the break of dawn the call to arms rang out, summoning the fighter to *jihād*, you would have seen him, a wolf on the back of his mount, shouting his war-cry while the entire battlefield resounded with it.[81]

Of the essays which follow, all were translated by Mehdi Abedi with the exception of Mutahhari's "*Shahīd*", which was translated anonymously, and parts of Shari'ati's "*Shahādat*", which were translated by Ali Asghar Ghassemy. The editing, footnotes and introduction were a collaborative effort by Mehdi Abedi and Gary Legenhausen.

Mehdi Abedi and Gary Legenhausen

Notes

1. G. H. Jansen, *Militant Islam* (New York: Harper and Row, 1979), p. 29

2. George Nader, "Interview with Sheikh Muhammad Hussein Fadl Allah", in *Middle East Insight* Vol. 4, No. 2, 1985, pp. 12-19. Also see Ayatollah Muhammad Hussein Fadl Allah, "Islam and Violence in Political Reality," *Middle East Insight* Vol. 4, Nos. 4 and 5, 1986, pp. 4-13.

3. Cf. fn. 1, below to Ali Shari'ati's "Discussion of *Shahadat.*"

4. References, such as this, to the Qur'an will be indicated in parenthesis with a colon between the numbers indicating *surah* and ayah. For information regarding the terms used in the Qur'an see Hanna E. Kassis, *A Concordance of the Qur'an* (Berkeley: University of California Press, 1983).

5. (4:69), (57:19).

6. (2:154), also (3:169).

7. Cf. (3:157-158), (3:170-171), (22:58-59).

8. In the Mosaic law there are, however, exceptions to the condition that women and children would be spared. Cf. Numbers 31, and Joshua 8. Cf. Michael Brown, "Is There a Jewish Way to Fight?" *Judaism*, Vol. 24 (1975), pp. 466-475.

9. Roland H. Bainton, *Christian Attitudes Toward War and Peace* (New York: Abingdon Press, 1960), p. 44.

10. LeRoy Walters, "The Just War and the Crusade: Antithesis or Analogies?" *The Monist*, October 1973, pp. 584-94. Cited in James Turner Johnson, *Just War Tradition and the Restraint of War* (Princeton: Princeton University Press, 1981), p. xxvi. In his seminal *Ideology, Reason and the Limitation of War* (Princeton: Princeton University Press, 1975) Johnson also argues that the classical just war doctrine of Vitoria and Suarez is inseparable from the idea of the holy war. Barrie Paskins and Michael Dockrill, in *The Ethics of War* (Minneapolis: University of Minnesota Press, 1979), support Johnson's analysis, claiming that the division between holy war and just war is "artificial and misleading." (p. 193).

11. *Op. cit.* p. 45.

12. J. T. Johnson, *Ideology.* The quote is from Johnson's own description of this work in the preface of his *Just War Tradition and the Restraint of War* (Princeton: Princeton University Press, 1981), p. ix.

13. See the discussion of Augustine's views in Frederick H. Russell, *The Just War in the Middle Ages* (Cambridge: Cambridge University Press, 1975).

14. James Turner Johnson, *Just War Tradition*, p. 94 f. Francisco de Vitoria (c. 1492-1546) wrote against the war of the Conquistadors against the Indians for religious reasons, though he did sanction the Spanish conquest on other grounds.

15. Ibn Khaldun, *The Muqaddimah*, tr. Franz Rosenthal, abridged and edited by N. J. Dawood (Princeton: Princeton University Press, 1981), p. 183.

16. In *Jihad in Mediaeval and Modern Islam* (Leiden: E. J. Brill, 1977), Rudolf Peters writes in his introduction: "The primary aim of the jihad is not, as it was often supposed in the older European literature, the conversion by force of unbelievers, but the expansion - and also defense - of Islam." p. 3. S. Abdullah Schleifer concurs that as traditionally understood, jihad may be waged to establish the shari'ah, but never for the sake of changing someone's personal faith, in "Jihad and Traditional Islamic Consciousness," *The Islamic Quarterly*, Vol. XXVII, No. 4, pp. 173-203.

17. Cf. Marshall G. S. Hodgson, *The Venture of Islam*, Vol. I (Chicago: University of Chicago Press, 1974), p. 201.

18. Rudolph Peters, *Islam and Colonialism: The Doctrine of Jihad in Modern History* (The Hague: Mouton, 1979), p. 149. The view of the doctrine of jihad as international law may be found in Muhammad Hamidullah *Muslim Conduct of State*, seventh ed., (Lahore: Sh. Muhammad Ashraf, 1977).

19. R. Peters, *Jihad in Mediaeval and Modern Islam*, p. 3-4. In *Islam and Colonialism,* (p. 122), Peters also argues that we are justified in speaking of jihad as *bellum justum.*

20. Cf. Ralph Lerner and Muhsin Mahdi, eds. *Medieval Political Philosophy* (Ithaca: Cornell University Press, 1978), and Hamid Enayat, *Modern Islamic Political Thought* (Austin: University of Texas Press, 1982).

21. Cf. Frederick H. Russell, *The Just War in the Middle Ages* pp. 11-12, and Lenn Evan Goodman, *The Case of the Animals versus Man Before the King of the Jinn* (Boston: Twayne, 1978), pp. 255-256.

22. S. Abdullah Schleifer, "Jihad: Modernist Apologists, Modern Apologetics," *The Islamic Quarterly*, Vol. XXVIII, No. 1 (1404/1984), pp. 25-46.

23. Muhammad Husayn at-Tabataba'i, *Al-Mizan* Vol. 3 (Tehran: WOFIS, 1402/1982), p.89.

24. See John Alden Williams, ed., *Themes of Islamic Civilization* (Berkeley: University of California Press, 1982), p. 269.

25. R. Peters, *Jihad in Medieval and Modern Islam*, p. 17. Majid Khadduri traces the idea that jihad can be justified solely on the grounds of religious differences to Shafi'i (d. 204/820), and comments on the controversy this provoked in *The Islamic Conception of Justice* (Baltimore: Johns Hopkins Press, 1984), pp. 165-66.

26. *Ibid.* p. 48. Cf. also p. 50 and p. 75, where it is argued that jihad is only permitted for defensive purposes.

27. Ayatullah Ahmad Jannati, "Defence and Jihad in the Qur'an", *Al-Tawhid*, Vol. 1, No. 3 (1404/1984), pp. 39-54, p. 42.

28. Muhammad Asad, *The Principles of State and Government in Islam*. (Berkeley: University of California Press, 1961).

29. R. Peters, *Islam and Colonialism*, p. 129.

30. Majid Khadduri, *The Islamic Conception of Justice* (Baltimore: Johns Hopkins University Press, 1984), pp. 169-70.

31. Hasan Al-Banna, *Five Tracts of Hasan Al-Banna* (1906-1949), Charles Wendell, tr., (Berkeley: University of California Press, 1978), p. 142 ff.

32. Sayyid Qutb, "Jihaad in the Cause of God," Ch. 4 of *Milestones* (Cedar Rapids: Unity Publishing Co., 1981), pp. 53-76.

33. S. Abul a'la Maududi, *Jihad in Islam* (Lahore: Islamic Publications, 1980), p. 5.

34. The injunction to "command the good and forbid evil" is Qur'anic: (3:104), (3:110), (3:114), (9:71). Muhammad Hamidullah, *Muslim Conduct of State* (Lahore: Sh. Muhammad Ashraf, 1977).

35. Ibrahim Amini, "Foreign Policy of an Islamic State in the Light of the Qur'an," *Al-Tawhid* Vol. II, No. 4, 1405/1985, p. 78.

36. On the brief caliphate of Hasan see S. H. M. Jafri, *The Origins and Early Development of Shi'a Islam* (London: Longman, 1979), p. 130 ff.

37. Ibn Abi Zayd al-Qayrawani (d. 386/996), "The Laws of Holy War," in John Alden Williams, ed., *Themes of Islamic Civilization* (Berkeley: University of California Press, 1982), p. 266.

38. Cf. Hamid Algar, *Religion and State in Iran: 1782-1906* (Berkeley: University of California, 1969); N. R. Keddie, *Scholars, Saints and Sufis* (Berkeley: University of California, 1972). For the challenge to claim that in the absence of the Imam, authority is held by the ulama, and for further references, see Said Amir Arjomand, *The Shadow of God and the Hidden Imam* (Chicago: University of Chicago Press, 1984) and Joseph Eliash, "Misconceptions Regarding the Juridical Status of the Iranian Ulama," *International Journal of Middle East Studies* (Feb. 1979), pp. 9-25. An interesting discussion of Shi'ite attitudes toward political authority can be found in Hamid Enayat, *Modern Islamic Political Thought* (Austin: University of Texas Press, 1982), and the review of this work and the discussion it has provoked by Dr. Wahid Akhtar in *Al-Tawhid*, Vol. II, No. 4, 1405/1985, pp. 165-189.

39. Cf. Gregory Rose, *"Velayat-e Faqih"* and the Recovery of Islamic Identity in the Thought of Ayatullah Khomeini," in Nikki R. Keddie, ed. *Religion and Politics in Iran* (New Haven: Yale University Press, 1983), pp. 166-188. Also see Farhang Rajaee, *Islamic Values and World View: Khomeyni on Man, the State and International Politics* (Lanham: University Press of America, 1983), pp. 9-23.

gation Organization,
P.O. Box 2782, Tehran, March 12, 1986.

50. A version of this story can be found in Rumi's *Mathnavi*.

51. John Alden Williams, ed., *Themes of Islamic Civilization* (Berkeley: University of
California Press, 1982), p. 269.

52. Majid Khadduri, *The Islamic Law of Nations* (Baltimore: Johns Hopkins Press,
1966), p. 155.

53. Muhammad Hamidullah, *Muslim Conduct of State* (Lahore: Sh. Muhammad
Ashraf, 1977), discussed in S. Abdullah Schleifer, "Jihad: Modernist Apologists,
Modern Apologetics," *The Islamic Quarterly* Vol. XXVIII, No. 1 (1404/1984), pp. 25-
46.

54. For the importance of the principle of double effect in Christian just war thinking
see Robert L. Phillips, *War and Justice* (Norman: University of Oklahoma Press,
1984), p. 30 ff. Phillips cites Aquinas for a succinct statement of the principle: "moral

acts take their species according to what is intended and not according to what is beside the intention, since this is accidental" (*Summa* 2.2, q. 64, art. 7). A similar statement is to be found in the frequently cited *hadith* according to which the Prophet of Islam declared that acts are judged by their intentions.

55. John Alden Williams, ed., *Themes of Islamic Civilization* (Berkeley: University of California Press, 1982), p. 269.

56. See the excellent discussion of modern literature on martyrdom by Hamid Enayat in his *Modern Islamic Political Thought* (Austin: University of Texas Press, 1982), pp. 181-94. Also helpful for an understanding of the importance of Husayn's martyrdom in Shi'ite culture is Michael M. J. Fischer, *Iran: From Religious Dispute to Revolution* (Cambridge: Harvard University Press, 1980).

57. Cf. Fischer, *Iran: From Religious Dispute to Revolution*, p. 26. The story is from the *Makhzan al-Buka*, a major work of *ta'ziya* (passion plays about Karbala).

58. Shaykh al-Mufid, *Kitab al-Irshad*, I. K. A. Howard, tr., (London: Muhammadi Trust, 1981), p. 367.

59. Majid Fakhry, *A History of Islamic Philosophy* (New York: Columbia University Press, 1983), p. 246.

60. A large number of books have been written which discuss the events preceding the downfall of Shah Muhammad Rez Pahlavi, and which document the importance of the writings and speeches of our authors. Some of these works are cited in the notes below.

61. This date is not agreed upon by all who report biographical information about Ayatulah Taleqani. Most writers claim he was born in 1910, but do not specify the date further. Hamid Algar, in the introduction to Ayatullah Sayyid Mahmud Taleghani, *Society and Economics in Islam* (Berkeley: Mizan Press, 1982), p. 9, gives the date Rabi'1 4, 1329/March 5, 1911. We assume that the majority of writers have erred in their intercalation from the Muslim to Gregorian calendars. Another point on which biographies differ is place of birth. A minority claim that Taleqani was born in the town of Taleqan near Yazd. Algar again gives more detailed information, specifying the town of Gelird in the *valley* of Taleqan, Cf. Buhram Afrasiyabi and Sa'id Dehqan, *Taleqani va Tarikh* (Taleqani and History), (Tehran: Nilufar Publications, 1981).

62. Sayyid Mahmud Taleqani, *Islam va Malikiyyat* (Tehran: Intishar, 1344/1972).

63. Abu Dhar was a companion of Prophet Muhammad who was famous for his insistence on equity and his opposition to the luxurious style of the Ummayyed court. Abu Dhar was one of the great heroes of Ali Shari'ati. Cf. Shari'ati's *Shahadat*, in this volume.

64. It is commonly believed that Shari'ati was born in Mazian, a village near Sabzavar. His family name was Mazinani, which he used on some occasions as a pen-name. Since his father had moved to Mashhad long before Shari'ati was born, there is reason to believe that he was born there, rather than in Mazinan.

65. See Shari'ati's *Kavir*, pp. 2-29, where an autobiographical sketch is given. See also the interview with Shari'ati's father in *Kayhan-e-Farhangi* No. 11, where his family tree appears.

66. His *Tafsir-e-Novin* has enjoyed wide popularity in Iran.

67. The letter is in response to Hopkins' invitation to Kashif al-Ghita to attend an anti-communist seminar. The latter refused, but instead sent a letter in which communism is pictured as a lesser evil than American imperialism.

68. In Yusuf Ali's translation this verse reads:

> God is the Light
> Of the heavens and the earth.
> The parable of His Light
> Is as if there were a Niche
> And within it a Lamp;
> The Lamp enclosed in Glass:
> The glass as it were
> A brilliant star:
> Lit from a blessed Tree,
> An Olive, neither of the East
> Nor of the West,
> Whose oil is well-nigh
> Luminous
> Though fire scarce touched it:
> Light upon Light!
> God doth guide
> Whom He will
> To His Light:
> God doth set forth Parables
> For men: and God
> Doth know all things.

69. *The Median School of Thought* is a section of *Tarikhe-e-Takamul-e-Falsafah* (The History of the Evolution of Philosophy), published in Shari'ati's *Collected Works*, No. 31, pp. 1-26.

70. Three students were killed in the demonstration protesting Nixon's visit to Tehran. They are known as the "16 Azar Martyrs", and the day is commemorated as *Ruz-e-Daneshju* (the Day of the University Students). A leftist magazine published abroad is named "16 Azar", drawing its name from the incident.

71. Cf. *Kavir*, pp. 78-84.

72. It is popularly believed among Shari'ati's supporters that he received two doctorates at the Sorbonne, one in sociology and the other in the philosophy of history or the history of Islam. Yann Richard recently found his dissertation in Paris, as is reported in a footnote in Nikkie Keddie, *Roots of Revolution*, (New Haven: Yale University Press, 1981), p. 294.

73. See Yazdi, *Yad Nameh Shahid Javid*, pp. 23 ff.

74. Massignon, *Salman Pak et les Primices Espirituelles del'Islam Iranien* (Paris: Societe des etudes Iraniennes, 1933).

75. A number of books have been published which criticise Shari'ati either from the viewpoint of the ulama, or from the left. Examples of the first kind are, Muhammad Ali Ansari's *Doktor Chemiguyad?* (What does the doctor say?) and Shyakh Qasim Islami's *Sokhani Chand ba Doktor Shari'ati* (A few words with Dr. Shari'ati). An example of leftist criticism is Ali Akbar Akbari's *Barrasi-e- Chand Mas'alah-e-Eftema'i* (Investigation of Some Social Issues).

76. A short autobiography is included in the preface to Mutahhari's *The Reason for Inclination toward Materialism.*

77. Tabataba'i is the most highly respected philosopher of Iran in recent history. His exegesis of the Qur'an, *Al-Mizan*, is already a classic, (The English translation of volumes one, three, four and five have been published by the World Organization for Islamic Services in Tehran in 1983. Also in translation is his summary introduction to Shi'ism. *Shi'ite Islam* (Houston: FILINC, 1979)). His philosophical reputation rests on a number of volumes on topics ranging from political philosophy to logic and metaphysics.

78. The practice of considering an expert of jurisprudence as a final authority on matters of the observance of religious law, a supreme source for emulation, *marja-i-taqlid*, began in the nineteenth century. Currently there are several ayatullahs who share this distinction. See Juan R. Cole, "Imami Jurisprudence and the Role of the Ulama: Mortaza Ansari on Emulating the Supreme Exemplar," in *Religion and Politics in Iran*, ed. Nikki R. Keddie, (New Haven: Yale University Press, 1983), pp. 33-46.

79. Shahrough Akhavi, *Religion and Politics in Contemporary Iran* (Albany: SUNY Press, 1980), p. 144.

80. Taleqani's eulogy of Mutahhari is available on cassette from the Book Distribution Center, P.O. Box 31669, Houston, Texas 77231.

81. Charles Wendell, tr. *Five Tracts of Hasan Al-Banna* (Berkeley: University of California Press, 1978), p. 82.

Jihad and Shahadat

I n the name of God, the Compassionate, the Merciful. Praise be
to God, the cherisher and sustainer of the worlds, creator of the
heavens and the earth. May divine peace and greetings be bestowed
upon all the righteous apostles, particularly upon the seal of the
prophets, the one who raised the flags of truth and the true religion,
and divine greetings upon his noble family and companions and
upon the infallible imams, martyrs, and truthful ones. I seek refuge in
God, from the cursed Satan.[2]

> Those who believe do battle for the cause of God and
> those who disbelieve do battle for the cause of *tāghūt*. So
> fight the minions of the devil. Lo! the devil's strategy is
> alweays weak.[3]

... Perhaps we can discuss this issue for a few minutes and reach a
conclusion. *Jihād* is among the most important and widely discussed
Islamic issues. By meditating upon the Qur'an, one discovers that
after every few *āyāt* related to issues of belief, society, ethics, and
jurisprudence, in various manners, there is the command to wage war
and carry out *jihād*. [On the other hand, the propaganda that has
been perpetrated in the past few centuries against Islam has been
primarily aimed at the issue of war, conquests, and the advances
made by Muslims. The scope of such evil propaganda has been
sufficiently broad as to more or less have engraved its mark upon our
youth and the educated. Fair and unbiased scholars, Muslim and
non-Muslim, have written in defense of Islam and the principles of its
just struggles. [They have investigated the following questions.]
What is the meaning of *jihād* in Islam? How has Islam progressed?
How many human casualties were caused by this great intellectual,

social, and moral revolution which appeared in the Arabian peninsula? Were the wars of the beginning of the Islamic era defensive or offensive? These questions in themselves are so extensive that if we decided to discuss them all in detail we would not have enough time to focus on the central issue itself.

Before being subsumed under religious or social concerns, defense falls among the intrinsic and natural characteristics of living beings. God has created a power in man's instinct which is called 'anger'. Anger also exists, more or less and in varying forms, in animals. Its function is to safeguard the right to live. Any living being, one way or the other, possesses a defensive power, which, at the proper time, moves from the instinct into the organs of defense. This power is bestowed by the Almighty. This defensive power even exists, more or less, in plants. Perhaps there are plants, the fruit and flower of which is to be used by others. There are yet other plants, the fruit of which is only for their own reproduction. People can only enjoy these visually. For this reason, some plants have big sharp thorns to warn the intruder, saying, "Since I am such a fragrant, beautiful being, this weapon must protect me from the harm of potential invaders." Yesterday a young man read some poetry, from which I recall a few lines. I don't know who the poet is, but it is an excellent piece:

> How long will you remain depressed as ice,
> Or drifting like a dead mouse in water?
> Contempt causes inner discord;
> Acceptance of repression invites humiliation;
> So like a rosebush, bear your weapon on your shoulder
> So you can also display your beautiful blossoms.[4]

The poem is miraculously eloquent and realistic. It is a fact that servility and lowliness ruin the harmony of man's faculties. [Those who live in such conditions may well perceive some facts, but they cannot express them with their tongues and hands. This is the meaning of discord: dissonance between a person's perceptive and practical mechanisms. If the rosebush wishes to preserve the freshness and beauty of its own roses, if it wishes to stand proudly, it must cut the hands of the intruders.] This is the same as what appears in the constitution of the animals, according to the law of evolution and instinct, exemplified by the development of the horn, talons, and teeth, and in man, is manifested in the emotion of anger. Since reason in man is the director of his other faculties, he utilizes anger as a weapon to defend his rights, territory, dignity, nationality, and what have you. Thus if a prophet or a law-giver decrees that war and defense is to be nullified in a nation, it is the same as decreeing that because lustful passion causes unfavorable social conditions, men and women have to cut off their procreative organs. Nay! Natural powers have their appropriate function; only they require proper guidance. By the same token that God has bestowed this same power upon man, he too must guide it toward its proper function — the procreation and preservation of mankind. As God has created the appetite for food, man must eat enough to protect his health and being. But the same appetite, overflowing its natural boundries, can be a destructive urge. Instead of living eighty or a hundred years, a gluttonous person may only live thirty of forty — suicide by over-satiation. Likewise, the sexual urge in man, if, instead of being used for procreation, is used in illegal, lustful ways, can cause social decay, due to factors including venereal diseases, such as syphilis and gonorrhea. Accordingly, when anger manifests itself in man, he takes up arms; and so he must, when his rights, honor, and dignity are [endangered]. If anger is not directed and utilized in the cause which God has determined, according to the law of creation, it becomes deviant. Then it results in wars of conquest waged for material expansion and the destruction of humanity. First, anger is a natural fact. Second, it must be guided by divine legislation.

If there were no religions, how else would the wise men and reformers of the world find a solution? Can we say that war should vanish from the face of the earth? This has indeed been an argument. Today this claim is still widespread. The institutions of peace and arms-limitation work day and night. They do in halls and rooms above the ground. Underground there are factories which are in a frenzy to create destructive, murderous weapons. Just below the people who brag about peace and disarmament, nuclear weapons are made. Then what is to be done? The real solution is that the natural instinct of anger is to be guided onto the straight path. This is what Islam says. Instead of war and killing, Islam has offered the concept of *jihād*. The term *jihād* is always attached to the locution *fi sabil Allāh* (in the way of God). What is the way of God? Which direction is it? Is it toward the heavens, toward Mecca, or toward Jerusalem? No. The way of God is the very path of the well-being and betterment of human society. It is the way of justice, truth, and human liberty. (It is the building of a world in which) a specific group or class does not dominate over the destiny of the people, in order to stop human intellectual movement or to stop people from utilizing the natural resources that God Almighty has created for the common use of humanity. As God has given natural powers and intellectual capacities to man, as God has created this atmosphere, light, and land for everybody, *sabil Allah* refers to the world in which all the people can develop their human capacities in order to obtain freedom. *"Jāhidū fī sabīl Allāh"* ("strive in the way of God") is the divine command. In Islamic jurisprudence, one volume is devoted to *jihad.* Interestingly enough, the volume appears in the portion known as *"'ibādāt"* ("worship"). Our jurisprudence is divided into two parts: *'ibādāt* and *mu'āmilāt,* the latter meaning "interpersonal relations." The difference between the two is that in *'ibadāt,* the intention of intimacy with God is a prerequisite. *Hajj,* prayer, fasting, almsgiving, exhortation to good deeds, prevention of evil deeds, and finally, *jihād* are all considered *'ibādat.* For example, if someone grabbed a sword and set off to fight the unbelievers without the intention of doing so for the pleasure of God, he would not be rewarded. If he were killed, he would not be considered a martyr. His act would be wasted as if he had committed suicide. Only one who has such a divine intention can take up arms for *jihād* and be rewarded by God. The duty of *jihād* has as a prerequisite the intention of *qurbat.* What does *qurbat* mean? It means intimacy, closeness. It is the same as *fī sabīl Allāh.* What is God, so that we can get near to him? God is the universal good, and it is God's will and attributes which have manifested themselves in the universe and in human society. God is wise, just and merciful. The realization of divine wisdom, justice, and mercy, and consequently the opening up of the doors of goodness to the people is *jihād fī sabīl Allāh. Jihād* is *'ibādat.* In examining the Qur'an and its *āyāt* one notices that wherever there is the command *"qātilū"* ("wage war") and *"jāhidū"* ("struggle"), there is also the locution, *fī sabīl Allāh.* In the *āyah* that I recited at the outset, the Almighty says:

> Those who believe do battle for the cause of God and
> those who disbelieve do battle for the cause of *taghut*. So
> fight the minions of the devil. Lo! the devil's strategy is
> always weak.[3]

The premise of this *ayah* seems obvious, that there is always war in
the world. Such a state is consistent with the nature of man. The main
point in the corollary is that the people of the world are of two types:
the ones who believe and therefore strive in the way of God, and the
ones who disbelieve and strive in the way of *taghut*. Whether we like
it or not, life is a struggle, it is warfare. But those who believe in a
supreme goal struggle in the way of God. Is there another way besides
the way of God? Yes. The way of *taghut*.

What is *taghut*? What kind of world is this? Do the ones who recite
the Qur'an pay the attention to this word which it deserves? *Taghut* is
a hyperbole from *tughyan* (deluge, rebellion, outburst). The sentence
"*tagha al-ma*" means "Water has overflowed; it left its natural bed. It
is destroying he neighboring houses and farms and uprooting the
nearby trees."This is the meaning of *tughyan*. *Taghut* is the one who
commits *tughyan*. *Taghut* is the selfish person. This word is a much
more meaningful term than that which the Greek philosophers have
coined, and following them, the social scientists have brought into
use: "despot, tyrant."[5] A tyrant can very well be only a tyrant over
himself. More clearly, his passions may dictate over and control him.
But *taghut* is the one who overflows from his rightful social limits. He
tramples social limits under his feet. It is as though a hurricane of
lusts has burst out, recognizing no limits. Some have mistakenly
thought that *taghut* means "idol." Of course, idols represent a kind of
taghut, but the two are not synonymous. The word *taghut* does not
necessarily mean and is not normally used to mean this.

Another *ayah* of the Qur'an reads, "... how they would go for
judgement (in their disputes) to *taghut* when they have been ordered
to renounce it ..."[6] If we take *taghut* to mean "idol," how can it make
judgements? It is obvious then, that the meaning of *taghut* is not idol.
The word "*taghut*" is repeated eight or nine times in the Qur'an.[7] In
surah two, in *Ayat al-Kursi*,[8] which is much recommended for
recitation after the required prayers, the term is repeated twice:

> There is no compulsion in religion. The right direction is
> henceforth distinct from error. And he who rejects *taghut*

and believes in God has grasped a firm handhold which will never break. God is Hearer, Knower. God is the Protecting Friend of those who believe. He brings them out of darkness into light. And for those who disbelieve, their patrons are *ṭāghūt*. They bring them out of light into darkness ...

There are only two possibilities, either man's existence and will come under God's control, the effect of which is that gradually the individual will come out of the darkness of selfishness and wrong-doing, and therefore, with the aid of knowledge and wisdom, his foresight will broaden; or *ṭāghūt* will possess him. It is either this or that. If the former is rejected as an alternative, the latter will occur automatically. Man cannot live without a *walī* (guardian); such a guardian is either God or *ṭāghūt*. [We say that] the Prophet and the imams are also guardians. If we say this, it is because they implement divine will. It is for this reason that they are *walī-Allāh* (divine guardians). Such guardians know the good of the people better than the people themselves do. The noble Prophet says, *"Alastu awlā bikum min anfusikum?* (Haven't I been closer to you than you to yourselves?")[9] "You were inclined to remain idol-worshippers, to be ignorant, weak, and down-trodden. But you witnessed that when I conquered you, you gained everything." This is how the divine Prophet delivered his ultimatum on the day of Ghadir,[10] when such a transformation had become obvious, and had reached a practical level. [Thus he asks] "Am I not closer to you than you to yourselves?" Thus if God and the divine guardians are not in charge, people will be possessed by *ṭāghūt*. What is the sign and the result of such possession. People will be taken out of light into darkness. That is, from the light of nature, the light of reason, and the light of perception, they will be dragged into the dark sphere of ignorance, lust, suspicion, and pessimism. As the *āyah* says, "Those who believe do battle for the cause of God and those who disbelieve do battle for the cause of *ṭāghūt* ..." Accordingly, the occurrence of war in the world is inevitable. Whenever there is no war, it will either be the end of the world, or there has to be another world, or human instinct must be completely transformed. If it is transformed, there will be a new form of life. But in the world as it is, our instincts necessitate war in one form or another. The main difference, however, is between the ones who believe, and therefore wage warfare in the way of God, and the ones who disbelieve and wage war in the way of *taghut,* in the way of the despots and tyrants, in the way of the ones who overflow their rightful limits. This is a second issue. Let me not forget the first: war is natural and instinctive and man cannot do without it. The second issue is that a religion, a perfect religion, unlike Christianity, recognizes the necessity of warfare. Christendom superficially claims that there must be no war. This is what the adherents of Christianity profess. They relate what they think are the words of Christ, "If someone slaps you on the cheek, offer the other cheek."[11] Has it been so in practice? Where have all these wars come from in this world? Did we Muslims create them? Who has been behind all these wars and massacres in this century? Further, Christendom recommends that those who want God's kingdom should not marry.[12] Has this been practical? Isn't "the Christian Europe" a center of lust as the result of reaction against such prohibitions? In the name of Christianity, groups of monks and nuns have locked themselves up in monasteries and convents; they imprison their vital faculties. If we were to suppose that there is a grain of truth in such legislation, we would have to hold that original Christianity was a temporary phenomenon or a false creed. But the Qur'an has confirmed Jesus, and we must believe that original Christianity was a true religion, and that such nonsensical regulations were attached to it later. [Regarding this, the Qur'an says]" ... But monasticism they invented — we did not ordain it for them ..."[13] Monasticism cannot be defined merely as remaining single. Huddling defenselessly in a corner and not defending one's existence and rights is indeed monasticism. It cannot be a universal law. Only a religion which recognizes the geometry of human instincts and makes a plan according to it can govern the world. Such religion tells man, "This instinct is within you; but do not use it for murdering, theft, lustful purposes, or military expansionism. Use it in its proper way. Defend your rights. Defend your dignity. Defend your country. Defend your religion. Defend human rights. By and by you have to channel this instinct into this proper path."

Let us return to the Qur'an. "And fight them until persecution is no more, and religion is for God. But if they desist, then let there be no hostility except against wrong-doers."[14] Or likewise, "And fight them until persecution is no more, and religion is all for God. But if they cease, then lo! God is seer of what they do."[15] This is *fī sabīl Allāh,* which has both a positive and a negative side. First it says, "Wage warfare"; then it says for what one should wage warfare. Does it say one should do so for expansionism or to obtain spoils? No. Do so in order to bring the voice of truth unto the ears of the people of the world. This is the meaning of *fī sabīl Allāh*: free the people! In other words, remove the obstacles to a truthful human life. Remove those 'powers' and 'classes' which are obstacles to the rights of the masses and which suppress public opinion. Abolish them. Liberate people from this suffocating environment, and familiarize them with God and the fountainhead of the universe. Do so "until there is no more persecution." Those centralized powers that deceive the weak masses set one group against the other, drive the masses away from divine truth into materialism, mislead the masses from the unity of God and drive them toward polytheism, idolatry, and the worship of humans. Fight them until these mischiefs are removed from the way of human evolution toward perfection. Do so until those particular classes which utilize public wealth for their own lust and violate the rights of millions of people — as did the Persian and Roman empires — are annihilated.

When that bare-footed Arab confronted the commander of the Persian army,[16] he was asked, "Did you come to conquer and to loot? Or did you perhaps come because of starvation or nakedness? If so, we will feed you; we will give you money; we will satisfy all of you, commanders and soldiers alike. Return to your land." [Rustam] thought his words had persuaded the man! Make note of what the man answered and how his words have been recorded in history. He said only one sentence, but a very meaningful one: "We have been given the mission of liberating the nations of the world from slavery to human laws and false religions which are for a particular class, and to lead them to the glory of Islam." This is the Islamic *jihād.* This is the meaning of *"jihād." "Jihād"* means "striving for truth"; it is not similar to war and murder. *"Jihād"* means "striving for truth," and that is why it is discussed in the volumes on *'ibādāt* (worship). It is conditioned by *fī sabīl Allāh.*

A man asked the noble Prophet, "Messenger of God! [What is the reward of] a poor person who goes to the battlefield for the sake of booty?" The Prophet repeated three times, "He has no divine reward." [Another person] asked the noble Prophet, "Is the one who goes to the battlefield in order to test his own courage or to see fame properly called *mujāhid fī sabīl Allāh* (striver in the way of God)?" "No! he replied. "Then who can properly be called *majūhid fī sabīl Allāh?*" The Prophet answered, "[The one who strives so] that God's word becomes the uppermost,"[17] meaning that God's will manifests itself and rules their wills. This is the meaning of "the way of God." This is the meaning of *"jihād* of Islam." There is not sufficient time available to discuss all the *āyāt* relevant to this topic.

A short while after the first generation of Islam, Muslims deviated. During the Umayyid caliphate, when every aspect of Islam was matamorphosized, the *jihād* of Islam remained no exception to the rule. It was metamorphosized as well. Let us recall the Englishman, Thomas Carlyle.[18] I am unable to quote him directly. When defending Islam from the accusation that it has advanced thanks to warfare and the sword, he suggests that one should look beyond these superficial matters. The real question is whether or not Islam is a true religion. If it is a true religion, if it is a religion teaching the unity of God and obedience to the one God, if it has laws and regulations useful to the world and it can make the people fortunate, such a religion has to advance. If there is no sword, it should advance with teeth and claws. One cannot ask why Islam has advanced with the sword. The real question is whether it is the truth or fallacy which has advanced. It is wrong to argue, as some do, that since it has advanced by the sword, it is false. If you are not prejudiced, if you do not wish to remain under illusion, and if you do not wish to paint a false caricature of Islam for the already prejudiced masses of Europe, why do you argue as such? Do you mean that since the Muslims have fought, Islam is a false religion? Isn't it more reasonable to say, that because Islam is a true religion, it has not disregarded the necessity of warfare, and on the contrary has given a commandment to that effect?

If a plant has no flower, there is no reason for it to have thorns. If man does not have a right to live and defend himself, if he does not have such a personal right, then what is the function of anger? If he has anger, it follows that he has rights. And if he has rights, he has to channel the power of his anger in the way of his rights, rather than channeling it in a false way. Man must defend his rights, to defend his dignity. This is the truth of *jihād,* and it is a necessary part of a true religion, which has laws. One cannot believe a religion which argues on the one hand that it is a true religion and has come to reform the world, but on the other hand does not have any dimension of defense, propagation, and advancement. Such a religion is not credible. If a religion is like this, we shouldn't accept its claim that it has come from God for the salvation of humanity and to lead people toward truth and salvation until the day of judgement.

Islam is a religion aimed at reforming humanity. It aims to save humanity from falling into the valley of animalistic passion. Islam has come to straighten man's stature, to direct his attention to God, and to establish justice and equity in the world. It has come to end war for the purpose of looting, murder, and expansionism — to end these wars instigated by world leaders, who use others as their tools in the name of nationalism and such in order to devastate them. The purpose of warfare, Islam says, is "so religion, all of it, is for Allah."[19] Such religion, indeed, has come. Is it then appropriate to assert that our religion merely says, "There is a God and there is an Apostle?" And if anyone asks you how the world can be reformed, can you tell them that the masses of the world should not fight the tyrants of the world, and push away the hands of those who rape the dignity, life, and rights of humanity?[20] Can you call this a true religion? Nay! If it is a true religion, it must take up the sword and advance. To what point should it advance? To the point that they either submit and say, "We are Muslims," in which case they become your brothers, or they say, "We will retain our own religion and will carry on our own way of worship; but we will follow the public law of Islam." In this case they become *dhimmi,* the protected minority. In such case, they again have equal rights with Muslims.

An Arab cannot say, "Because the religion has come from my country, I am superior to the non-Arab." Once Muslim, there is no difference between Arab and non-Arab. The criterion for superiority is piety.[21] The more pious, the more superior. The law is universal. Whether the person in question is Chinese, Roman, black or white, as soon as he accepts Islam, he is a Muslim. Muslims have equal rights. One cannot say, "Because I am Arab and I accepted Islam before you did, I am superior to you, a non-Arab whom Islam reached later." The deviations which originated from the beginning of the Islamic era stemmed from this misperception. The Arab prided himself by claiming his priority and thus superiority in Islam. "Islam has come from our country, and thus we have right over others." This caused them to violate the rights of Iranians and to push them aside. Thus the reaction manifested itself in a sort of nationalism.[22] The suspicions that contemporary representatives of foreigners are utilizing to divide the Muslims and to establish walls among them have been derived from that period. If only we had maintained that we are all brothers, all equals, all waging warfare to liberate the people of the world, as our forefathers did at the beginning of Islam!

Can there be a religion in the world which is a Godly faith and yet lacks principles of advancement and defense? We cannot even properly hypothesize such a religion. Now, whom shall one fight with? Against whom should we wage war? *Jihād* with whom? The first issue of *jihād* is that Islam has to declare its invitation. Since Islam is a natural religion, the people of the world, the natural people, the ones who love freedom, the masses of people, will welcome it. The ruling classes and those whose profits lie in turning the masses away from the truth and from joining any truth will cause trouble. Consequently war will flare up. In this war the parasite social layer, which had hampered man's aptitude, will wither away. Was this not the case in Iran?[23] If we read two pages of history, we see that the masses of people welcomed the invitation of Islam. Only the military men, who were dependent on the treasures of the ruling class resisted the Muslims. The lower layers of society helped them, and showed them the way. There is plenty of evidence in history that the masses of Rome and Iran cooperated with the Muslims, saying, "Come, if your slogan is *'Allahu Akbar'* (God is the Greatest), if you believe that all people are equal in God's sight, we are ready to help." Thus the masses began fighting until this corrupt and rotten layer, which had been obliterating the talents, was removed. Suddenly the Iranian talent blossomed. Read two pages of history, one page before Islam and one pager after! Suddenly there are many poets, writers, scholars, and orators![24] What a transformation took place in this country! These were the consequences of Islam which washed away that corrupt layer.

So, as long as there is an obstacle, Islam says it has to be removed.
Truth must be declared to the people. If the other side attacks, war
will take a defensive form. Otherwise, since it is a divine religion, it
will be for the purpose of announcing *risalāt*[25] to the masses of the
people. If the other side caused trouble and created obstacles, defense
becomes necessary. If they attack a country under Islamic rule, all the
Muslims must rise for defense. There are then two types of wars thus
far, [wars of advancement and wars of defense]. There is, however,
another *jihād,* which we can call internal. If a religious minority,
which is under the protection of Islam, breaks the rules of protection
[what is to be done?] In a country where the law is derived from
Islam, its government is Islamic, the laws and regulations of Islam
are implemented, and its taxpayers are Muslims, how does Islam
deal with the Jewish and Christian minorities who live there? Islam
commands, "If they practice according to the regulations of the
protected minority, they are, just like Muslims, free to worship
according to their practice. They have to pay their *jizya* (poll-tax). In
such case, their lives, belongings, and rights are to be protected. No
one can intrude upon their property and their dignity, just as with
Muslims. But if they break the conditions of their protection, they
are considered *muhārib* (hostile). [War against them] is another type
of *jihād.* Muslims have to fight with them, because they have rebelled
against the law. One has to fight them within the boundaries of
Islamic society, until they submit to truth and law, until they bow
their heads down, until they properly come under Islamic
government and law.

Now let us see what Islamic jurisprudence instructs concerning the
limits of a protected minority. Please pay attention. We want to see
to what limit Muslims have a duty to deal with them as protected
minorities. This portion is in all our books on jurisprudence, and I
have extracted it from *Al-Mukhtasar al-Nāfi'* of Allamah Hilli.[26] He
lists five conditions of *dhimmah* (protection): (1) One has to pay the
jizyah. In order for this rights to be protected and in order to be
immune from the harm of Muslims, one has to pay a kind of poll-tax
to the Muslim *bayt al-māl* (public treasury). (2) One must not harm
the Muslims, must not have any sexual engagement with Muslim
women, must not steal the property of Muslims, and must not

cooperate with the enemies of Islam. (3) One must not be flagrant with prohibited things, such as intoxication, adultery, and incest. (4) One must not build new churches or temples and must not sound church bells. If they build a new church, it must be destroyed. (5) One must not build a building taller than the buildings of the Muslims. This would be disgraceful to the Muslims.[27]

Who owns the fifteen story building at the corner of Lalehzar and Islambul? Who are the ones in this country cooperating with the enemies of Muslims? This is the law of Islam. This is the jurisprudence of Islam. I demand a confession from you yourselves. Who are the ones who steal the property of Muslims and help the Israelis and international Zionists? Who are the ones who take Muslim women out of the boundaries of chastity? Are they protected minorities? Or hostile ones? An expert of jurisprudence must rule. I grant that such things, God willing, should not happen in our country. Taking into consideration that Muslims, and particularly Shi'ite scholars, have clarified these issues, if a government — we hypothesize that, God willing, such is the not the case in our country — had certain cooperative links with these, what is the duty of the Muslim people toward such government? I don't want to appear prejudiced. [But look,] on the one side they push Muslim masses into the deserts and rape the boundaries of Islam; and on the other hand, they take Muslim properties by different means in order to promote evil-doing, rather than employing them in productive spheres. If a government opens an embassy for them without naming it as such,[28] and then the authorities go there and have a great deal of fun, what is the duty of the people toward such a government? You determine the duty of the people. Should a government which does not submit to the laws of Islam rule over the Muslim masses? You tell me, your excellency! If everything I say is false, they should deny it. If it is true, it is not in accordance with Islamic ordinances. Let me tell you, today Zionism is the second hide of colonialism. Colonialism is the hide of Zionism. Zionism has crept into the hide of Israel. Israel has taken a new form in our country, and has appeared as Baha'ism.[29] In all the ministries and key offices of the Shi'ite Islamic government, to which a great deal of hail and praise is due, and all of its authorities are protectors of Islam, [the Baha'is] have infiltrated everywhere. Oh you overt and covert governmental agents who are present here, this is what Islam says. This is what religion says. I don't care if the reference is to the prime minister or someone above him, or someone under him. You ask why I say these things? You are bitter about it? Then stop me. If you do so, I will no longer have duties. But as long as I am here, I am obliged to preach the laws and regulations of Islam. I am nobody's employee. I am nobody's hireling. I don't want the governmental apperatus to inflate me with air or to give me a position. I am what I am, whether you like it or not.

Yesterday they made me angry. A group of Muslim youths assembled in Dezashib yesterday afternoon. Behold the buffoonery of the governmental agents. Tell me clearly and all at once, "Do not go on the pulpit and speak." This is why my nervous system is exhausted. Whatever I say, I myself am totally responsible for it. Tomorrow you should not come and arrest the sponsor of this assembly, put him on trial, and take his life away. It has nothing to do with him. [Whatever you wish to say,]tell me. Tell me that I am a liar, that I speak against religion, that I am an agitator, that I have connections with foreign embassies. Tell me all you want. Open a file on me. The masses of people know what I am. Is this what you call an Islamic country? Are these the protectors of Islam? In al-Mu'tamar al-Islāmī (the Islamic Conference), we could not raise our heads when they showed us the document of relations.[30] Dear Minister of Agriculture, isn't there a Muslim advisor in this country? Don't we have engineers? If not, bring some from Switzerland or India or Germany. Why does the chief advisor of land distribution have to be a Zionist Jew? From where shall I begin my criticism? I say these things and I have documents. You tell me I am a liar. I know about the party of a month ago. I know where it was held, and I know who were in charge of the celebration. I even know their names. I know the advisors as well. They told me about it, and I said, "It doesn't concern us." Then you see that if a certain fellow travels, there is so much noise in the newspapers about him. About Al-Mu'tamar al-Islāmī, they wrote not a single world. They mentioned nothing about what was said at the Islamic conference in Jerusalem. They said nothing about who was there and what was discussed. Whose fault is it except that of the agents of Israel, who are uprooting the tree of chastity of this country, who are destroying the economy and life of this country, who scatter the harvest of this country to the wind? As

Mr. Muttahhari mentioned, the danger of these is greater than any other danger. Tonight I warn you, my Muslim brothers, scholars, and dignitaries, about this danger. You know your duty. The government has to deny all this and say that they are all lies and propaganda, so that we shall not be ashamed in front of the Muslims of the world.

Here is another phase of *jihad.* Thus far [we have mentioned] three kinds of war commanded by Islam: *jihad* with foreigners for the advancement of Islam, *jihad* for the defense of Islam and Islamic countries, and *jihad* so that a protected minority does not become hostile. Another type of *jihad* is waging war against the despots, so that no one can reign as a tyrant, as a *taghut* in a Muslim country. [...][31] It is the duty of every Muslim to invite the despots onto the straight path. In a benevolent manner, one must tell him, "Dictatorship and despotism is not good for you, for the country, or for the society. No dictator has gone to his grave with a whole head." Yes, one has to advise him. If he does not accept, then one must arrange a militant stand against him.

Perhaps you Muslims will question why the scholars of Islam do not say these things concerning *jihad.* Why is the information we receive such as it is? We look at the beginning of Islam. We see that the commander of the believers, Ali, would personally participate in *jihad.* Not only did he approve of *jihad,* but he would personally help. In some wars, he even sent his own sons. What happened later? Mu'awiyah[32] took charge. Then Yazid.[33] According to our sources concerning *jihad,* one condition is that the imam or sultan must be just. This clearly indicated in our sources. *Jihad* cannot be for the sake of strengthening the government of a tyrant, sultan or imam. But is is recommended for us to fight alongside a just sultan and to defend him.

How was the situation at the time of our Imams? True, that if the Muslims would go to fight, the Muslim empire would expand; but for what purpose? What good would it have been for Muslims to conquer China and the revenue to go to Abdul Malik ibn Marwan,[34] Sulayman ibn Abdul Malik,[35] or to an Abbasid Caliph?[36] Has Islam desired such things? No! It is for this reason that the locution *"Sultan adilun"* ("a just sultan") has been repeated in our Islamic sources.

Such is the fact of the matter. Consider, for example, the narrations concerning Friday prayer. If Shi'ites had been instructed to say the prayer with others it would have meant the government was approved. It would have meant approval of the government of the usurping caliphs, such as Walid ibn Abdul Malik[37]. It would have meant approval of the government of Mutawakkil.[38] It would have meant approval of the government of such and such an Ummayyad child. Why? Because the Imam of Friday prayer was the representative of such governments. Friday prayer is not like other prayers. It is for this reason that (our imams) would decree that if one finds a just imam, one should say the prayer. Otherwise one should not. This means that one should not approve of such governments. But if the Muslims themselves would assemble without any connection to the government, there is no reason that Friday prayer should not be considered *wājib* (obligatory). If we investigate the jurisprudential sources of Friday prayer, we see its similarity to the issue of *jihād.* Our Imams would question for what purpose one should wage *jihād.* For the purpose of having more booty? For the purpose of giving Harun al-Rashid[39] more means of indulgence? So that instead of one thousand female singers, one might have five thousand? Such "Islam" is not desired.

When 'Umar ibn 'Abdul 'Aziz[40] became caliph and wanted to conduct some reforms and to cut off the hands of thieves and looters, opposition arose. From somewhere in Turkistan, the governor wrote to him, "People are converting to Islam, group by group, so they will not have to pay the *jizyah.* Please permit us to refuse their conversion, so that we can collect this tax from them." Umar ibn Abdul Aziz sent his agent there with the instruction to hit the head of the governor with a whip. He sent a letter saying, "God Almighty has appointed Muhammad, peace be upon him, as a guide to the people. He did not appoint him as a tax-collector." It was written from Egypt, "The Coptics have been converting to Islam in order to avoid paying the poll-tax. Please let us circumcise them. The ones who refuse the circumcision should pay the poll-tax." The caliph sent his agent with a letter saying, "God Almighty appointed Muhammad as *khātam* (seal of the prophets); he did not appoint him as *khātin* (circumcisor)! You blankety-blank fellow!" This is the character that Muslim conquests had taken.

Because of this characteristic, Muslims were not even spared. One Muslim nation would be taken, stolen, and consumed. This is why our Imams emphasized *imāmun ʿādilun* or *sulṭānun ʿādilun*. Some experts of jurisprudence have mistaken the term *"imāmun ādilun"* for *"imamun masūmun"* (infallible imams). There is a difference between *ʿadālat* (justice) and *ʿiṣmat* (infallibility). To be more precise, every *maʿsūm* is *ʿadil*. Every *ādil* is not necessarily *maʿsūm*. Thus if we see a just individual ruling Muslims, *jihād* is required on all of us. This is a topic in itself. I demand that great scholars and orators investigate this matter. In a true religion in which there are systematic laws and regulations, one cannot do everything one chooses. They have drained our religion of its vitality.

Let me tell you an historical account I have just recalled. The fourth Imam, al-Sajjad[41], is going to *Ḥajj* pilgrimage. A fastidious fellow, Abbad Basri, after greeting him, states, "You left behind the difficult task of *jihād* and have undertaken the easy task of *ḥajj,* while the Almighty says,

> Lo! Allah has brought from the believers their lives and their wealth because the Garden will be theirs: they shall fight in the way of God and will slay and be slain. It is a promise which is binding on Him in the Torah and the Gospel and the Qur'an. Who fulfills His covenant better than God? Rejoice then in your bargain that you have made, for that is the supreme triumph. (9:111).

Our Imam politely asked him to complete the *āyah,* because indeed it does not end right there. Thus he recited:

> (Triumphant) are those who turn repentant (to God), those who serve (Him), those who praise (Him), those who fast, those who bow down, those who fall prostrate (in worship), those who enjoin the right and forbid the wrong and those who keep the limits (ordained) by God
> — And give glad tidings to the believers. (9:112).

Thus the condition of *jihād* is that the *mujāhid* (participant in *jihād*) must first be repentant for his sins. He must worship God and leave behind his material possessions. He must genuflect and prostrate himself unto God. He must enjoin good deeds and proscribe evil deeds. He must be a man who guards divine ordinances. The fourth Imam, peace be upon him, told Abbad, "If you see people with these characteristics, then *jihād* alongside them is superior to *ḥajj.*" *Jihād* with whom and for whom? Such was the question at the time of our Imams. One has to properly understand the logic of the language of these Imams concerning the issue of *jihād.* Did they really mean that Muslims must be cut off from their defensive power? Should they become lowly and helpless? Or did they mean that one should not get oneself killed without sufficient reason? When truth was distinguished from fallacy, when the person in charge of *jihād* was known and the inevitable result of *jihād* became clear, when intentions became pure and channeled *fī sabīl Allāh,* people had to rise for *jihād.*

As much as Islam has emphasized *jihād* and warfare, it has also valued human life. One is not to get himself killed in emotionalism due to someone's agitation or to those "ism's" that they make today: "Sir, come and defend your country on the basis of your national feeling." For what? So that a bunch of thieves and looters can ransack the land? Am I crazy? But if it is said, "Do it for God, do it for truth," I am ready. I will make my chest the shield. But for such and such material-"ism"? This is sheer madness. The wise men of the world, the most superior of whom are under the command of Islam, have to do such things for truth and for the way of God. These are the ways which have been established, and they will be with us forever.

The following are the final words of Husayn[42] in his last days upon entering Karbala: (Abu Mikhnaf al-Tabari[43] has narrated this from Uqbat ibn Abi al-Ayzarat, and Majlisi narrates it from al-Manaqib[44]). I apologize for the length of my speech; I myself am tired, too. (I am not sure whether or not what I am about to narrate will be digestible for some people.) In one of the caravan stations, apparently that of Baydah, in which the army of Hurr [ibn Yazid al-Riyahi][45] was present, the Imam paused and spoke these words, "Oh you people, the Apostle of God, peace and greetings be upon him, said ..." The Imam narrated from the Apostle of God, and such was the manner of the Imams when they spoke to an audience composed of non-Shi'ite elements as well as Shi'ites. If the audience were only composed of Shi'ites, they would speak on their own authority, without necessarily quoting the Apostle. Husayn continues:

"... Oh people! This is from the Apostle of God, who said,
    'If anyone notices a ruthless sultan encroaching upon

God's boundary, breaking His covenants, opposing the traditions of the Prophet, and behaving indecently among the people, one must stand in opposition to him, by action and word. Otherwise it is God's right to take him to his proper place. One must first advise him, and if this fails, must use force. Whoever endorses such sultan's actions through silence, God will take him to hell as an accomplice. O people! Watch and beware that they (this government and its followers) have chosen obedience to Satan, have forsaken God's obedience, have manifested corruption, have abrogated God's ordinances, have appropriated public funds, have permitted what God has prohibited and have prohibited what God has permitted. If all Muslims have chosen silence, I am the first responsible to alter this situation. You wrote to me and I received your letter and your message. Your representatives came to me. You made a covenant to help me and not to leave me alone. If you remain steadfast in your commitment and pact, you will have become mature. I am Husayn, son of Ali and Fatimah, the daughter of the Prophet. My life is with your lives and my family is with your families.[46]

[By the last portion of this speech, Husayn means to say:] "We do not see ourselves separate from you and expect no special treatment. We are with the people, and whatever is for the people is for us. Whatever is for us is for the people. We are all one. We do not desire to be exalted as rulers. We are one, like any other individual. Our family is like any other family." Wasn't this attitude shown in practice in the few years of Ali's government? If someone would see Ali on the street or in the market-place, they would not recognize him as being different from a common man. Was his house different from any typical house? Was his wife or daughter treated as special? This is the pattern we have to follow. This is the pattern of Islamic government and of the Islamic governor. This is not the rule of one person. This is the rule of God.

Radically speaking, there is no *ḥukūmat* (government) in Islam. *In al-hukmū illā li-Allāh.*[47] (The rule belongs to no one except God.) Government belongs to God, the Apostle, and the Imam. After the

Imam, it is the *mujtahid*[48] and then the masses of Muslims who are all
the executive power of divine law. It is for this reason that Husayn
says, "My life is with your lives, and my family is with your families."
[He means to say:] "Do not think that I want to sacrifice others in
order to save myself and my family." The difference between Ali and
Muawiyah was this indeed, that Muawiyah would sit behind the
battle-fronts, leaning on pillows and sitting on soft cushions. In front
of him were all sorts of edible delicacies. He would eat and laugh. The
poor people had to go and confront the swords. He would tell them,
"Go and get killed." Ali, on the other hand, would command for
jihād, and he himself would be in the front row of the battle.

Let us imagine the battlefield of Siffayn.[49] We see Muawiyah
sitting in his special place, heartily laughing at the people, thinking to
himself, "How wonderfully am I playing with these folks. Using lies,
emotionalism, and false propaganda, I am decimating them in order
to rule over them." In contrast, Ali, when he commands in battle, is
the first to step ahead. This is the meaning of "My life is with your life
and my family is with your families."

Husayn continues, "... If you have broken your covenant, if you
feel regret for having made such a covenant with me, such is not
unexpected from you. You did so with my father, my brother, and
the son of my paternal uncle, Muslim.[50] Poor is the one who relies on
your covenant. If you do not fulfill your promise, you have denied
yourself intellectual growth, but you have not harmed us. '... So
whoever breaks his oath, breaks it only to his own harm ...' (48:10).
Soon God will make me needless of you, and he will place me in the
vicinity of his mercy."

In *Biḥār al-Anwār,*[51] it is narrated from *Manāqib:*[52] "When Hurr
ibn Yazid, by the command of Ubayd Allah,[53] halted Husayn in the
desert of Karbala, confronting him with one thousand horsemen,
Husayn picked up pen and paper and wrote a message to the Shi'ite
nobles and leaders of Kufah, (which I paraphrase): "This is a letter
from Husayn ibn Ali to Sulayman ibn Surad, Musayyib ibn
Najabah, Rifa'ah ibn Shaddad, Abdullah ibn Walin, and the other
believers.[54] He wrote to the Shi'ite leaders who were either in prison
or in exile and were unable to be present to help him. Notice the
locution "you know" in this letter, indicating the unquestionability of
the issue. The [important part of the] letter begins as follows:

You know the Apostle of God said, "If anyone notices a ruthless sultan encroaching upon God's boundary, breaking his covenants, opposing the traditions of the Prophet, and behaving indecently among the people, one must stand in opposition to him, by action and word. Otherwise it is God's right to take him to his proper place. Beware that they (this government and its followers) have chosen obedience to Satan, have forsaken obedience to God, have manifested corruption, have abrogated God's ordinances, have expropriated public funds, have permitted what God has prohibited and have prohibited what God has permitted. I am primarily responsible to alter this situation. You wrote to me and I received your letter and your message. Your representatives came to me. You made a covenant to help me and promised not to abandon me. If you remain steadfast in your commitment and pact, you will be shown to have become mature. I am Husayn, son of Ali and Fatimah, the daughter of the Prophet. My life is with your lives and my family is with your families. For you there is a pattern in me. If you do not [remain steadfast], and you break your covenant, and annul your acceptance of my leadership, by my soul, this would come as no surprise. You did the same to my father, to my brother, and to the son of my paternal uncle, Muslim ibn 'Aqil.[50] The loser is the one who relies on you. You have ruined your own fortune. "... So whoever breaks his oath, breaks it only against his own self..." (48:10).[55]

Perhaps Husayn quoted the entire sermon for the people of Kufah in this letter.

A discussion of *jihād* cannot be complete without an elaboration of the meaning of *shahīd*, which is in itself a great topic. There is not much time left. In short, anyone who has understood this truth and divine goal and has stood for it, sacrificing his life, is called *"shahīd"* in the terminology of the Qur'an and jurisprudence. The *shahīd* is the one who has experienced the *shuhūd* (vision) of truth. The sacrifice of his own life is not based on illusion or agitation of his emotions. He has seen the truth and the goal. That is why he has chosen to wallow in the blood and the dust. Such a person does so with the intention of intimacy with God, not on the basis of fantasies and personal desires. He is above these worldly matters. He has understood the value of truth in a deserved way. This is why he annihilates himself, like a drop in the ocean of truth. This is the true meaning of the esoteric term *"fanā fī Allah"* (self-annihilation in God). *Fanā* is not what the Sufi does in the *khānaqāh,*[56] shouting "Hu! Hu!" and then imagining that he has reached God. The real meaning of *"fana"* is exhibited in the following poem:

From head to toe, God's light you'll radiate,
If in His cause, you self-annihilate!

If a person has reached the stage of readiness for self-annihilation through the vision of truth, for the sake of establishing truth, his title is *shahīd*. Thus one cannot call everyone *"shahīd."* If someone mistakenly or for a worldly and illusive cause gets killed, he has lost both worlds, this and the hereafter. A *shahīd* is the one who understands religion, knows his God, and believes in the hereafter as well as in eternal life. He must realize the goal. Then because he has seen the truth, he has no fear of death. Death is easy for him. Some Sufis argue that in prayer, one has to consider one's *quṭb,*[57] because the *quṭb* is the manifestation (of God); and because man is a physical material being, he cannot perceive the absolute except via manifestations. This is a wrong notion. Of course one can perceive the absolute. [He can do so gradually and by breaking the boundaries.] In our prayer, we recite: "You alone we worship; you alone we ask for help. Show us the straight path, the path of those whom you have given property? Power? [No.] Here is another *ayāh:* to whom you have given blessings of such-and-such. The ones to whom you have given property? Power? (No.) Here is another *ayah*: "Whoever obeys God and the messenger, they are among those whom God has favored, of the prophets, the saints, the martyrs, and the righteous. They are the best of company!" (4:69)

Al-shuhadā (pl. of *shahīd*), that is to say, the ones who die in the cause of God, have a great status. *Ṣāliḥūn* (the righteous) are those who follow them. There are altogether four groups upon whom God has completed his blessing. Those who obey God are one of these. Because they have experienced an internal revolution and have envisioned the truth, the *shuhadā,* once martyred, have been guaranteed the sure gift of eternity by God.

Aren't you surprised? A group of people in one corner of the world assembled.[58] The enemy did not allow their voices to be heard. They were besieged, killed, and then mutilated. No one remained from them to being their news to the town. But the system of creation has recorded their names and their deeds. Isn't this a miracle? Isn't this a vision of truth? Isn't it for us to ponder upon? [We even know] the names of their fathers, mothers, wives, and horses; [and we even know] their utterances. Everything has remained. From where has all this reached us and why have these men remained in history? It is because through self-annihilation, they travelled to eternity. The supreme movement toward perfection is based upon this principle: vegetation is eaten by the lamb; it changes into flesh and bone. Man eats the flesh of the lamb; the flesh turns into thought, energy, and faith — a chain of sacrifice toward evolution. [As Rumi[59] has put it]:

> From the inanimate I died and I became vegetation,
> From vegetation I died and I became an animal,
> From an animal I died and I became human.
> I am not afraid of death; death has never made me lesser.
> Once more I shall die as a human being,
> And I shall fly as an angel;
> Then once again I shall fly from the angelic,
> And I will become something unimaginable.
> I will become nothing, nothing, because the harp
> Tells me: "Unto Him we shall return."

[As if the companions of Husayn] had grown wings on the day of Ashura,[60] as if their bodies had become too small for their spirits, one of them would beg Husayn to permit him to go to the battle field earlier than the others. Another would beg for a similar honor, saying, "My chest has contracted due to worldly life." What kind of people were they? They had wives, children, kin, and businesses as well. Zuhayr ibn Qayn al-Bijili[40] was a man who, until a few days before, having been effected by the propaganda of the government of Muawiyah, was seeking blood-revenge for Uthman[62] and had contempt for Ali and his family. Suddenly, on the way (to Karbala) he made a decision to join the camp of Husayn. What wonderful words were exchanged between them! What did he say and what did he hear? It was as if lightning destroyed all his worldly attachments.

One hour ago Zuhayr had cows, lambs, and cattle. He was attached to his tribe and to his property. Now he has realized himself. He has experienced transfiguration.

Why are we all so depressed? Because we don't have any goal in life; because we have no goal in our life, we think that what counts is money and power obtained by any means. Because we don't get what we want, we are bitter. We are depressed. The businessman or beaurocrat goes home in the afternoon so shattered and depressed that he does not wish to talk to his family. Why? Because he has not achieved what he had planned to do. What did he want? If he is a military man, he is depressed because he did not receive the promotion that his colleagues did. If he is a businessman, he is depressed because his income is not as great as he had expected. The economy is bad and everyone is depressed! We are depressed because we are confined to this base world. The *shahīd* is the one who operates above this lowly world. The believer is the same. Zuhayr was depressed because he was a skeptic. He did not know the meaning of life. He didn't know who right, Ali or Muawiyah. He was under an illusion. Worldly wishes and attachments had surrounded him. With a sudden flash of lightning, the illusion went away. The worldly attachments were cut off and he became a *shahīd* even before he became a martyr. Life became easy for him. Once he had envisioned the truth, nothing else was important. Life and death were the same to him. He told his wife, Bint Amrw,[63] "Farewell. I am finished. You go and take care of the camels, cattle, and lambs. I give everything to you. I have found what I wanted." When Truth revealed itself, nothing else had any value. It was the night before Ashura. Then there came the morning of Ashura, and then the afternoon. Blood was dripping from his body, and he was very thirsty. He came to say 'farewell' to Husayn by tapping on his shoulder and saying, "May my life be sacrificed for you, you guided one, you guide. You are my savior. You are my liberator. You freed me from this deceptive world." While blood was pouring out of his wounds, he said, "I am no longer worried." His wife is becoming a widow, his children orphans, and he says, "I am no longer worried." This is power! Then he chants:

> Today I shall meet your grandfather,
> And the wonderful Ali, with whom God was pleased.

[He is saying,] "The distance between me and them will vanish as soon as my soul leaves my body." He is so certain about the eternity of truth and the secret of humanity. [He says], "I am going to meet your brother and your father." Then he falls in front of Husayn and dies. It is famous that his wife went to Kufah, waiting for her husband to return. The news reached her that they had all been killed with Husayn. She gave a shroud to her slave and ordered him to go and bury her husband. The slave came back without having done so. When he was asked, he replied that he had been unable to do it because he saw the bodies of the children of the Prophet mutilated in the middle of the sand and the blood of the warm desert of Karbala.

There is no change nor power except by God, the Sublime, the Great. "God is sufficient for us! Most excellent is He in whom we trust!" (3:173).

God Almighty, we ask You by your Great and Sublime Name, ALLAH.

God Almighty, lighten our hearts with the light of faith and truth. Strengthen our steps in the way of the good of the Muslim nations. Uproot the wicked tree of suspicion from among the Muslims. God Almighty, guide us to the straight path. Lord, guide our power to the path of happiness and prosperity. God Almighty, forgive our deceased ones. Grant assistance and success to anyone who defends the dignity of the Muslims by any means and supports the Muslims. Those who by any means commit treason against the Muslims and the Muslim world, may the Almighty cleanse the world of their existence. Oh Lord, grant triumph to our Algerian Muslim brothers[64] and save them from the claws of oppression of these blood-thirsty and criminal pseudo-civilized ones. Lord, awaken the Muslim world, particularly this Islamic country. Fortify our ranks. God Almighty, Lord, grant us death as pure Muslims. Make assemblies such as this one a means for good in this world and in the hereafter.

May the peace, mercy, and blessings of Allah be upon you all.

Notes

1. This piece is one of the speeches delivered by Ayatullah Taleqani which was delivered impromptu to the public in Tehran. From the pulpit where he spoke, a poor and somewhat incomplete cassette recording was made. The speech was then transformed into written text and was published the same year. The Persian text has been published twice outside Iran, in 1976 by the Book Distribution Center of Houston, Texas, and in 1978 by Islamic Book Services, London. A valuable, yet incomplete translation was prepared in 1982 by my friend and colleague, Dr. Fatollah Marjani, which I have used with his consent as an aid to the present translation. A great deal of credit is due to him, particularly since he was the first to faithfully undertake this challenge.

In the same year a complete and eloquent translation by R. Campbell, edited by Hamid Algar, appeared in *Society and Economics in Islam: Writings and Declarations of Ayatollah Sayyed Mahmud Taleghani* published by Mizan Press. Unfortunately, this translation contains a number of errors which have been corrected in the present version. This translation has been prepared from the cassette recording, using the Persian transcription as an aid. Brackets [...] are used herein to indicate additions by the translator. Parentheses (...) are used to clarify ambiguities of Arabic words and locutions. Braces [...] are used to indicate text which is not recorded on the tape, but which has been reliably reconstructed in the Persian transcription.

This translation is dedicated to the memory of my mother.

M.A.

2. Much in this salutation is formulaic. According to Islamic belief, there will be no prophets after Muhammad, that is, as it is put in the Qur'an (33:40), Muhammad is the seal of the prophets. According to Shi'ite orthodoxy, the Prophet of Islam was succeeded by twelve infallible leaders or *imāms*. The phrase "I seek refuge in God from the cursed Satan" is an ejaculation uttered before one recites the Qur'an.

3. (4:76). Those who have translated the Qur'an into English have varied concerning the interpretation of the term *tāghūt*. J. M. Rodwell uses the word untranslated. J. Dawood, and A. J. Arberry have translated it as "idols." M. H. Shakir has used another Arabic term, *"Shaytān"* (Satan). Yusuf Ali has chosen the term "evil." Hashim Amir-Ali translates it as "devil."

Arthur Jeffery, in *The Foreign Vocabulary of the Qur'an* (Baroda: Oriental Institute, 1938), pp. 202f., claims that *"tāghūt"* came into the Arabic from an Ethiopic term used to designate idols. A. Ben-Shemesh notes in his translation, *The Noble Quran* (Tel Aviv: Massada, 1979), p. 44, that *"taghūt"* corresponds to the Hebrew *"ta'uth"* mentioned in the Talmud and Midrash.

Mahmoud M. Ayoub, in *The Qur'an and its Interpreters* Vol. 1 (Albany: State University of New York Press, 1984), p. 255 cites differences among Muslim experts of *tafsir*:

> Commentators have differed regarding the meaning of the *tāghūt* (idols). This word is usually coupled with the word *al-jibt*. Tabari interprets the word *tāghūt* to mean satans, idols, or soothsayers *(kuhhān)* to whom satans come and reveal lies and wickedness. Tabari takes the word in its general sense to mean all of these and anything else that may be worshipped instead of God ... Ibn Kathir reports on the authority of 'Umar ibn al Khattab that *al-jibt* is sorcery and *taghut* is Satan ... Zamakhshari explains *tāghūt* as either Satan or idols ... Shawkani, citing al-Jawhari, a well-known lexicographer, says that *"tāghūt* is the soothsayer, Satan, or every leader into error." Shawkani

adds idols as well ... Tabarsi relates on the authority of the sixth imam
that *ṭāghūt* is Satan. He concludes, "It is intended that anyone who
rejects faith by opposing God's command" is *ṭāghūt* ...

Taleqani's interpretation is supported by Raghib al-Isfahani's *Mufradāt al-Qur'ān*,
a reliable Qur'anic lexicon. In the lexicon, *Al-Munjid* (Beirut: Dar al-Mashirg, n.d.)
the following entry is given: "*al-taghiyah: al-jabbar al mutakabbir*, (the egotistical
despot')" and it is mentioned that "despot" was a title used by the Byzantine emperors.
The lexicon also notes that "*ṭāghūt*" may be used for any assailant or aggressor, for the
sources of misguidance, or for the devil *(al-shayṭan)* which turns one away from
righteousness.

The popular Pakistani scholar and activist, S. Abul a'la Maududi, provides
essentially the same discussion of *ṭāghūt* as does Taleqani in his 1939 address *Jihad in
Islam* (Lahore: Islamic Publications, Ltd., 1980), p. 9.

4. The poem was written by Abu Muhammad Ilyas ibn Yusuf ibn Zaki (1140-1203
C.E.), known as Nezami, one of the greatest poets of Iran. His famous book, *Khamsah*
contains twenty-eight thousand couplets.

5. It is not clear which term Taleqani has in mind. He uses the Arabic *mustabidd*,
"self-willed." "Despot," "dictator," and "tyrant" are possibilities. For Plato and
Aristotle, the despot is one whose power is unlimited by law. While it is possible for a
despot to use his absolute rule benevolently, the tyrant is never benevolent. The
subjects of a tyrant are considered to be no better off than slaves. In Plato's *Gorgias* it
is argued that it is better to suffer than to do injustice, and that the tyrant is therefore
the unhappiest of men.

6. (4:60).

7. It appears eight times, once in each of the following *āyāt*: 2:256, 2:257, 4:51, 4:60,
4:76, 5:60, 16:36, and 39:17.

8. *Āyat al-Kursi*, the *āyah* of the Throne, is *ayat* 255-257 of *sura* 2. In Arberry's
translation this reads as follows, with "*ṭāghūt*" substituted for Arberry's "idols":

God
there is no god but He, the
Living, the Everlasting.
Slumber seizes Him not, neither sleep;
to Him belongs
all that is in the heavens and the earth.
Who is there that shall intercede with Him
save by His leave?
He knows what lies before them
and what is after them,
and they comprehend not anything of His knowledge
save such as He wills.
His Throne comprises the heavens and earth;
the preserving of them oppresses Him not;
He is the All-high, the All-glorious. (255)

> No compulsion is there in religion.
> Rectitude has become clear from error.
> So whosoever disbelieves in *taghut*
> and believes in God, has laid hold of
> the most firm handle, unbreaking; God is
> All-hearing, All-knowing.
>
> God is the Protector of the believers;
> He brings them forth from the shadows
> into the light.
> And the unbelievers — their protectors are
> *taghut*, that bring them forth from the light
> into the shadows;
> those are the inhabitants of the Fire,
> therein dwelling forever.

9. Cf. (33:6).

10. The day of Ghadir is the eighteenth of the month of *Dhul-Hajjah,* on which date, by the command of God, the Apostle of Islam nominated Ali to succeed him. For reference to the importance of this event and a list of historical sources relevant to it, refer to notes 6 and 7 of Allamah Sayyid Muhammad Husayn Tabatabai's *Shi'ite Islam,* ed. and trans. by Sayyid Husayn Nasr (Houston: Free Islamic Literature, Inc., 1979). Also see the report of the incident in Shaykh al-Mufid, *Kitāb Al-Irshād,* tr. I. K. A. Howard (London: Muhammadi Trust, 1981), p. 123 ff. Note that there is an error in Campbell's translation *(Society and Economics in Islam,* pp. 81-82). It is the Prophet Muhammad who makes the speech at Ghadir Khum, not Ali.

11. Cf. Matthew 5:39 and Luke 6:27-29. Of course, it is only a minority of Christian sects which have taken the Sermon on the Mount to imply pacifism.

12. Very few sects, such as the Shakers, have required the celibacy of all those who would enter heaven. However, there are no celibate religious orders in Islam, as there are in Catholicism. Marriage with at least a prescribed minimum amount of sexual intercourse is in fact required according to the jurisprudents, for those who are physically and economically capable of it.

13. (57:27).

14. (2:193).

15. (8:39).

16. Taleqani imagines the meeting of the representative of the Muslim army with Rustam Farrukhzad. In 637, during the caliphate of Umar, Rustam was killed and his army defeated in the battle of Qadisiyyah.

17. Cf. (9:40).

18. Thomas Carlyle (1795-1881). The exact words of Carlyle to which Taleqani refers

are from *On Heroes, Hero-Worship, and the Heroic in History.* ed. Archibald MacMechan, (Boston: Ginn & Company, 1901), pp. 69-70:

> Much has been said of Mahomet's propagating his Religion by the sword. It is no doubt far nobler what we have to boast of the Christian Religion, that it propagated itself peaceably in the way of preaching and conviction. Yet withal, if we take this as an argument of the truth or falsehood of a religion, there is a radical mistake in it. The sword indeed: but where will you get your sword! Every new opinion, at its starting, is precisely in a *minority of one.* In one man's head alone, there it dwells as yet. One man alone of the whole world believes it; there is one man against all men. That *he* take a sword, and try to propagate with that, will do little for him. You must first get your sword! On the whole, a thing will propagate itself as it can. We do not find, of the Christian Religion either, that it always disdained the sword, when once it had got one. Charlemagne's conversion of the Saxons was not by preaching. I care little about the sword: I will allow a thing to struggle for itself in this world, with any sword or tongue or implement it has, or can lay hold of. We will let it preach, and pamphleteer, and fight, and to the uttermost bestir itself, and do, beak and claws, whatsoever is in it; very sure that it will, in the long-run, conquer nothing which does not deserve to be conquered. What is better than itself, it cannot put away, but only what is worse. In this great Duel, Nature herself is umpire, and can do no wrong: the thing which is deepest rooted in Nature, what we call *truest,* that thing and not the other will be found growing at last.

19. Cf. (2:193), (8:39).

20. Cambell's translation of this passage contains an error due to a mistake in the transcription. The oral sermon uses the word *"najangand"* (should they not fight), while the transcription has *"bejangand"* (should they fight).

21. "Oh mankind, We have created you as male and female, and have made you nations and tribes so that you may know one another. Certainly the noblest of you, in the sight of God, is the most pious." (49:13).

22. This makes reference to the Shu'ubiyah, a literary movement of the third century (A.H.), led by men such as Abu 'Ubaydah (of Persian Jewish origin — d.c. 825), who pointed out how uncouth the tribal Arabs had often been, and how poorly some Arabs had treated the Prophet of Islam. Cf. H. A. R. Gibb, "The Social Significance of the Shu'ubiyah," in *Studies on the Civilization of Islam,* ed. Stanford Shaw and William Polk (Boston: Beacon Press, 1962).

23. It is famous among Iranians that during the Muslim conquest of the Persian Empire, even in the capital, Tisfun, masses of people distributed bread and dates among the Muslim warriors, who had come to overthrow the Sassanid monarchy.

24. Cf. Martyr Murtada Muttahhari, *Khadamāt-e-Mutaqābel-e-Islām va Īrān* (Mutual Contributions of Islam and Iran), (Tehran: Sherkat-e-Enteshar, 1970), (Persian), an English translation by Mehdi Abedi is scheduled to be published by IRIS in 1987.

25. The traditional meaning of *"risālat"* is "messengership, message," but Taleqani interprets it also to mean "freedom."

26. Abul Qasim Najm al Din, better known as ''Al-Muhaqqiq al Hilli'' or ''Al-Muhaqqiq al Awwal'' (602/ 1205-676/ 1277). It is his student and successor, Jamal al Din Abu Mansur Hasan ibn Yusuf ibn Mutahhar (d. 726/ 1325), who is known as "Allamah Hilli." The former scholar first wrote the monumental treatises of Shi'ite jurisprudence, *Sharāyiʻal Islām* and *Al-Nafiʻfī Mukhtaṣar al Sharāyi,ʻ*known as *"Al-Mukhtaṣar al Nāfiʻ"* Several pages of the former work concerning *jihād* and the status of the dhimmis have been translated by John Alden Williams and are included in his *Themes of Islamic Civilization,* (Berkeley: University of California Press, 1982), pp. 268-272.

27. For a modern treatment of the issue of protected minorities, see Ayatullah Khumayni's *Tahrir al-Wasilah,* Vol. 2, pp. 497-507.

28. At the time this sermon was read, Israel had recently opened an "informal" embassy in Tehran.

29. As an offspring of the Babi movement in Iran, Baha'ism was established by Mirza Husayn Ali Nuri (1817-1892), known as Bahaullah, and then promulgated by his eldest son, Abbas Effendi (1844-1921). The rumor was wide-spread that Baha'is had infiltrated all levels of the Iranian government, despite their profession of political non-involvement. The link between them and international Zionism is normally substantiated by the fact that their holy city, Haifa, is in Israel. According to Hamid Algar, in his footnote 15, p. 106, in *Society and Economics in Islam,* "The relevant documents are due to be published in Iran. There is also a mass of evidence pointing to the high-level involvement of numerous Baha'is in the administrative and repressive apparatus of the Shah's regime." For the historical background of the campaign against the Baha'is by the ulama see Shahrough Akhavi, *Religion and Politics in Contemporary Iran,* (Albany: SUNY Press, 1980), p. 76 ff.

30. At an Islamic conference held in 1961 in Jerusalem, to which Taleqani had been a representative, it was revealed that the government of the Shah had supported Israel in the Arab-Israeli dispute.

31. One sentence is missing, because the first side of the tape ended here.

32. Muawiyah ibn Abi Sufyan (r. 661-680 C.E.) is the founder of the Umayyad dynasty, the first monarchy established in the name of Islam. The capital was Damascus. Before his reign, he had been governor of Syria for ten years (634-644) under the reign of Umar, and for twelve years (644-656) under Uthman. He was expelled from his position of governor by Imam Ali. Muawiyah refused to step down and waged war against Ali (Siffayn, 658). After the martyrdom of Ali, he usurped the leadership of the Islamic world.

33. Yazid ibn Muawiyah (r. 680-683 C.E.) was the second Caliph of the Umayyad dynasty. Imam Husayn ibn Ali refused to approve his rule, and the conflict led to the battle of Karbala in 680 which has become a symbol of the anti-tyrannical movement in Shi'ite history, particularly in revolutionary Iran.

34. Abdul Malik ibn Marwan was the fifth Umayyad Caliph (r. 685-705 C.E.).

35. Sulayman ibn Abdul Malik was the seventh Umayyad Caliph (r. 715-717 C.E.).

36. The Abbasid dynasty (750-1258 C.E.) followed the Umayyad dynasty. They were descendents of Abbas, the uncle of Prophet Muhammad. They came to power with the help of the Iranian Abu Muslim al-Khurasani, and they were finally overthrown by the Mongol king Halaku Khan.

37. Walid ibn Abdul Malik (r. 705-715 C.E.) was the sixth Umayyad caliph.

38. Al-Mutawakkil (r. 847-861 C.E.), son of al-Mutasam, was the tenth Abbasid Caliph. He moved his capital from Baghdad to Damascus. His death signaled the decline of the Abbasids.
   In the two sermons of the Friday prayer, the sermonist is required to mention the name of the supreme religious authority. During the Umayyad and Abbasid dynasties, it was the name of the caliph which was to be mentioned. Thus those who were silently present would technically affirm, by their presence, the legitimacy of the usurping caliph. For this reason, the Shi'ite Imams, in some instances, boycotted the sham Friday prayer, which was serving the opposite of its rightful function.

39. Harun al-Rashid (r. 787-809 C.E.), son of al-Mahdi, was the fifth Abbasid Caliph. He came to power after his brother, al-Hadi, (r. 785-786). He died in Tus, Iran.

40. Umar ibn Abdul Aziz ibn Marwan (683-720 C.E.), the eighth Umayyad caliph, reigned from 717 until his death. He is famous for his piety, justice, and knowledge of jurisprudence. He is known as Umar II.

41. Ali ibn al-Husayn, al-Sajjad, is the fourth Imam of the Shi'ites (38/658-95/713) and the only male survivor of the battle of Karbala. The collection of his prayers, a masterpiece of eloquence and devotion, has been translated by Sayyid Ahmad Muhani as Imam Zain al-Abidin's *Al-Sahifah Al-Sajjādiyyah,* (Tehran: Islamic Propagation Organization, 1984).
   For the sources of this narration, refer to Al-Hurr al Amili, *Wasa'il al-Shi'ah,* Vol. XI, pp. 232-4; al-Kulayni, *Al-Kafi,* Vol. III, p. 333; al-Tabarsi, *Al-Ihtijaj,* p. 171; *Tafsir al-Qummi,* p. 281; al-Tusi, *Tahdhib,* Vol. II, p.45.

42. Husayn (4/626-61/680) is the third Shi'ite Imam.

43. Lut ibn Yahya al-Tabari, was a famous historian (d. 158/774).

44. *Al-Manāqib* was written by Rashid al Din abu Ja'far Muhammad ibn Ali (d. 588/1192). There are also books with the same title by Khawarazmi and others. We have not been able to determine to which of these Taleqani refers here.

45. Al-Hurr ibn Yazid ibn Najiyah ibn Qanab ibn Hurr al-Tamimi al-Riyahi was a well-known nobleman of Kufah and leader of its cavalry who joined Husayn and was killed with him. As an experienced warrior, he was selected by Ibn Ziyad, Yazid's commander-in-chief, to command a contingent against Husayn. He was the one who obstructed Husayn's way near Kufah. He was under the assumption that Husayn was

not going to be killed. When he discovered Yazid's decision to martyr Husayn, he joined Husayn's camp and he was martyred.

46. Al-Tabari, Vol. IV, pp. 304-5; ibn Athir, *Al-Kāmil,* Vol. III, p. 280; Muhsin al-Amin, *A'yān al-Shī'ah,* Vol. IV, part one, pp. 228-9.

47. Cf. (6:57), (12:40), (12:67) and similarly, (6:62), (28:70, (28:82) and (40:12).

48. A *mujtahid* is an expert in jurisprudence, one who is sufficiently qualified to perform *ijtihad,* to deduce rulings on the basis of the Qur'an and *sunnah.* Cf. Juan R. Cole, "Imami Jurisprudence and the Role of the Ulama: Mortaza Ansari on Emulating the Supreme Exemplar" in *Religion and Politics in Iran,* ed. Nikkie R. Keddie (New Haven: Yale University Press, 1983), pp. 33-46.

49. Siffayn (or Siffin) is a place near the Euphrates River, close to the Syrian border. At this place, in 657 C.E., there was a famous battle between Imam Ali and Muawiyah. In this battle, Muawiyah attempted to defeat Ali politically by treachery referred to as *"hakamiyah."* When it appeared as if he would lose the battle, Muawiyah ordered his men to hoist copies of the Qur'an on their lances in an apparent appeal to Muslim unity. This led to an arbitration which was imposed on Ali at which he was not ably represented.

50. Muslim ibn Aqil ibn Abitalib, the deputy of Husayn to Kufah, was martyred in Kufah before the battle of Karbala.

51. *Bihār al-Anwār,* by Muhammad Baqir al-Majlisi (1627-1700 C.E.) is an encyclopedia of Shi'ite theology, containing more than one hundred volumes.

52. Cf. fn. 44.

53. Ubayd Allah ibn Ziyad was governor of Iraq at the time of the battle of Karbala.

54. Sulayman ibn Surad al-Khuza'i, a leading member of the Kufan Shi'ah, died leading a revolt to avenge the blood of Husayn in 65/683. Al-Musayib ibn Najabah, Rifa'ah ibn Shaddad al-Bajali, and Abdullah ibn Walin were also leading Kufan Shi'ites, the latter being a messenger of Husayn. Indeed these men had written the following letter to Husayn:

> In the Name of God, the Merciful, the Compassionate.
> To al-Husayn B. Ali, peace be upon him,
> From Sulayman b. Surad, al-Musayyib b. Najaba, Rifa'a b.
> Shaddad al-Bajali, Habib b. Muzahir, and the believers and
> Muslims of his Shi'ah among the Kufans.
> Greetings, we praise God before you, other than whom there is no deity.
> Praise be to God Who has broken your enemy, the obstinate tyrant who
> had leapt upon this community, stripped it of its authority, plundered
> its *fay'* (booty for distribution) and seized control of it without its
> consent. Then he had killed the choice members of it and had preserved
> the wicked members of it. He had made the property of God a state
> (divided) among its tyrants and wealthy. He was destroyed as Thamud
> were destroyed. (Now) there is no Imam over us. Therefore come;

through you, may your God unite us under truth. Al-Mu'man b. Bashir is in the governor's palace and we do not gather with him for the Friday (service). Nor do we accompany him (out of the mosque) for the Festival service. If we learn that you will come to us, we will drive him away until we pursue him to Syria, if God, the Exalted, wills.

This is quoted by Shaykh al-Mufid in the *Kitab al-Irshād,* (Elmhurst: Tahrike Tarsile Qur'an, 1981), pp. 303-4. What Husayn writes is apparently a reply to this.

55. Ayatullah Taleqani has paraphrased this narration, as it is appropriate for oral speech. In this second reference, it is quoted directly from the sources listed in note 46.

56. A *"khānaqah"* is a Sufi center. The term is Persian, and means, "the house of feeding." It is where the Sufi receives physical and spiritual nourishment.

Fanā is the 'passing away' of consciousness of self, and is contrasted with *baqā,* the 'remaining' consciousness of God. Some sufis have claimed that *fanā* is the ultimate stage of spirituality, while others, like al-Junayd (d. 910 C.E.), have held that there are stages of spiritual development beyond *fana.* Similarities and differences between Sufi *fana* and Buddhist *nirvana* are discussed in R.A. Nicholson, *The Mystics of Islam,* (New York: Schoken Books, 1975), 16-27.

The opposition of the Shi'ite ulama toward Sufism dates from the Safavid period. Modern Shi'ite critics of Sufism deprecate the otherworldliness of Sufism, in contrast to politically activist Shi'ism. However, Shi'ism has not always taken an activist role in politics, and the Sufi orders have sometimes been politically active, e.g. in the Sudan and in Soviet central Asia.

57. A *qutb* or *pir* is a saint or leader of a mystic order. *"Qutb"* is a Persian term for "pole." The most eminent Sufi of the age is considered a pole about which the spiritual world of the adept revolves.

58. The reference here is to the battle of Karbala.

59. The great poet and mystic known in the west as "Rumi" is Mawlawi Jalal al-Din Muhammad al-Balkhi (1207-1273 C.E.). He was born in Balkh in northeastern Iran, studied under his father, travelled a great deal, and was devoted to his master, Shams al-Din Tabrizi. Mawlawi is considered by many as the greatest of the Sufi poets. The Mevlevi dervishes of Turkey consider themselves his followers, but he is revered as a source of Islamic wisdom by members of all Muslim sects. He is the author of the eight volume *Mathnawi,* and other volumes of poems. The passage quoted by Taleqani is from the *Mathnawi* (Vol. III, 11. 3901-07). For other passages which make a similar or related point see the selection by William C. Chittick, *The Sufi Path of Love,* (Albany: SUNY Press, 1983), p. 79ff.

60. Ashura is the tenth of the month of *Muharram.* This day is observed as a commemoration of the battle of Karbala in Shi'ite communities.

61. He was a noble chieftain of this tribe, having great influence in Kufah. He was first attached to Uthman, but once, while returning from *hajj,* he met Husayn. The meeting caused him to become a devoted Shi'ite.

62. Uthman was the third caliph (r. 644-656); he succeeded Umar. He came from the tribe of the Umayyads, who were for a long time enemies of the Prophet of Islam. During his reign, he gave many governmental positions to his relatives, and strengthened the position of Muawiyah. Hodgson's account of the death of Uthman is as follows:

> A group of Arab soldiers, come back from Egypt to claim what they felt were their rights, seem to have been cozened by Uthman's associates into returning home with false assurances of redress; when they discovered their leaders were to be executed instead, they returned mutinously. After a period of general negotiation and counterplotting, in which the non-Umayyad leading families at Medina seem to have been largely neutral, the mutineers broke into Uthman's house and murdered him. (His power like that of Abu Bakr and Umar had rested on pious prestige alone; he did not even have a private bodyguard.) — from Marshall G.S. Hodgson, *The Venture of Islam,* Vol. I. (Chicago: University of Chicago Press, 1974), pp. 213-214.

The followers of Ayishah (a widow of the Prophet) and the followers of Muawiyah accused Ali of responsibility for the assassination , and at the very least for harboring the assassins. Ali claimed innocence of the murder, and ignorance of the murderers.

63. History has recorded the name of his wife as "Daltham, the daughter of Amrw."

64. The Algerian revolution was in progress at the time this sermon was delivered.

Jihad in the Qur'an

The First Lecture
Questions about Jihad

In the Name of God,
The Most Merciful, the Most Compassionate

> Fight against those who have been given the Scripture
> but do not believe in God and the last day, do not forbid
> that which God has forbidden through His messenger,
> and do not follow the religion of truth, until they pay the
> *jizyah* (poll tax) readily, being brought low. (9:29)

This *ayah* of the Qur'an concerns the People of the Book, referring to those non-Muslims who have a tie to one of the heavenly books, such as the Jews, Christians, and perhaps the Zoroastrians.[1]

The *āyah* speaks of war with the People of the Book, but does not command us to fight against the People of the Book per se, but rather against those of them who have no faith in God or the Last Day, who do not adhere to the prohibitions of God, allowing what He has forbidden, and who are not religious in accordance with the religion of truth. It is these People of the Book whom we must fight until they pay the *jizyah* (poll tax). In other words, when they pay the tax and are humble before us, we are to fight them no more.

From the content of this *āyah,* many questions arise which must be answered with the help of other Qur'anic *āyāt* relating to *jihād,* which we will set apart and review.

The first of these questions concerns the exact meaning intended by the words, "Fight against those who ... do not believe in God." Do these words mean that we are to drop everything and start fighting, or is it meant that we should fight them the minute they issue from their territory and violate ours? In the terminology of the learned of Islam, this is an unconditional *ayah* which, if there are similar *ayat* that are conditional, must also be interpreted as conditional.

The term "conditional" is a very important one, and I wish to explain it to you, for otherwise it will be difficult for you to grasp the full meaning of the *āyah* under discussion. Any commandment (even that of a human) can be given in one context with no conditions and then again in another context with conditions attached. In such case we immediately realize that whoever issued that commandment or introduced that law intended the same meaning in both instances. Now, having made this realization, what is the next step? Is it prudent to adhere to the unconditional commandment and assume that the conditional was given only for that special instance? Or should we interpret the unconditional as the conditional, which means adhering to the conditional?

Let me cite a special example. On two separate occasions, for instance, we are given a commandment by someone having authority to command us and whose commandments we respect. One time we are told that we must respect such and such a person, which is an unconditional commandment. Another time he gives the same commandment but modifies it, saying that we must respect that person if he does such and such a thing, like taking part in our meeting. The second time the commandment contains an "if." The commandment is now conditional. The person making the commandment did not simply state that such and such a person is to be respected. He said that "if he takes part in the meeting, he is to be respected." The first commandment had no condition. We were simply told to respect him, and assuming we had ears and could hear his commandment, it would have meant to us that we were to respect that person whether he came to the meeting or whether he was too lazy to bother. But if we also hear the other commandment, we understand that we are to respect the person provided he comes to the meeting, and if he refrains from coming to the meeting, we are not to respect him.

The scholars say that the rule requires us to interpret the unconditional as the conditional, meaning that we must assume the aim of the unconditional to be exactly that of the conditional.

Now, among the unconditional ayat of the Qur'an related to *jihād* is that which was cited initially:

> Fight against those who have been given the Scripture
> but do not believe in God and the last day, do not forbid
> that which God has forbidden through His messenger,
> and do not follow the religion of truth ... (9:29)

In another *āyah* we are told, "Fight in the way of God against those who fight against you..."(2:190) What are the meanings of these *āyāt?*

Do they mean that we must fight against such people, regardless of whether they are about to attack us? Is the commandment unconditional that we must fight them whether they are intending to fight us or not?

There are two possible views. One is that the commandment remains unconditional: "The People of the Book are not Muslims so we are allowed to fight them. We are allowed to fight anyone who is not Muslim until we subdue them. If they are neither Muslim nor People of the Book, we should fight them until either they become Muslim or we kill them. If they are People of the Book, then we should fight until they either become Muslim or agree to pay us tribute."

The other view is that the unconditional must be interpreted as the conditional. Someone with this view would insist that the other Qur'anic *āyāt* concerning the legality of *jihād* should lead us to the conclusion that this ayah is not at all unconditional. Accordingly, the conditions for the legality of *jihād* include the following: that the other side intends to attack us; that it creates a barrier against the call of Islam by negating its freedom and becoming an obstacle to its diffusion, whereas Islam stipulates that such barriers are to be destroyed; or that a group of people are subject to the oppression and tyranny of a group from among themselves, in which case Islam says that we must fight those tyrants so as to deliver the oppressed from tyranny. This duty has been expressed in the Qur'an in the following words: "Why should you not fight for the cause of God and the cause of the *mustad'afīn* (oppressed) ...?" (4:75) Why indeed shouldn't we fight for God and the oppressed men, women and children, subject to torture and tyranny?

This second question is related to the fact that the *ayah* does not fundamentally state that we are to fight with all the People of the Book, but tells us that we should fight only against those who do not believe in God or the last day, who count as permitted that which God has forbidden, and who are not religiuis in accordance with any true religion. The second question explores the real meaning of these stipulations. Does it mean that all the People of the Book — all the Jews, all the Christians, and all the followers of the various sects — lack faith in God, in the last day, in God's ordinances, and in any true religion, such that any one of them who claims to believe in God must be a liar? Is the Qur'an actually saying this in regards to all of them? Should we determine that, since the Christians claim that Jesus is the son of God, they really don't believe in God? Or because the Jews say things about Jacob and the other Prophets which are not in accordance with divine truth, they have no more faith than the Christians? Or that those who say, "God's hand is fettered ..." (5:64) cannot be believers in God along with the rest of the People of the Book?

If we think in these terms, it means we believe that the Qur'an does not recognize any faith in God or in the resurrection other than the faith of Muslims. If we are asked why, we will say that the Qur'an states that the beliefs of the People of the Book are in disorder. A Christian recognizes the existence and even the unity of God, but at the same time, even if he is a learned Christian scholar, he holds some idea about Jesus or the Angel Gabriel that blemishes his belief in divine unity. This is the view of some of the exegetes, that when the Qur'an tells us we must fight against the People of the Book, it means that we are to fight against all the People of the Book, because every one of them lacks valid faith in God, in the resurrection, and in what God has permitted and forbidden. What these commentators believe is that the word "messenger" in this *āyah* refers to the Seal of the Prophets, Muhammad, and that "religion of truth" refers to the religion which mankind today has the duty to accept, rather than a religion which was the duty of people to accept during some particular period of the past.

A different group of exegetes, however, considers that the Qur'an implies that the People of the Book belong to two classes and that some of them really do believe in God, in the last day, and in the laws of God, and we are to leave these alone. We are to fight those People of theBook who are such in name only but who in reality have no valid belief at all and who do not consider forbidden that which God has forbidden, even in their own religion. So it is not with all the People of the Book, but only with a certain group of them, that we are to fight.

The third question relates to the term *jizyah* (poll-tax). We are told to fight them until they pay it or until they accept Islam. There is no doubt that the Qur'an distinguishes between the People of the Book and the polytheists, or *mushrikūn,* those who formally worship idols and have no ties to any divine book. Nowhere in the Qur'an does it say that we are to fight the *mushrikūn* until they pay the *jizyah* and then to cease conflict. This is a clear difference.

This point raises the question of exactly what *jizyah* is. There is debate about the word itself. Some insist that it is not an Arabic word, having no root in Arabic, but has come from the Persian root of *gazyeh,* the name of a tax introduced by Anushirvan[2], a Sassanid king of Persia. This tax, however, was a capitation tax on the people of Persia themselves and not on anyone else and it was collected for war. They claim that the use of the word then spread from Iran to Hirah, a town situated on the site of present day Najaf (in Iraq) and from there it was adopted by the rest of the Arabian peninsula, where it came into common usage.

Others disagree, claiming that, although *jizyah* and *gazyeh* are close, the former is actually an Arabic word from the root *"jaza"* — and this is the view held by most etymologists.[3] The real interest, however, is not in the nature of the word, but in the nature of the essence the word denotes. Is *jizyah* the extortion of "protection money" and *danegeld,* a kind of blackmail? Is Islam telling us to fight until we receive the blackmail payment and then to stop our aggression? A poet has even written:

> We are such that we have taken tribute from emperors,
> Then have even taken their crowns and maces.[4]

If the meaning of *jizyah* is a kind of blackmail, the question arises as to the meaning of the entire commandment. Is this instruction merely a law of brute force? What kind of basis in human rights and justice can it have, if Islam not only gives Muslims permission, but makes it obligatory for them to fight the people of other religions until they either accept Islam or buy the Muslims off?! Both of these alternatives present problems, for the former means imposing Islam on them and the latter means exacting wealth from them. Thus we must conduct a detailed examination to discover if *jizyah* is really blackmail or protection money or if it is something else.

Here we must set aside the meaning of this *āyah* and the questions that arise from it and examine other issues that must be separately analyzed and discussed in preparation.

The first issue concerns the reason for *jihād* being an element in Islam. Some believe that there should not be any *jihād* and law of war in religion and that religion should oppose war as bad, rather than establishing it as law. But we know *jihād* to be one of the principle duties of Islam. When we are asked what the principle duties are, we say, "There are ten: prayer, fasting, *khums, zakāt, hajj, jihād,* etc."[5]

One of the arguments that Christians propagate in an extraordinary fashion against Islam is this: first they ask why such a law exists in Islam, and then they state that due to this legal permission Muslims have started wars with various people and forcibly imposed their will on them. They claim that the Islamic *jihāds* were all fought for the imposition of Islamic beliefs. It is due to this permission that Muslims impose Islam by force, which they claim is how Islam has always spread. They say that the principle of *jihād* in Islam and one of the basic rights of man, freedom of religion, are in eternal conflict. This is one of the issues to be discussed.

A second issue is the difference that Islam has maintained in the law of *jihad* between the *mushrikin* — the polytheists — and the monotheists. There is a provision for living in harmony with the People of the Book that is not applicable to the polytheists.

Another issue is whether Islam differentiates between the Arabian peninsula and the rest of the world. Has Islam appointed for itself a place, the Arabian peninsula, as its headquarters, its center, where no one from the polytheists or People of the Book is admitted, whereas Islam is not so severe in other places and Muslims live in harmony with *mushrikīn* and People of the Book? In short, is the Arabian peninsula different from other places in these terms?

The answer is that between Mecca and other places there is without doubt a distinction, and in the *āyah* preceding the one under discussion we are told, "The idolators are unclean, so do not let them come near the Inviolable Place of Worship ..." (9:28).

The fourth issue concerns agreements with the polytheists. Is a Muslim allowed to make agreements with such people? And if he does, is the agreement to be honored?

The last issue concerns the conditions of war. When Islam has legalized warfare, what kinds of warfare, in terms of the particular conditions of war, does Islam consider legal or forbidden? For example, does Islam consider genocide legal or forbidden? Is it permissible to kill those who have not lifted the sword: old women, children, or men who are peacefully engaged in their jobs and trades? These five issues need discussion.

The first issue for discussion concerns the very legality of *jihad,* whether or not it is correct for a law of war to exist within the context of religion and the texts of its commandments. Protestors say, "No, war is evil, and religion must always be opposed to evil, so religion must always be opposed to war. It must always support peace, and intending to support peace, it must not contain any laws concerning war, and it must never itself go to war." This is the kind of propaganda that Christians conduct, weak and limpid, with no ground to stand on.

War - is it always bad? If in defense of a right, against oppression, is it still bad? Obviously not. We must regard the conditions and motives of war and consider for what motive and aim the war is fought. There are times when war is aggression: when, for example, a group of people or a nation sets its greedy eyes on the rights of others, on the lands of others, or on the common wealth of a people, or when it falls prey to over-ambition, to lust for pre-eminence or superiority, claiming that, "Of all races, ours is the most outstanding, superior to other races, and thus we must rule over those races." War for these reasons is obviously wrong. Whether a war is waged to take possession of land, to seize ownership of national wealth or due to contempt for others and to notions of racial superiority — for example, "Those people are of an inferior quality, while we are of a superior one, and the superior must govern over the inferior" — it is a war of aggression. These types of wars are certainly evil, and there can be no denial. There is another type of aggressive war that will be discussed later, war for the imposition of belief.

But if a war of defense is undertaken in the face of aggression, such as in the case that others have occupied our land or cast their sights on our wealth, property, freedom, and self-esteem, wishing to replace this with the esteem of themselves, what is religion to say? Should it say, "War is evil, laying hands on a weapon is evil, and picking up a sword is evil," advocating peace? And vis-a-vis someone who has attacked and wants to destroy us, must we abstain from war — which would mean failing to defend ourselves — on the pretext of peace?

This would not be peace, this would be surrender.

In such an event, we cannot say that, being the advocates of peace, we are absolutely opposed to war. This would mean that we are advocates of misery and surrender. Make no mistake, peace and surrender are as similar as chalk and cheese. Peace means honorable co-existence with others, but surrender is not honorable co-existence; it is absolutely dishonorable on one side and in fact is not truly honorable on either side. On one side the dishonor is of aggression and on the other it is the dishonor of surrender in the face of *zulm* (injustice and oppression).

So this fallacy must be eradicated, and a person who declares himself to be opposed to war, saying that war is totally bad — be it injustice or be it defense and resitance in the face of injustice   has made a grave mistake. War that is transgression is utterly bad, while war that means standing erect in the face of transgression is utterly good and is one of the necessities of human life.

The Qur'an also indicates this matter, and in fact illuminates it. In one place it tells us: " ... And if God had not repelled some men by others, the earth would have been corrupted ..." (2:251) and in another place, " ... For had it not been for God's repelling some men by means of others, cloisters and churches and oratories and mosques, wherein the name of God is mentioned often, would surely have been pulled down." (22:40) So if God did not prevent some people by means of other people, ruin and corruption would overtake all places. Furthermore, it is for this reason that all the countries of the world find it necessary to maintain armed forces for their defense. The existence of armed forces, the duty of which is to prevent aggression, is an absolute necessity. Now please do not assert that, given two countries with armies — one for aggression and the other for defense — the one with the army for defense is merely weaker, or it too would become aggressive. This debate is of no concern here. The relevant fact here is that the existence of an army for defense is essential for every nation in order that it may be strong enough to repel aggression against it.

Thus the Qur'an tells us: "Make ready for them all that you can of force and tethered horses, and thereby you may dismay the enemy of God and your enemy, and others besides them whom you do not know ..." (8:60) The statement about tethered horses is made because in the past, the strength of armies consisted mainly of horses, but naturally each age has its own characteristics. What the Qur'an is saying here is that in order for our strength to dismay the hearts of the enemy, as opposed to suggesting the idea of aggression to them, we are to build an army and make ourselves strong.

It is said that Christianity has the distinction of lacking any type of warfare. We claim, in contrast, that Islam has the distinction of having the law of *jihād*. If we look closely, we see that Christianity has no *jihād* because it has nothing at all.[6] By this I mean that there is no Christian structure of society, no Christian legal system, and no Christian rules by which a society is to be formed which elements could contain a law of *jihād*. There is no substance to Christianity; it consists of no more than a few moral teachings that form a system of advice such as "tell the truth; do not tell lies; do not consume the wealth of others" and so on. How can it see a place for a law of *jihād*? Islam is a religion that sees its duty and commitment to be the formation of society. Islam came to reform society and to form a nation. Its mandate is the reform of the whole world. Such a religion cannot be indifferent. It cannot be without the law of *jihād*. In the same way, its government cannot be without an army. While the range of Christianity is extremely limited, the range of Islam is extremely wide. While Christianity does not cross the frontiers of advice, Islam is the religion which covers all the activities of human life. For the governing of society, it has economic and political laws. It came to organize a state and a government. Once that has been done, how can it be without an army or a law of *jihād*?

It is determined that whatever a group says about religion always having to be opposed to war and having to advocate peace, because peace is good and war is totally bad, is a mistake. Religion certainly must advocate peace, and the Qur'an says, "Peace is better ..." (4:128),[7] but it must also advocate war. For example, if the opposition is not prepared to co-exist honorably, and due to its being an oppressor it intends to trample on the face of human dignity and honor, and we submit, then we have welcomed misery and have accepted dishonor. Islam says: "Peace, if the other side is ready and willing to accept it. If not, and it turns to war, then war."

The second issue concerns the conditions in which Islam says one must fight. The first revelations of the Qur'an that were revealed concerning *jihād,* in the accepted view of all the commentators, are these *āyāt* from *Sūrah* 22:

> Truly God defends those who are true. Truly God does
> not love each treacherous ingrate. Sanction is given to
> those who fight because they have been wronged, and
> God is indeed able to give them victory; to those who
> have been unjustly driven from their homes merely
> because they said, "Our Lord is God — For had it not
> been for God's repelling some men by means of others,
> **cloisters and churches and oratories and mosques,**
> wherein the name of God is mentioned often, would
> surely have been pulled down. Truly God helps the one
> who helps Him. Truly God is strong, Almighty — and
> those who, if We give them power in the land, establish
> worship, pay the *zakat,* enjoin kindness, and forbid
> iniquity. And God's is the sequel of all events. (22:38-41)

These amazing *āyāt* are the first revealed concerning the legislation of *jihād.*

Before we can analyze these *āyāt,* however, something else must first be examined. As we know, the first revelation was brought down to the Prophet in Mecca when he was forty years old. The Prophet lived for the next thirteen years in Mecca, during which years either he or his companions were terribly oppressed by the pagans of the Quraysh, the ruling houses of Mecca, so much so that a group of them were forced to seek permission from the noble Prophet to migrate. They left Mecca and went to Ethiopia. Repeatedly the companions asked the noble Prophets to allow them to defend themselves, but during the whole of their thirteen year stay in Mecca, he did not do so — for which there was a good reason — until at last his task took a solid shape and Islam spread, among other places, to Medina. There, a small group of Medinans had become Muslims, had gone to Mecca, had paid their allegiance to the Prophet, and had made a covenant promising, should he go to Medina, to support him. So he and the Muslims migrated to medina and there for the first time, an independent Muslim base was brought into existence. During the first year, permission for defense was still not given. It was during the second year of the *hijrat* that the first *āyāt* of the

Qur'an related to *jihād*, these same *āyat* (in the above paragraph), were revealed. The tone of the *āyat* is this: "Truly God defends those who are true ... God does not love the treacherous ingrate." This indicates that the polytheists had been treacherous to the Muslims, had betrayed them, had transgressed against them, and had rejected God's blessing upon themselves. Then it declares, "Sanction is given to those who fight because they have been wronged ..."; which means, "Oh Muslims, now that the polytheist ingrates have come to fight against you, fight them!" In reality this is a state of defense. This permission has been given because the oppressed must defend themselves! Then comes a promise of assistance: " ... and God is indeed able to give them victory; to those who have been unjustly driven from their homes merely because they said, 'Our Lord is God.'" Notice to what extent the tone of the *āyat* is one of defense. They next explain the whole reasoning of *jihād*. The Qur'an is amazing in the way it discloses realities and brings to mind all their details. Here a particular *āyah* is presented just as if the Qur'an had been confronted with all the questions and problems raised by Christians of today, who say, "Oh Qur'an! You are supposed to be a divine book and a religious book, so how can you give permission to fight? War is a bad thing, so always proclaim, 'Peace! — Purity! — Worship!'"

But the Qur'an tells us: if the other side becomes aggressive toward us and we do not defend ourselves, not one stone will be left upon another. All the houses of worship will be destroyed. "... For had it not been for God's repelling some men by means of others, cloisters and churches and oratories and mosques, wherein the name of God is mentioned often, would surely have been pulled down." Some people would commit such transgression that no one would find the freedom in which to worship God.

The Qur'an then makes a promise of help: "Truly God helps the one who helps Him. Truly God is Strong, Almighty." Helping God means helping real truth and justice.

Now notice how God describes those whom He helps. God helps the people who defend themselves, the people who, when they establish a government, form one according to these lines: "those who, if We give them power in the land, establish worship, pay the *zakāt* ..." — Prayer is the correct spiritual bond between man and

God, and *zakat* (poor-due, purification tax) is the correct spiritual bond of cooperation between human individuals ... the people who worship God in sincerity and help one another — " ... enjoin kindness, and forbid iniquity ..." — who consider themselves to be under a bond to promote what is good and combat what is evil. "And Allah's is the sequel of all events ..."

What has been presented so far is that the Qur'an has fundamentally defined *jihād* not as a war of aggression, of superiority, or of domination, but of resistance to aggression.

Of course, the forms of aggression to be resisted are not always on the lines of one party invading the territory of another. Perhaps a form of aggression will be on the lines of the adversary in its own territory subjecting to torture and tyranny a group from within its own people, a group that is weak and powerless, who, in Qur'anic terminology, are called *mustaḍ'afīn* (the meek, the oppressed). In such conditions, Muslims cannot remain indifferently aloof. Muslims have a mandate to free such afflicted people. Or perhaps the adversary has created such a terrible state of repression that the call of truth, love, and justice is not allowed to flourish, has created a dam, an obstacle — which must be destroyed! All these are types of transgressions. Muslims must free mankind from the chains of the bondage. In all these conditions, *jihād* is an urgent necessity; and such a *jihād* is defensive, in resistance to transgression, injustice, and oppression. The word *difā'* (defense) in its general meaning refers to resistance against an existing transgression, injustice, or oppression; but the types of transgression against which *jihād,* in the view of Islam, is necessary are still to be discussed.

The Second Lecture:
Defense or Aggression?

Previously we said that one of the points that the Christian world considers to be a weak point of Islam is the Islamic *jihād,* which prompts it to claim that Islam is a religion of war rather than a religion of peace, which Christianity holds itself to be. It says that war is totally bad and peace is good, and any religion that is divinely founded must advocate peace, which is a good thing, and not advocate war, which is a bad thing. Until recently Christianity looked at issues from the perspective of morality exclusive to itself, advocating "turning the other cheek," which fosters weakness. But Christianity today has switched positions. It has changed its face. It now perceives things from a different perspective and carries on its propaganda through a different channel, that of essential human rights and particularly that of freedom, and they perceive war as being totally opposed to the right of freedom, to freedom of belief, of will, and of choice concerning religion, nationality, and other things. But Muslims look at the issue from both perspectives of morality and human rights. The answer to this matter was stated in the previous lecture. It is self-evident and clear that what the Christians say is not at all valid.

There is no doubt that peace is good. And warfare, for the sake of aggression against other people who have no intentions against the aggressor or that aggressive society, war for the sake of occupying that unsuspecting nation's lands and of grabbing their property, or for the sake of making them slaves and subjecting them to the aggressor's influence and laws, is undoubtedly bad. That which is bad is transgression and aggression. But all war, on all sides, is not always aggression. War can be aggression but it can also be a reply to aggression, for such reply must sometimes be given through force. There are times that force is the only feasible reply.

Any religion concerned with society must give thought to what it will do on that day when it is faced with aggression, or let us suppose, it is not itself faced with aggression, but another people are. It is for

such a day that religion must have a law of warfare. The Christians
say that peace is good, and we agree. But what about submission,
humiliation, and misery? Are these also good? If one power is faced
with another power and they both advocate peace, both desiring, in
today's terms, to live in peaceful co-existence, without either side
intending to attack the other, both wishing to live in a state of peace
with reciprocal rights and mutual respect, then this is called peace
and is good and essential. There is a time, however, when one group
is an aggressor and, on the pretext of war being bad, the other group
submits to the humiliation of having to tolerate the imposed
aggression. The proper name for this is not peace, but willing
acceptance of humiliation and misery. Such a submission in the face
of force should never be called peace. There is a difference between
the advocation of peace and the acceptance of humiliation. Islam
never gives permission to be humiliated, while at the same time it
strongly advocates peace.

What I want to stress is the importance of this issue which
Christians and others have used to attack and protest against Islam,
claiming it to be Islam's weak point, adding that Islam is a religion of
the sword; that Muslims raised the swords over people's heads,
saying, "Choose Islam or die"; and that people chose Islam in order
to stay alive. Therefore, it seems necessary that this issue be discussed
thoroughly and minutely, and one must investigate not only $\bar{a}y\bar{a}t$ of
the Qur'an, but also confirmed traditions of the Prophet and
glimpses from his life. First the Qur'anic $\bar{a}y\bar{a}t$ shall be discussed.

It has presumably been shown that some of the Qur'anic
instructions concerning *jihād* against the *kuffār* (disbelievers) are
unconditional, such as those that state only this: "Oh Prophet! Strive
against the *kuffār* and the hypocrits." (66:9); or in the case of another
$\bar{a}yah$, that after a period which is given to the polytheists (four
months), if they have not adopted Islam or migrated from Mecca,
then they are to be killed; or in that very *ayah* with which we began
our discussion and which is about the People of the Book; or another
$\bar{a}yah$: "Oh Prophet! Strive against the *kuffār* and hypocrits and be
harsh with them." (9:73). Thus anyone with ears to hear these $\bar{a}y\bar{a}t$
would say that the instructions of the Qur'an are no less than that
Muslims must be in a state of war with the *kuffār* and hypocrits and
must never be in a state of peace with them, that Muslims must fight

them as vehemently as they can. And if one speaks thusly, it will become evident that the Qur'an instructs Muslims to fight against non-Muslims.

It has already been stated, however, that there is a scholastic rule that when both a conditional and an unconditional commandment exist, that is, when there is an instruction that in one place is unconditional but in another place has a condition attached to it, then in the language of the scholars, the unconditional must be interpreted as the conditional. The *āyāt* I have just recited are unconditional. Other *āyāt* exist that are conditional implying that Muslims should strive against the polytheists for the reason that they are in warfare or aggression against you and thus definitely have the right to fight against them. Thus it becomes clear that where the Qur'an says, "Oh Prophet! Strive against the *kuffār* and the hypocrits ..." it means that we must fight against those *kuffār* who are fighting us and who will continue fighting if we fight them.

In Sūrah 2, the Qur'an tells us: "Fight in the way of God against those who fight against you, but do not begin hostilities. Truly God does not love aggressors." (2:190) So you who have faith, fight those who are fighting you, because they do so, but do not violate the limit. What does not violating the limit mean? Naturally its obvious meaning is that it is those who are fighting us that we are to fight, meaning that we are to fight with a certain group of people and that group is the soldiers that the other side has sent, the military men whom they prepared for war with us and who are fighting us. It is these whom we are to fight, and in ordinary language, we should not turn chicken on the battlefield and run away. We must cross swords, exchange bullets, and fight. But with people who are not men of war, who are not soldiers, and who are not in a state of combat, such as old men, old women — in fact all women, young and old — and children, we must not interfere and we must not do any of the other things that are counted as transgression. We must not cut their trees and ruin their economic resources, and we must not fill their canals. Such things are all transgression.

One should not be misled by the fact that sometimes in the course of war, there is no option but to damage houses, etc. True, but such occasions, when it is not possible to fight without such occurrences, are a separate issue. But for tis kind of activity to be itself a part of the activities of war is forbidden.

Another conditional *āyah* is that which has been discussed from *Surah* 22, which in fact consists of five or six consecutive *āyāt* and is the first ayah revealed concerning *jihād*. The content is that, because the other side has drawn their swords against us, we have permission to do the same thing.

In another *āyah* from *Surah* 9, it is stated, "Wage war on all of the idolators as they are waging war on all of you." (9:36)

Before discussion of these two *āyāt,* something else must take precedence. It has been stated that the permission for *jihād* is subject to some conditions. One is that the adversary must be in a state of aggression. They are attacking us, and thus we must fight them. Beyond this condition, suppose the adversary does not propose to attack us but is guilty of a gross injustice to another group of humans, and we have it within our powers to save that group from the aggressor's clutches. If we fail to save them, we are in effect supporting the aggressor's oppression against the victim. We may be in a situation whereby a party has not transgressed against us but has committed injustice against a group from another people, who may or may not be Muslims. If they are Muslims — as in today's plight of the Palestinians who have been exiled from their homes, whose wealth has been seized, and who have been subjected to all kinds of transgression — whereas for the moment the transgressor has no intentions against us, it is permissible for us to give assistance to those oppressed Muslims and deliver them. This is not only permissible, but obligatory, because they are Muslims. Such action would not be a case of commencing hostilities, but rather of rushing to the defense of the oppressed in order to deliver them from the clutches of oppression.

But if the oppressed person or party is not Muslim, then the tyranny can be of two types. There is a case where the oppressor has positioned a people in a vacuum and blocks the call of Islam. Islam reserves the right to spread its message throughout the world, but this depends upon there being the freedom for it to spread.

Imagine some government that says to the Muslims who are delivering the call of Islam to a nation, "You have no right to say what you are saying. We do not allow it." In these circumstances it is not permissible for us to fight with that nation, with those people who are blameless and unaware. But against that corrupt regime which props itself up with a putrid ideology that it uses like a chain around the necks of the people to imprison them in a blind alley, isolated from the call of truth — this is also permissible in the view of Islam, for us to fight that regime and remove that obstacle, that prison of oppression. In the view of Islam, this is permissible, for this itself would be a form of revolting against injustice and oppression. It may be that the *mazlūm,* the oppressed, are not aware of the nature of the injustice and have not requested our help, but is not actually necessary for them to request it.

The requesting of help is yet another issue. It is permissible or moreover obligatory for us to render aid to the oppressed regardless of whether they apply to us for help. The simple fact that the oppressed are oppressed, that an oppressive regime has erected a barrier for its own well-being, preventing a nation from becoming aware of the call wherein lies the prosperity and happiness of that nation, which call they are sure to accept if they hear and become aware of it, prompts Islam to say that we can break that barrier, which exists in the form of a repressive government, separating those people from Islam.

Many of the wars of early Islam were fought for the very reason just mentioned. The Muslims who went to war used to say that they had no quarrel with the peoples of the world and that they were fighting governments in order to rescue people from the misery and slavery imposed on them by those governments. When the Persian commander Rustam Farrukhzad asked some Muslim warriors what their goal was, they replied, "To transport people from the worship of mortals to the worship of God ... Our aim is to free these creatures of God, these people whom, by your tricks and violence you have placed under the yoke of slavery and bondage to yourselves. We will deliver them, set them free, and make them devotees of God, the Sublime, the devotees of their Creator, rather than devotees to others created by the One who created them."[8]

In the letters that the noble Prophet wrote to the People of the Book, he particularly used to include this *āyah*:

"Say: Oh People of the Book! Come to an agreement
between us and you: That we shall worship none but God,
and that we shall ascribe no partner unto him, and that
none of us shall take others besides God as lords."(3:64).

This *āyah* instructed the Prophet to invite the People of the Book,
those same people about whom the instructions of *jihād* were
revealed, to accept an agreement that would be the same with respect
to them as to the Muslims. It does not say that they are to accept an
agreement which only benefits the Muslims. They are to accept what
is equal for all and is the concern of all.

If, for example, Muslims should say to a people, "Come you
people, accept our language," then those people have the right to ask,
"Why? We have our own language, so why should we come and
accept yours?" Or Muslims might say, "Come and accept our special
habits and customs." And they might reply, "Why should we do so,
when we have our own habits and customs?" But if Muslims say,
"Come and accept this which is neither exclusively ours nor yours,
but everyone's. God is the God of us all, so accept Him," this no
longer relates just to Muslims. When Muslims say, "Worship Him
who is the Creator of both of us and you, Him who is the Creator of
all," then this is the same for Muslims and non-Muslims. The Qur'an
says, "Come to an agreement between us and you." Only God, the
Creator of us all, is to be worshipped. And another principle that is
supremely profitable both for Muslims and non-Muslims is, "...that
none of us shall take others besides God as lords," which means that
the social order of master and servant is abolished and the order of
equality between human beings is established.

This *āyah* reveals that, if we fight, we do so for what is the same in
regards to all mankind. This having been stated, it can now be said
that one of the conditions which the unconditional *āyah* can be
subjected to is that if a people are bearing the oppression of a certain
group, it becomes permissable for us to fight to free those people.

Now there are two other *āyāt* that I wish to recite, the first being
(8:39): "And fight with them until there is no more *fitnah* (discord),
and religion is all for God." This means that we are to fight those who
create discord among us and who seek to cause Muslims to relinquish their religion. Muslims are to fight with these until the discord

they cause has been eliminated. This itself is another condition. A further condition is contained in (4:75): "Why should you not fight for the cause of God and of the *mustadafin* (oppressed) among men, women, and children."

These five *ayat* that have been discussed here have demonstrated that, if the instructions of Islam concerning *jihad* given in some places are unconditional, in other places they are conditional, and, in the terms of the scholars, the unconditional must be interpreted as the conditional.

In the Qur'an there is a group of *ayat* which specify that religion is to be accepted freely and not due to the application of force, and this fact confirms the claim that it is not the view of Islam that its followers should use force, telling people to either become Muslims or die. These *ayat* illuminate those unconditional *ayat* in a different way.

One of these is a part of "*Ayat al-Kursi*" (2:255-7) and is well-known: "There is no compulsion in religion. The right direction is henceforth distinct from error." (2:256). This *ayah* means that we must explain clearly the right path to people and its own reality is distinct. There is no place for the use of compulsion in religion and no one must be obliged to accept the religion of Islam. This *ayah* is explicit in its claim. In the Islamic commentaries, it is written that a man of the Ansar[9] who had previously been a polytheist had two sons who had become Christians. These two sons had become fascinated by Christianity and were very devoted to it, but their father was now a Muslim and was upset that his sons had become Christians. He went to the noble Prophet and said to him, "Apostle of God! What can I do to these sons of mine that have become Christians? No matter what I have tried, they still do not accept Islam. Do you grant me permission to force them to leave their religion, and become Muslims?" The Prophet replied, "No, *La ikraha fid-din*. (There is no compulsion in religion)."[10]

Concerning the circumstances in which this *ayah* was revealed, it is also written that there were two tribes, the Aws and the Khazray, who were living in Medina, an who were the original inhabitants of Medina. At the dawn of Islam they were living there together with several large Jewish tribes who had come to Medina at a later period. One was the tribe of Bani Nazir and another was the Bani Quaryzah, while there was yet another large tribe of Jews that lived on the fringes of the city.

The Jews, due to their religion and their possessing a heavenly book, had more or less become respected as the literate individulas of that society, while among the original inhabitants of Medina, who were polytheists and generally illiterate, there had recently come into existence a small group who were also literate. The Jews, because their culture was more advanced and the range of their thought was broader, exercised quite an influence on this group. Thus, despite the fact that the religion of the Aws and the Khazraj was different from that of the Jews, they were becoming progressively more subject to Jewish ideas. As a result, they would sometimes send their children to the Jews to be educated, and while under the Jewish influence, the children would now and then renounce their pagan religion of polytheism and become Jews. Thus, when the noble Prophet entered Medina, a group of these boys of Medina were being trained by the Jews and had chosen Judaism for themselves as their religion, which some refused to renounce. The fathers and mothers of these children became Muslim, yet the children continued to adhere to Judaism. Later when it was settled that the Jews should leave Medina, as punishment for the discord they had instigated, those children also left with their fellow Jews. Their fathers came to the noble Prophet, asking permission to separate their sons from the Jews, to force them to relinquish Judaism and become Muslims; but the Prophet did not permit this. They appealed, "Apostle of God! Please give us permission to force them to leave their religion and accept Islam." But He told them, "No! Now that they have chosen to go with the Jews, let them go." The commentators claim that it was then that the *āyah* (Q. 2:256) was revealed.[11]

Another *āyah* decrees, "Call unto your Lord's way with wisdom and fair exhortation, and reason with them in the better way." (16:125). This *āyah* has also introduced clearly the only way for Islam to be accepted.

In another *āyah* it is stated, "The truth is from the Lord of you all. Then whosoever will, let him believe, and whosoever will, let him disbelieve." (18:30) So this *āyah* has also stated that faith and rejection, *īmān* and *kufr*, can only be chosen by oneself and cannot be forced on others. So Islam does not say that others must be forced into Islam, that if they become Muslims, good, but otherwise they are to be killed, according to their choice. Instead it says that whoever wants to believe will do so and whoever does not want to believe will not.

Another is as follows: "And if your Lord willed, all on the earth would have believed together. Would you then compel men until they are believers?" (10:100) The *āyah* is addressed to the Prophet who really loved the people and wanted them to be true believers. The Qur'an says that the use of force in such matters is meaningless. If force were a valid method, God Himself with His own power of creation would have made believers of all the people, but belief is what people must choose for themselves. Thus for the same reaons that God, with all His powers of creation and omnipotence has not forced mankind to be believers and has given them the free will to choose among the options, so the Prophet likewise was to leave the people free to choose. He whose heart has the desire will become a true believer, and He whose heart lacks such desire will not.

Another *āyah* addressing itself to the Prophet states, "It may be that you torment yourself because they do not believe. If We wished We could send down to them from the sky a portent such that their necks would remain bowed before it." (26:3-4). It in effect says, "Oh Prophet, it is as if you intend to kill yourself because they have not believed, as if you desire such suicide. Do not be so full of grief for their sakes, We, with Our power and might, could have easily forced the people to belief if We so desired." God says that if He wanted to send down from the sky a sign or affliction to tell the people that they must either convert or be destroyed, then all the people under compulsion would become believers, but He did not do so because He wants all the people to choose for themselves.

These *āyāt* further clarify Islam's view of *jihād*, that the aim of Islam by *jihād* is not that which some self-interested parties have said it is. These *āyāt* clarify that Islam's aim is not compulsion, that it does not command Muslims to raise the sword over the head of whoever is not a Muslim and offer the simple choice of Islam or death. Indeed this is not the purpose of *jihād*.

There is another series of *āyāt* in the Qur'an which deserves mention. On the whole, Islam gives much importance to the issue of peace. In one *āyah* it is clearly defined: "Peace is better." (4:128). Though, as stated, peace is not the same as submission to an oppressor. In another *ayah* it is stated, "O you who believe, come, all of you, into *silm* (peace, submission to God)." (2:208)[12]

But clearer than these *āyāt* is this one: "And if they incline to peace, you should also incline to it, and trust in God." (8:61). These *āyāt* clearly show that the spirit of Islam is that of peace.

In another *āyāt* from *Sūrah 4,* the Prophet is told, "So if they hold aloof from you, do not wage war against you, and offer you peace, God allows you no way against them." (4:90).

In the same *Sūrah* it is further stated, this time about the hypocrites, "If they turn back, then take them and kill them wherever you find them, and choose no friend or helper from among them, except those who seek refuge to a people between whom and yourselves there is a covenant or who come unto you because their hearts forbid them to make war on you or on their own folk." (4:89-90).

Thus four series of *āyāt* have been presented. One of these consists of *āyāt* that state unconditionally to fight, so those who hear these and no others may assume that Islam is a religion of war. The second series consists of *āyāt* giving the order to fight but with certain conditions, such as the opposing side being in a state of war with us, or a nation of Muslims or non-Muslims being placed under the heels of a group from within itself which has trampled on their freedom and rights. The third series makes it perfectly clear that the call Islam is not sounded with the force of arms. And finally in the fourth series Islam decisively announces it love of peace.

The Third Lecture
Defense — the Essence of *Jihad*

One of the points that now comes in question is that of the Islamic view of the essence of *jihād*. On this point there is complete agreement among scholars that the essence is defense, meaning that not one of them even suspects *jihād* or any kind of fighting — motivated by aggression, by lust for the resources of the other side, aimed at the harnessing by an aggressor of a people's economic or human resources — to be in any way permissible in the view of Islam. In Islam's view, fighting with such motives are types of tyranny and oppression. *Jihād* is only for the sake of defense, and in truth it is resistance against some kind of transgression, and certainly it can be lawful. Of course there is also the third possibility that one fights not for the sake of aggression, nor in defense of oneself or a human value, but for the expansion of a human value, and this is to be discussed. Leaving this point aside, however, it is clear that in the basic definition of *jihād* there is no difference of opinion and all the scholars are agreed that *jihād* and war must be for the sake of defense. The differences of opinion that do exist are minor ones and concern the question of what it is that has to be defended.

The opinions of some on this matter are limited. They say that defense means self-defense, that war is lawful for an individual, a tribe, or a nation in defense of itself and its property. According to this view, if the lives of a people are exposed to danger from another region, then fighting in defense of their lives is lawful for that people. In the same way, if their property is subject to aggression, then from the point of view of human rights, they have the right to defend that property which is their material right. Likewise, if people are faced with the aggression of another nation that wants to take possession of their wealth and in some fashion carry it away, then those people have the right to defend their wealth, even by force.

Islam says, "Whoever is killed for his property or principles is a martyr."[13] So in Islam, defending one's principles is like defending one's life or property. In fact is is superior; it is defense of one's honor. For a nation to defend its independence is undeniably lawful. So when a group wants to take away the independence of a nation and place that nation under its own mandate, if the people of that nation choose to defend themselves and take up arms, what they do is lawful, and in fact praiseworthy and admirable. So ... defense of life, defense of wealth, property, and lands, defense of independence, and defense of principles are all lawful. No one doubts the fact that in these cases defense is permissible, and as shown, the view that some Christians put forth about religion having to advocate peace and not war and that war is absolutely bad and peace is absolutely good, has no reasonable means of support. Not only is fighting in defense not bad, it is extremely good and one of the necessities of human life. This is what is meant in the Qur'an where it states, "And if God had not repelled some men by others, the earth would have been corrupted." (2:251) and in another place: "For had it not been for God's repelling some men by means of others, cloisters, churches, oratories, and mosques, wherein the name of God is often mentioned, would surely have been pulled down." (22:40). Up to this point all the scholars are more or less in agreement.

There exists the question, however, of whether the things we are allowed to defend are only these — individual, group, and national rights — or whether it is legitimate for us to defend other things as well. Do there exist things, the defense of which is obligatory, that do not pertain merely to the rights of humanity as a whole? Is it lawful or unlawful to fight in response to a transgression against a basic human right?

Perhaps someone may wonder, "What is fighting for the sake of humanity?" or may think, "I do not have any reason to fight for any rights except my own, or at the most, those of my nation, so why should I be concerned about the rights of humanity?" But this mode of thinking is in no way valid.

There exists something superior to the rights of the individual or nation. Something more sacred, the defense of which in accordance with the human conscience is higher than the defense of individual rights. And that something is the rights of humanity. In other words, the value of fighting in defense lies not in defending one's self, but in defending "the right." When one's cause is "the right," what difference does it make whether it is an individual right or a general right of humanity? Indeed, defense of the rights of humanity is more sacred, although no one wishes to admit it.

For example, freedom is reckoned as one of the sacred values of humanity. Here freedom is not limited to an individual or a nation. Now, if it is neither one's personal freedom nor that of one's country, but freedom in another corner of the world that pertains to the right of humanity which is being infringed upon, is the defense of that right of humanity lawful for Muslims or not? This question should be pondered. If it is lawful, then defense is not limited to the actual individual whose freedom is in danger, but it is lawful, even obligatory, for other individuals and other nations to rush to the aid f liberty and fight against liberty's negator and repressor. So what is the answer? No one should have any doubts that the most sacred form of *jihād* and war is that which is fought in defense of humanity and of human rights.

During the period in wich the Algerians were at war with the French colonialists, a group of Europeans helped them in their war, either by actually fighting alongside the Algerians or otherwise. Does it seem that only the fighting of the Algerians themselves was lawful, because only their rights were transgressed, and that the people who came from the farthest corners of Europe to take part in the battle for the benefit of the Algerian nation were no more than oppressive aggressors? Perhaps they should have been told, "Stop interfering; what business is it of yours? No one has transgressed your rights, so why are you fighting here?" Or is it rather the case that the *jihād* of such people was in fact even more sacred than that of the Algerians, because the Algerians were defending their own rights, whereas the cause of the others was more ethical and sacred. Obviously the second assumption is the valid one.

Freedom lovers — both real and pretend ones — have earned general respect among the different nations due to their having presented themselves as defenders of human rights, rather than merely their own individual rights, or those of their nation or even continent. If they were ever to transcend the use of the tongue, the pen, letters, and lectures, and actually go to the battlefield and fight, for the Palestinians, for example, or the Viet Cong, then the world would consider them to be even more sacred. It would not reproach them, saying, "Why do you interfere where you have no business? No one is bothering you!"

The world considers war, whenever it is for the sake of defense, to be sacred, and even more so if it is in defense of one's nation, for the cause has grown from a personal one to a national one, and the individual is not merely defending himself, but is also defending the other individuals that make up his society. And if the cause should transcend national interests to humanitarian interests, it again reaches a more sacred plane.

Here then is the nature of the dispute concerning *jihād,* and it is only a minor dispute. The dispute is not over whether or not *jihād* is lawful only in defense. In reference to this major point, there is unanimous agreement that it is only lawful in defense.[14] The dispute arises over the actual definition of defense. This minor dispute concerns whether *jihād* is limited merely to self-defense, or at most to defense of one's nation, or whether it should also include defense of humanity.

Some claim, and rightly so, that the defense of humanity is a legitimate defense, so that the cause of those who rise to "enjoin the good and proscribe what has been prohibited" is a sacred one. It is possible that a person is not directly transgressed against; he may even be highly respected with all the necessities of life available to him, and similarly for his nation; but, from the perspective of human ideals, a basic human right is being transgressed. Within his society, although neither the material rights of that society or his own individual rights have been transgressed, yet a task presents itself which is related to the highest interest of humanity, namely, when good and bad are in opposition, to establish the good and abolish the bad from that society. Thus if a person sees that the good, recognized (by God), has been relegated to the position of the bad, forbidden (by God), and vice versa, and he stands for the sake of enjoining the good and prohibiting the bad, then what is he defending? Neither his own personal rights nor the material rights of the society, but a spiritual right that is particular to no single person or nation, related to all the world's human beings. Obviously we are not to condemn but are to consider sacred the *jihād* of that man, for it is in defense of a right of humanity.

Concerning the question of freedom, one can see today that the very people who combat freedom, in order to delegate to themselves a mark of respectability, ironically claim to be the defenders of freedom, for they know that the defense of freedom is tacitly understood as being sacred. If they were truly fighting for the defense of freedom, their claims would be valid, but they aply the name "defense of freedom" to their transgressions. Yet in this they acknowledge the fact that the rights of humanity are worthy of defense and that war for the sake of those rights is legitimate and beneficial.

An important matter must now be discussed concerning *tawḥīd*, *"Lā illāha illa Allāh"* (There is no God except God.) Does *tawḥīd* (monotheism) pertain to the rights of humanity or of the individual? Here it is possible for a Muslim to assert that it does not pertain to the rights of humanity, but only to those of the individual, or at most, to the internal affairs of a nation. Thus he himself may be a monotheist, and has the right to choose such if he wishes, and now that he has chosen to be a monotheist, no one has the right to persecute him for it, for it is his personal right, but if someone else chooses to be a polytheist, that is likewise the right of that person. As for *tawḥīd* being the right of a nation, the same person is saying that any single nation in its laws can hold one of three positions. One of these is that it chooses monotheism and adopts it as the official religion and does not accept any other religion. Another is that a form of polytheism is established as the official creed. And the third is that the nation allows one to choose whatever religion or sect one desires. If monotheism is embodied in the law of a nation, then it is one of the rights of that nation, and if not, no. This view is one perspective of the way things are. There is another perspective, however, which regards monotheism as similar to freedom itself and thus pertaining to the rights of humanity. In discussing freedom, it was said that the meaning of the right to freedom is not simply that the freedom of an individual not be threatened from any quarter, for it is possible that it be threatened by that very individual. So if a people should fight for monotheism by combating polytheism, their fight is motivated by defense rather than by subjugation, tyranny, and transgression. This difference of opinion is the essence of the minor dispute in question. There are even two views among the learned of Islam. Some of them have expressed the former view and some adhere to the latter, but which is correct?

I intend to state my own view on this subject, but initially it is necessary to speak on yet another issue, and thus perhaps when a conclusion is reached the two views shall be united. This issue is that some affairs can be accepted due to duress and under compulsion, whereas the very nature of certain other affairs is that they be freely selected.

Imagine, for example, becoming dangerously infected with an illness and having to accept an injection. In such case it is possible for individuals to be forced to accept the injection, and if a person is unwilling, others can use force and restrain him, or at last resort, administer it while he is unconscious. This is something that the person accepts under duress. But the nature of some other things is that they cannot be accepted under compulsion, for they can only be accepted by choice and selection. Among such things is the purification of the self or the refinement of one's behavior. If one chooses to refine others so that they come to recognize and accept virtues and evil as they are, the latter being faults in humanity to be abstained from, so that they come to be repelled by the false and attracted by the truth, such cannot be done by the whip or by force.

With the violence of the whip, it is possible to prevent someone from stealing, but it is impossible to make that person's spirit trustworthy. If such things were possible, then, for example, if a person's self was in need of purification and his personal behavior needed morals and ethics, he would simply be taken and given one hundred lashes of the whip, thus making him highly civilized. In place of all that comprises a good education, the teachers would simply use the whip and pronounce something like, "In the interest of the life-long attraction to truth and the repulsion from falsehood, this person receives one hundred lashes and thus never again will tell a lie."

With this example in mind, it is to be asserted that faith, regardless of whether it is a basic right of humanity or not, is by its very nature not something that can be administered by force. Imagine that we wish to create faith — this is impossible. Faith means belief and inclination, attraction to and acceptance of a thought, and for such attraction, two conditions must be met. One condition is that the matter must accord with intellectual standards for human thought and reason; and the second is that it must have the special quality that appeals to the human heart such to engender natural attraction. Neither of these conditions is within the jurisdiction of force. The first condition is not, because thinking is ruled by logic. If it is desired that a child be taught the solution to a mathematical problem, he must be taught by means of logic so that he will find credence in it; he cannot be taught by the whip. His reasoning will not accept the matter solely due to force, however much he is beaten. The same applies to the second condition, the possession of a quality that stimulates inclination, attraction and sentiment.

According to this line of reasoning, there is a huge difference between monotheism as a right of humanity and matters other than monotheism, such as freedom. Freedom can be given to people by force, because transgression and oppression can be prevented by force. Intrinsically the people are free. So a nation can be freed by force when transgression is checked by force. But living freely and a freedom-loving spirit cannot be imposed by force. It is impossible to force a person to accept a belief or to forcibly create faith in a certain ideal which is within the heart. Such is the meaning of: "There is no compulsion in religion." When the Qur'an says this, it does not mean that, whereas religion could be imposed by force, one ought not do do so and should leave people to adopt any religion of their choosing. The Qur'an is saying that religion cannot possibly be imposed by compulsion. That which can be imposed under such condition is not religion.

To the Bedouin Arabs who had recently accepted Islam without having perceived the nature of its essence and without Islam having influenced their hearts, who were claiming to have faith, the Qur'an gave this reply:

> The wandering Arabs say, "We believe." Tell them, "You
> do not believe, but should rather say, "We submit," for
> the faith has not yet entered into your hearts." (49:14)

In Qur'anic terms, "the Arabs" means the desert nomads who came to the noble Prophet claiming to have faith. He was instructed to tell them that they did not have true belief or faith and that they should merely claim to have become Muslims, that is, to have made the verbal declaration, to have done that which entitled them to be superficially rated as Muslims, to have recited, *"La ilāha ill Allāh, Muḥammadan-rasūl Allāh,"* and were thus availed the same rights as other Muslims. He was instructed to advise them that what is called true faith had not yet entered their hearts. This ayah specifies that faith is a matter of the heart.

Another factor that supports our claim is that Islam does not permit blind following in the principle beliefs of religion and counts independent research as essential. The principle beliefs of religion are of course related to sincere belief and faith, so that it becomes clear that, in the view of Islam, faith is a product of unshackled thought, free from the captivity of blind following, force and power. The faith that Islam seeks cannot be produced by such means.

So now the two views of the Islamic scholars closely approach each other. The view of the one group is that monotheism pertains to the individual right of humanity, and as it is undeniably legitimate to defend such rights, it is by analogy legitimate to defend monotheism and to fight against other people for its sake. Whereas the meaning of the other group's claim is that there is no legitimate way to defend monotheism, and if a nation is polytheist, one is not permitted to fight them on that account. The proximity of these views lies in the fact that, even considering monotheism to be a universal right, one can still not fight against another nation to impose that right, for it is demonstrated that, by its very essence, monotheism is not something that can be accepted due to compulsion. There is however another point, that if we reckon monotheism as a right of humanity, and if we seek the best interests of humanity and the best interests of monotheism, then it is possible that we can fight with a nation of polytheists, but not to directly impose monotheism and faith on them, for it is clear that such is impossible.

Muslims may, however, fight with the polytheists in order to pluck out the fundamental roots of evil from that society. Ridding a society of these evil, polytheistic beliefs is one thing, whereas imposing belief in monotheism is another.

According to the belief of those who consider monotheism to pertain to the rights of an individual or, at most, of a particular nation, it is said that to do this is not permissible. The predominant line of thought in the west, which has also penetrated the ranks of Muslims, is exactly this.

Such issues as monotheism are regarded by the Europeans as strictly personal issues and not at all central to life, being more or less customs which each nation has the right to choose. On this basis, it is held that even for the sake of cutting out the root of the evil, no one has the right to combat polytheism, because polytheism is not iniquity, and monotheism is a purely personal issue.

If, on the other hand, one considers monotheism to be a universal issue, one pertaining to the rights of humanity and one of the conditions for humanity's general prosperity and welfare, then we see it as permissible to commence war with the polytheists to allow access to monotheism and in order to cast out the root of the iniquity, even though war directly for the sake of imposing the monotheistic belief is not permissible.[15]

Another issue is raised here, which is whether fighting for the freedom of the "call" is permissible or not. To fight for the freedom of the call means that Muslims must have the freedom to propagate their special beliefs and ideas in every nation. This does not refer to the generally current spreading of propaganda, but to explanation, and nothing more. And whether or not one considers either or both freedom and monotheism to be universal human rights, to propagate thusly is definitely lawful. Now if a barrier hinders the call, such as some power having arisen as an obstacle, denying permission and claiming that such propagation will impair the thinking of its nation — and it is obvious that most governments consider impaired any thinking which, once adopted, may lead to the people ceasing their subjugation to that government — then it is permissible to fight against it until it falls and the barrier against the call crumbles. This would be for the cause of defense, and thus would be in the category of *jihād* which is for that aim.

So far it has been demonstrated that the essence of *jihād* is defense. There is now just one issue that remains, which is whether, in our view, monotheism pertains to the universal rights of humanity, or merely to the personal rights of an individual, or at most, to the rights of a nation. What must be done is to examine the criteria for personal rights to determine what they are. In some aspects, all humans are the same, whereas in others they are all different. There are so many differences that even two people cannot be found who are exactly the same in every detail, and just as this is true in physical characteristics, so it is in spiritual characteristics. *It is the interests that are related equally to all human beings that are the basis of the universal rights of humanity.* Freedom means the absence of obstacles to the flowering of the natural potential of the human individual, and it is related to all of humanity. Freedom for one person has exactly the same value as for another; but between different individuals, there exist many distinctions, and these pertain to "personality," because they are personal differences. Just as there exist differences in skin-tone and body-type between two people, so there exist distinctions in personality: preference in color or style of clothing, in choice of town to live in or favorite area, in choice of home decorations, or in which subject to study — all are personal issues, and in these no one should bother anyone else. Thus no one has the right to compel anyone to marry a certain person, for this is a personal issue and everyone has his own taste in such choice. Islam in fact asserts this. These interfering Europeans who claim that no one must be bothered in the name of monotheism or faith say so because they think that these are among the personal concerns of the individual, issues of personality and taste. They think that individuals need to amuse themselves in life with a certain past-time that is called religion. In their view, it is like art. One likes Hafiz, another likes Sa'adi, another Mawlawi, Khayyam, or Ferdowsi.[16] They say that religion is just like this. One person may like Islam, while another chooses Christianity, Zoroastrianism, or none of these. No one must be troubled. Religion in the view of these Europeans is unrelated to the core and path of human life. This is their basic supposition, and between their line of thought and ours, there is a world of difference. Religions such as their own must indeed be as they say, but according to our view, religion means the "straight path" of humanity, and indifference to religion means indifference to the real path of progress of humanity. We say that monotheism is the pillar of the well-being, prosperity and happiness of mankind, rather than merely the personal concern of an individual or of this group or that group. Accordingly, the truth lies with those who count monotheism as pertaining to the rights of humanity. If at the same time we claim that war for the sake of imposing monotheism is not permissible, this is not because it does not pertain to humanity's general rights, but because the very nature of monotheism does not allow it to be imposed, as the Qur'an affirms: *"La ikrāha fiddīn."*

There is still another issue that needs to be discussed here, which is the distinction between "freedom of thought" and "freedom of belief." Human beings have the power of thought which allows them to calculate and deduce conclusions on the basis of logic and reason. But belief means being connected and firmly bound to the object of belief. And so many beliefs have absolutely no basis in thought, being sheer imitation, upbringing, and habit, and these impose on human freedom. That which is here presented from the point of view of freedom, with the claim that mankind must have it, is freedom of thought. Yet there are some beliefs that are not in the least rooted in thought, that are mere dormancy and stagnation of the spirit handed down from generation to generation and that are the essence of bondage — so that war fought for the elimination of such beliefs is war fought for, not against, the freedom of humanity. If a man prays for his needs in front of some idol that he himself has made with his own hands, then in the terms of the Qur'an, that man is more misguided than an animal![17] The actions of that person have not the slightest foundation in thought, and if his thinking were shaken up, he would not perform such a deed. His actions are merely a reflection of the dormancy and stagnation that have appeared in his heart and soul, rooted in blind imitation. This person must be forcibly freed from the internal chains that enshackle him, so that he may think. So those who recommend the freedom of imitation and the freedom of possessing chained souls and minds are mistaken! That which we advocate in accordance with the rule of the *āyah* — *"Lā ikrāha fid-dīn"* — is the freedom of thought.

The Fourth Lecture
The Question of Abrogation

The discussion thus far has concerned Islamic *jihād*. There are now three issues to be examined, one of which has a Qur'anic basis, one of which has reason as a basis, and one of which has both a Qur'anic basis and a historical one.

The first issue is in connection with the *āyāt* of *jihād*. It has been shown that some of the *āyāt* of *jihād* are unconditional, while others are conditional. The meaning of the unconditional *āyāt*, those with which the command to fight the polytheists or People of the Book was issued without any conditions is the same as that of the conditional *āyāt*, those which have given the command attached to special conditions. For example, it has been stated that we must fight with them if they are fighting or in a state of war with us, or if we are fearful and have some evidence that they have decided to attack us. As to whether the unconditional or the conditional *āyāt* are to be observed, it was said that in the view of the scholars there exists no difference of opinion to leave a margin of doubt, for if one is aware of the rule and examines both types of *āyāt* together, it becomes clear that the conditional *āyāt* are explanations of the unconditional. So, accordingly, one must derive the meaning of *jihād* from what is explained by the conditional *āyāt*, precluding the recognition of any *āyāh* of *jihād* as obligatory without conditions.

Yet some commentators have thought up the issue of abrogation.[18] They agree that many *āyāt* of the Qur'an set conditions for fighting against the non-Muslims, but they say that other *āyāt* have been revealed that abrogate all those instructions and conditions. Thus it is necessary to discuss abrogations, both that which abrogates and that which is abrogated. Some think that the first *āyah* of Surah 9 — which gives the complete command of *jihād* and conditions for the immunity of the polytheists, fixing a period for them to stay in Mecca, after which they would no longer have the right to remain and the Muslims would beseige them in their fortifications and hiding places and kill them, and which, furthermore, was revealed in the ninth year of *hijrat* — in one blow abrogated all the instructions previously received concerning *jihād.*

This view is incorrect for two reasons. One is that one *ayah* should only be considered abrogator of another when it is in complete disagreement with it. Imagine that an *āyah* was revealed with the order not to fight at all with the polytheists and then another is revealed with the order thereafter to fight. The meaning of this would be that God had cancelled the first instruction. Such is the meaning of abrogation, that the first instruction is annulled and another is put in its place. Thus the second instruction must be such that it is one hundred percent opposed to the first. However, if collectively the contents of the first *āyah* and the second *āyah* are compatible, so that one is the clarifier of the other, then there is no further question of one abrogating the other.

The *āyāt* of *Sūrah* 2 are not such that they can be considered to annul the *ayat* that had arrived previously and which attached conditions to *jihād.* This is because, considering all the *āyāt* of *Sūrah* 9 together, it is clear that they collectively tell one to fight the polytheists for the reason that they pay no observance to one of the essentials of humanity — loyalty to one's promises — which the nature of every human realizes must be kept, even if the law of one's particular nation does not stress this point or even include it. Thus the *āyāt* tell us to fight if one has concluded an agreement with them and they, whenever they see the opportunity to violate it, do so and strive to destroy or annihilate us. Reason dictates that if we determine that a people are going to destroy us at the first opportunity, we should not wait for them to act before reciprocating, or they will succeed in destroying us. In today's world one may see that one nation attacks the other side because it has made the clear decision that the other nation intends to attack them, and when this happens, the whole world will agree that it is permissible and right. No one would say that, although they may have had clear evidence that the enemy intended to attack on a certain day, yet they had no right to attack that enemy today, but should have waited with folded arms for the attack and only then should have retaliated.

The Qur'an in those same *āyāt* of *Sūrah* 9, the most militant *sūrah* of the Qur'an, says, "How is this — when if they have the upper hand over you, they disregard honor and pact in respect to you? They satisfy you with their mouths while their hearts refuse." (9:8). So these *āyat* are not so unconditional as has been thought. What they actually say is, in the circumstances of sensing danger from enemy territory, to fold one's arms and wait would be a mistake. Thus one must not consider that these *āyāt* are completely out of accord with the other *āyāt* and they should not be considered as abrogators. This is the first of the reasons why these *āyāt* are not abrogators.

The second reason is something which the scholars of *uṣūl al-fiqh*[19] say, and if it can be explained, then it will explain the second reason.

The scholars say, *"There is no general rule without an exception,"* *and this is absolutely right.* One is told to fast, but not if one is ruled as travelling or sick. There are the same kind of exceptions in prayer and other matters. There is no generality that has no exception. Even this very generality has exceptions. But there are in fact some generalities that really have no exceptions and admit none.

The point of this is that some issues refuse to be abrogated, because their tone admits no exceptions. For example, the Qur'an states, "... if you are thankful, He is pleased with it for you." (39:7), and to this there can never be any exceptions. It is not possible that there will come a time when a person will be sincerely grateful to God and He will not be pleased. This is something that will not be different in any circumstances, unless the person becomes ungrateful.

Similarly in the matter of abrogation, some *āyāt* are such that abrogation is fundamentally not applicable to them because the meaning of abrogation is that the abrogated order was temporary. Thus certain things cannot be temporary. If they are now, they must always be. An example will demonstrate why.

There is an *āyāh* of the Qur'an which states, "... but do not begin hostilities. God does not love aggressors." (2:190). This has a generality in regard to individuals and a continuity in regard to time. It is not possible for one to maintain exceptions to this generality, to say that God does not like aggressors except some of them. The holiness of divinity and the filth of transgression are not two things that go together for one to be able to claim that God does not love transgressors except this Mr. X or that Mr. Y. This is a generality with no exceptions. It is unlike fasting, where one fasts unless one is in a certain condition. Regarding fasting, one might be in a certain condition wherein one must not fast, but transgression is not such a thing where it can be claimed that in one condition one must be unjust, whereas in another condition one must not. Wherever there is injustice and oppression, it is wrong, irrespective of who has committed it. Even if those who do it should be Prophets of God, their act is still blameworthy, sin, and disobedience. God loves no one who is disobedient. One cannot say, "... except the disobedience of His Prophets." Even this is unacceptable. Even if Prophets — God forbid — committed sins, they would not be loved by God. The difference between the Prophets and others is not that they committed sins and God loved them anyway, but they they never committed sins, in contrast to others. This, then, is a generality that admits no exceptions. It is also the same from the point of view of time. It cannot reasonably be claimed that this fact pertains only to a certain time and, for instance, after ten years God changes His mind, cancels His original commandment, and says that thereafter He loves transgressors.

The first *ayāh* concerning *jihād* in the Qur'an has such a tone: "Fight in the way of God against those who fight against you, but do not begin hostilities." (2:190). Fighting against aggression, so as to eliminate aggression, is not aggression, but fighting against anything but aggression is aggression and unlawful. This rule admits no abrogation. It is possible, for example, that permission for *jihād* and self-defense be withheld for awhile in our own best interests, for us to endure and persevere for awhile, and then, later, the instructions for *jihād* be received, meaning that the command to be patient is cancelled because it was only for a limited period. The intention of the commandment that was annulled is that from the very beginning it was appointed to be temporary.

According to this distinction, the Qur'an limits *jihād* strictly to a kind of defense and only permits it in the face of aggression. But in the last lecture it was stated that *jihād* for the expansion of human values, even if they are not in danger, cannot be condemned, and it was also pointed out the meaning of aggression is a general one, such that it does not necessarily have to be against life, property, principles, land, or even against independence and freedom; if a group transgresses against values that are counted as human values, then this is aggression.

It is desirable to cite a simple example. In the contemporary period, huge efforts are being made to pluck out the roots of various diseases. So far, the primary causes of some diseases like cancer have not been discovered and thus the methods of cure are likewise still unknown. But at the moment there exists a series of medicines which people use to temporarily allay the effect of these diseases. Supposing that an institution discovers the cure for one of these diseases, and that the other institutions that profit from the existence of that illness, those factories that produce those medicines useful for that illness alone, in order to prevent their market from collapsing — in which case they would lose millions or billions of dollars — destroy that newly discovered cure which would be so beneficial for humanity, destroy those connected with it, and destroy the formula so that no one else can know about it. This would be indefensible. One is unable to say that no one has attacked one's life, property, principles, independence, or territory, but merely that some fellow in one corner of the world has made a discovery and another in a different part of the world wants to rub him out, and it has nothing to do with us. On the contrary, this is not the place for "what has it got to do with us?" This is a place where a human value is exposed to danger and aggression has taken shape against it. If one takes a stance of resistance and war, one shall not be considered an aggressor, but one who has risen to oppose aggression and fight the aggressors.

So when it is said that the basis of *jihād* is defense, this does not mean defense in the limited sense of having to defend oneself when one is attacked with the sword, gun, or artillery ball. It means that if one's being, one of one's material or spiritual values, or anything that mankind values and respects and which is counted as a condition of mankind's prosperity and happiness is aggressed against, then one should mount a defense against this.

Once again the topic arises concerning whether monotheism is a personal issue or whether it is one of the values of humanity. If it is the latter and must be defended, such that if among a set of laws there is one that states that monotheism must be defended on the principle of it being a basic human value (as in Islam, for example) this does not mean that aggression is considered lawful. It means that monotheism is a spiritual value and the meaning of defense is so wide that it includes spiritual values. To repeat, Islam does not say that one must fight to impose monotheism, for, being of faith, it cannot be imposed. Faith is built on discernment and choice, and discernment is not influenced by force. The same applies to choice. *"Lā Ikrāha fid-dīn"* means one must not compel anyone, for faith is not something that can be compelled. It is not the meaning of this phrase, however, that one is not to defend the rights of monotheism. It does not mean that if the slogan, "There is no deity but God," is in danger from some direction, one cannot defend it. Not at all!

That religion must not be imposed on the individual and that people must be free in their choice of religion is one matter. That belief, however, in the current phraseology, must be free, is quite another. Many beliefs have "thought" as a foundation, meaning that many beliefs have been discerned and found to be true and have been freely chosen. The alignment and commitment of an individual's heart to his belief in many cases is built on thought, discernment, and selection, but is that true of all human beliefs, or are some merely built on a sentimental basis? An example the Qur'an cites on the subject of the imitation by one generation of the previous is: "Truly we found our fathers following a religion and we are following in their footsteps." (43:23). The Qur'an puts great stress on this point, and the same applies to a belief that is formed by the imitation of the patricians of a society. In such places the phrase "freedom of belief" is completely without meaning, for freedom means the absence of obstacles to the activities of an active and advancing force, whereas this type of belief is a constriction and a stagnation. Freedom in constriction is similar to the freedom of a prisoner condemned to a life sentence or a man bound in heavy chains, and the only difference is that he who is physically enchained senses his condition, while he whose spirit is in chains is unaware of it. This is what is referred to when it is said that freedom of belief founded on imitation and the influences of the environment, rather than on freedom of thought, is totally meaningless.

The final issue of concern in this discussion is that of *jizyah*. In the content of the *āyah* it has been revealed that one is to fight the People of the Book, either with or without attached conditions, until they pay the *jizyah*. It could be assumed that *jizyah* connotes a type of protection money or danegeld and that Muslims in the past have taken extortion; but protection money, in any shape, is oppression and the Qur'an negates this in all its forms. *Jizyah* is from the foot JZA, which in Arabic is used for both reward and punishment. If *jizyah* in this context means the recompense of punishment, then it can be claimed that its meaning is indeed protection money or danegeld, but if it means a reward, which it does, then the meaning changes.

It has already been said that some claim that *jizyah* is fundamentally a non-Arabic word, that it is the Arabicised form of the Persian word *gazyeh* the name of a head-tax first introduced by the Persian king, Anushirvan, and that when this word arrived among the Arabs, the "G" was changed into a "J" in accordance with the normal rule, so that the Arabs, instead of calling it *gazyeh* called it *jizyah*. Thus *jizyah* means a tax, and paying taxes is not the same as paying extortion money. The Muslims must also pay kinds of taxes, and the only differenceis between the actual type of taxes paid by the Muslims, versus that paid by the People of the Book. There is, however, no proof for this idea that the word is not Arabic, and furthermore, there is no immediate importance in this word. Whatever the root of the word may be, what must be done is to discover the nature of *jizyah* from the laws that Islam has introduced for it and by which it is practically defined.

To put this in a different way, it is necessary to examine whether Islam considers *jizyah* to be a reward or a punishment. If in return for the *jizyah,* Islam makes certain undertakings, gives certain services, then the payment of the *jizyah* is its reward. If, however, it takes the *jizyah* without giving anything in return, then it is a kind of protection money. Taking protection money means taking the right to use force. It means that the strong tell those who are weaker to give an amount of money so they won't bother them, interfere, or destroy their security. If on the other hand, Islam says that it places an undertaking before the People of the Book and in return for that undertaking they are to pay to Islam *jizyah,* then in this case the meaning of *jizyah* is a reward, regardless of whether it is a Persian or an Arabic word. It is the nature of the law that is important, rather than the nature of the word.

When the essence of this law is perceived, one notices that *jizyah* is for that group among the People of the Book who live under the protection of and are subject to the Islamic state. The Islamic state is charged with certain duties towards its nation and likewise charges its nation with certain duties towards itself, and the first of these is to pay taxes for the state budget to be maintained. These taxes include that which is taken as *zakāt* and otherwise in the forms of various taxes that the Islamic government introduces in accordance with the best Islamic interests. All these must be paid by the people, and if they were not to do so, the Islamic government would automatically fall into disorder. There is no government that has a budget which is not, either in part or whole, subsidized by the people. Any government that wants a budget must meet its budget either directly or indirectly from taxes.

The second of the citizen's duties is to be charged with the responsibility of providing soldiers and undertaking sacrifices for the sake of the state. It is possible that a danger will arise and the individuals that comprise the citizens of the state must help in its defense. If the People of the Book are living under the protection of the Islamic state they are not bound to pay those Islamic taxes and are not bound to take part in *jihād,* even though any advantage from the *jihād* will also benefit them. In accordance with this, when the Islamic government secures the safety of a people and places them under its protection, whether or not they are its own people, it requires something from them, financial or otherwise. From the People of the Book, instead of *zakāt* and other taxes, it requires *jizyah.* So in the early days of Islam, whenever People of the Book volunteered to come and fight in the ranks of the Muslims to the advantage of the Muslims and the Islamic state, the *jizyah* was given back to them, since the *jizyah* was collected because they were not bound to provide soldiers, but, as they had come forth to fight, the money was theirs and the Islamic state could not rightfully keep it. In the commentary on the Qur'an, *Al-Minār*[20] there are many accounts from various history books of how the People of the Book used to be told that, since they were living under the protection of the Islamic state and of the Muslims, themselves sending no soldiers (the Muslims would sometimes not accept them), then instead of sending soldiers they had to pay the *jizyah.* And if once in ahile the Muslims in certain instances found confidence in them and accepted their soldiers, they no longer took *jizyah* from them.[21]

Accordingly, whether *jizyah* is Persian or Arabic, whether it is from j.z.a. or from *gazyeh,* this much is clear: it is technically a reward to the Islamic government from its citizens who are non-Muslim People of the Book, in return for the services that it performs for them and in return for their not having to provide the state with soldiers and not having to pay taxes.

Now the first problem of how and why Islam stops its *jihād* for the sake of *jizyah* becomes clear. The answer is illuminated in response to the question, "Why does Islam desire *jihād*?" It does not desire it for the sake of the imposition of belief, but for the removal of barriers. When the other side says that it has no quarrel with Muslims and will not create a barrier to the call of monotheism, then when it does not create such barrier, it is to be ruled in accordance with the *ayah*: "And if they incline to peace, you should also include ot it." (8:61). If they have been humbled, and manifest a heart and mind of peace and compromise, then Muslims are no longer to be militant. They are not to say, "Oh no! We do not want peace; we are going to fight." Now that they have come forward to live in peace and concord, Muslims must also declare the same. Of course, now that they wish to live under the Muslim protection but do not have to pay any of the Islamic taxes, nor provide any soldiers, and neither is there confidence in their soldiers on the part of the Muslims, then in turn for the services and protection of the Muslims, a simple tax is taken from them called *jizyah.*

Notes

1. Zorastrians are a religious minority living in Iran, where they are known as "Zartoshti," and in India, where they are called "Parsis." The prophet of this religion is Shat Zartosht Espantoman, known in the West as Zoroaster or Zarathustra. While many scholars accept the opinion of R. C. Zaehner, that Zarathustra lived from about 628 to 551 B.C., in her recent work, Mary Boyce argues that he may have lived between about 1700 and 1500 B.C. See Mary Boyce, *Zoroastrians: Their Religious Beliefs and Practices* (London: Routledge and Kegan Paul, 1979). The issue concerning Zoroastrians in Muslim jurisprudence is whether they are monotheists, and whether Zoroaster was a divinely inspired prophet who brought a scripture from God. The unresolved issue has caused some Muslim experts of jurisprudence to consider them as merely "attached" to the People of the Book, thus Mutahhari's use of "perhaps." The word "*Majūs*" in (22:17) is taken by the exegetes to refer to them. Tabataba'i makes the following comment *(Al-Mizān,* Vol. 14, p. 358):

> It is well known that the Magi are believers in Zoraster and their sacred book is the Avesta. [Zoraster's] life history and the precise time of his mission are ambiguous due to scattered information. [9](The Zorastrians[0] lost their book as a result of Alexander's domination of Iran, but it was recollected during the reign of the Sassanids [c. 224-640 C.E.]. This makes for difficulty in understanding their religion. It is certain, however, that they believe in two origins of good and evil. [Yazdan and Ahriman — Light and Darkness], and they respect the angels and seek refuge with them without making idols for them as the idolators do. They venerate the basic elements [Earth, Air, Fire and Water], with special emphasis on Fire, dedicated to which were their fire temples in Iran, China, India, and other lands. They believe in Ahura-Mazda as the creator of all things.

2. Chosro I (r. 531-579 C.E.) was a famous Sassanid king known as "Anushirvan the Just" (sometimes used sarcastically because he had the Mazdakites massacred).

3. *Jazā,* from the root JZY, means to recompense, to give satisfaction.

4. A poem by the famous Iranian poet, Adibul Mamalik Farahani (1860-1917).

5. The ten principles are: (1) *salāt* (prayer), (2) *sawm* (fasting), (3) *hajj* (pilgrimage), (4) *zakāt* (tax), (5) *khums* (one fifth tax), (6) *jihād,* (7) to enjoin the good, (8) to forbid evil, (9) association with the righteous, (10) disassociation from the unrighteous. Sometimes these are counted differently, cf. Shari'ati's *"Shahādat"* fn. [78]

6. Unfortunately Mutahhari does not consider the Christian doctrine of the just war. Christianity is often caricatured for polemical effect. Cf. Taleqani's remarks concerning celebacy in Christianity, and Shari'ati's discussion of the difference between the Islamic and Christian view of martyrdom at the beginning of his "Discussion of *Shahādat.*"

7. The phrase is from (4:128) in the context of settlement between husband and wife. Yet it is taken by both Mutahhari and Tabataba'i (in *Khulasa-e-Ta'ālim-e-Islam,* p. 179) as having general application.

8. Cf. Taleqani's *"Jihād* and *Shahādat"* in this volume, where a similar point is made.

9. The *Ansar* were the residents of Medina who helped the Prophet and the other Muslims who emigrated from Mecca, the *Muhajirun*.

10. See Tabarsi, vol. II, p. 363; Ibn Kathir, vol. I, p. 256; Tabataba'i, vol. II, p. 347.

11. See Tabataba'i, vol. II, p. 347; Tusi, vol. II, p. 311.

12. The root, SLM, from which the word "Islam" is derived means both peace and submission. This may appear to contradict the point made earlier in the text, that peace and submission are not the same. However, according to Muslim belief, one should submit to nothing less than God, and it is only this ultimate submission which may be identified with peace.

13. In accordance with the idea that there should be no dichotomy between the sacred and the profane, in Islam, anyone killed in the defense of a right, material or otherwise, is a martyr. There are, however, degrees of martyrdom. One who dies on the field of battle is not washed and dressed for burial, rather he is to go to his grave wearing the bloody garment which testifies to his dedication to Islam. According to Shari'ati (see his *"Shahadat"*), the highest form of martyrdom is to engage in battle, knowing that one will be killed, in order to expose injustice.

14. This is somewhat of an overstatement. See the section of the introduction on just cause.

15. Cf. Tabataba'i, *Al-Mizan*, (English), Vol. 4, p. 171ff.

16. These are all famous Iranian poets: Abulqasim Firdowsi (d. 1020 C.E.), Umar Khayyam (d. 1122 C.E.), Mawlawi (Jalaluddin Rumi)(d. 1273), Muslihuddin Sa'di (d. 1292 C.E.), Hafiz of Shiraz (d. 1389 C.E.).

17. Cf. (7:179), (25:44).

18. "Abrogation" *(naskh)* here is *"naskh al hukm dun al tilawah"* (abrogation of the ruling of an *ayah* without the abrogation of its wording) which is the only mode of abrogation acceptable in Shi'ite exegesis. See Nu'mani (Arabic), pp. 6-11; *Itqan* (Arabic) vol. II, pp. 20-27; Kamali Dezfuli *Qanun-e-Tafsin* (Persian), pp. 350-383; and (in English) John Burton, *The Collection of the Qur'an* (London: Cambridge University Press, 1977) pp. 68, 113.

19. *Usul al-fiqh* is the study of the principles of jurisprudence.

20. Reference is made here to the commentary on the Qur'an by Muhammad Abduh and Rashid Rida, *Tafsir al-Qur'an al-Hakim* 11 vols. Cairo: 1325/1907-1353/1934.

21. See Tabataba'i, vol. IX, pp. 240, 242, 252.

Ayatullah Murtada Mutahhari

4.

Shahīd

There are certain words and expressions to which, in general use or particularly in Islamic terminology, a certain sense of dignity, and sometimes even sanctity, is attached. "Student," "teacher," "scholar," "inventor," "hero," "reformer," "philospher," "preacher," "believer," "pious person," *"mujāhid,"* "truthful one," *"walī,"* "Imam," and "prophet" are some of the words of this category.[2] A sense of dignity, even sanctity, is attached to these words in general usage, especially in Islamic discourse. It is evident that a word as such as no sanctity. It becomes sacred because of the sense which it conveys. The sanctity of a sense depends on a particular mental outlook, and on values which are cherished generally, or by a particular group of people.

In Islamic terminology there is a word which has a special sanctity. When anyone familiar with the Islamic modes of expression hears this word, he feels it to be invested with a special glory. This word is *shahīd.* A sense of grandure and sanctity is associated with it, in its use by all the people. Of course the standards and the criteria vary. At present we are only concerned with the Islamic usage of this term.

From the Islamic point of view, only that person is regarded as having secured the status of *shahīd* who Islam recognizes as having acted according to its own standards. Only he who is killed in an effort to achieve the highest Islamic objectives and is really motivated by a desire to safeguard true human values attains this position, which is one of the highest to which one can aspire. From what the noble Qur'an and *hadīth* say about the *shuhadā,* it is possible to infer why Muslims attach so much sanctity to this word, and what the logic behind it is.

With respect to the proximity of the *shahīd* to God, the noble Qur'an says: "Think not of those who were slain in the way of God as dead. Nay, they are alive, finding their sustenance with their Lord." (3:169)

In Islam, when a meritorious person or deed is to be exalted, it is said that particular person has the status of *shahid,* or that a particular act merits the reward of *shahādat.* For example, a student who seeks knowledge with the motive of finding out the truth and gaining the favor of God is said to die the death of a *shahīd* if he dies during the course of his studies. This signifies the high status and sanctity of a student. Similarly, a person who endures pain and labors strenuously for the support of his family is said to be like a fighter in the cause of God. It may be noted that Islam is severely opposed to lethargy and parasitism, and regards hard work as a duty.

All those who have served humanity in one way or another, whether as scholars, philosophers, inventors, or teachers, deserve the gratitude of all mankind. But none deserves this to the extent that the *shuhadā* do, and that is why the people of all sectors of the society have a sentimental attachment to them. All other servants of humanity are indebted to the *shuhadā;* whereas the *shuhadā* are indebted to none. A scholar, a philosopher, an inventor or a teacher requires a congenial and conducive atmosphere in order to render their services, and it is the *shahīd* who with his supreme sacrifice provides that atmosphere.

The *shahīd* can be compared to a candle whose job it is to burn out and get extinguished in order to shed light for the benefit of others. The *shuhadā* are the candles of society. They burn themselves out and illuminate society. If they do not shed their light, no organization can shine. A man who works in daylight or in candlelight or in lamplight will pay attention to everything but the source of the light by which he works, although it goes without saying that without that light he can accomplish nothing. The *shuhadā* are the illuminators of society. Had they not shed their light on the darkness of despotism and suppression, humanity would have made no progress.

The Qur'an uses a delightful expression for the Prophet. It has compared him to an illuminating lamp. This expression combines the sense of burning and enlightening. The Qur'an says: "O Prophet! Surely we have sent you as a witness *(shahid)*, a bearer of good news and a warner; and as a guide to God by his permission and as an illuminating lamp." (33:45-46)

There is no doubt that in Islamic terminology *"shahid"* is a sacred word and that for those who use an Islamic vocabulary, it conveys a sense higher than that of any other word.

Islam is a juridical religion. Every Islamic law is based on a social consideration. According to Islamic law, the corpse of every Muslim must be washed ceremonially, and shrouded in neat and clean sheets. Thereafter prayers have to be performed and only then is it buried. There are good reasons for doing all this, but we need not discuss them in the present context. There is an exception to this general rule. The body of a *shahid* is neither to be washed nor shrouded. It is to be buried in those very clothes which the *shahid* was wearing at the time of his death. This exception has deep significance. It shows that the spirit and the personality of a *shahid* are so thoroughly purified that his body, his blood and his garments are also affected by this purification. The body of a *shahid* is spiritualized, in the sense that certain rules applicable to his spirit, are applied to his body, blood and clothes. The body and the garments of a *shahid* acquire respectability because of his spirit, virtue and sacrifice. One who falls *shahid* on a battlefield is buried with his blood-stained body and blood-soaked clothes without being washed. These rules of Islamic law are a sign of the sanctity of the *shahid*.

What is the basis of the sanctity of *shahadat?* It is evident that merely being killed can have no sanctity. It is not always something of which to be proud. Many a death may even be a matter of disgrace. Let us elucidate this point a bit further. We know that there are several kinds of death:

(1) Natural Death: If a man dies a natural death, after completing his normal span of life, his death is considered to be an ordinary event. It is neither a matter of pride nor of shame. It is not even a matter of much sorrow.

(2) Accidental Death: Death as the result of accidents or an epidemic disease, like small-pox or plague, or due to natural disasters, such as earthquake or flood, is considered to be premature, and hence is regarded as regrettable.

(3) Criminal Death: In this case, a person kills another in cold blood simply to satisfy his own passion or because he considered the victim to be his opponent or rival. There are many instances of such murders. We often read in the daily newspapers that a particular woman killed the small child of her husband because the father loved the child while the woman wanted to monopolize his attention, or that a particular man murdered the woman who refused to accept his love. Similarly we read in history that a certain ruler massacred all the children of another ruler in order to foil the chances of any future rivalry. In such cases, the action of the murderer is considered to be atrociously criminal and heinous, and the person killed is regarded as a victim of aggression and tyranny, whose life has been taken in vain. The reaction which such a murder creates is one of horror and pity. It is evident that such a death is shocking and pitiable, but is neither praise-worthy nor a matter of pride. The victim loses his life unnecessarily, because of malice, enmity and hatred.

(4) Self-murder: In this case, the death itself constitutes a crime, and hence, it is the worst kind of death. Suicidal deaths and the deaths of those who are killed in motor accidents because of their own fault come under this category. The same is the case of the death of those who are killed while committing a crime.

(5) *Shahādat: Shahādat* is the death of a person who, in spite of being fully conscious of the risks involved, willingly faces them for the sake of a sacred cause, or, as the Qur'an says, *fī sabīl Allāh* (in the way of God).

Shahādat has two basic elements: (a) the life is sacrificed for a cause; and (b) the sacrifice is made consciously. Usually in the case of *shahādat,* an element of crime is involved. As far as the victim is concerned, the death is sacred; but the action of the killers is a heinous crime. *Shahādat* is heroic and admirable, because it results from a voluntary, conscious and selfless action. It is the only type of death which is higher, greater and holier than life itself.

It is regrettable that most of the preachers who narrate the story of Karbala call Imam Husayn the *Sayyid al-Shuhadā,* although they have little analytical insight into the question of *shahādat.* They describe the events as if Husayn lost his life in vain. Many of our people mourn Imam Husayn for his innocence. They regret that he was a victim of the selfishness of a power-hungry man who shed his blood, through no fault of Husayn's. Had the facts really been this simple Imam Husayn would have been regarded merely as an innocent person to whom a great injustice was done. But he would not have been called a *shahīd,* let alone the *Sayyid al-Shuhadā.* That Imam Husayn was the victim of selfish designs is not the whole story. No doubt the perpetrators of the tragedy committed the crime out of selfishness, but the Imam consciously made the supreme sacrifice. His opponents wanted him to pledge his allegience, but he, knowing fully well the consequences, chose to resist their demand. He regarded it as a great sin to remain quiet at that juncture. The history of his *shahādat,* especially his own statements, bear witness to this fact.

The sacred cause that leads to *shahādat* or the giving of one's life has become a law in Islam. It is called *jihād.* This is not the occasion to discuss its nature in detail, nor to say whether it is always defensive, or offensive, and if it is only defensive, whether it is confined to the defense of individual, or at most of national, rights, or if its scope is so wide as to include the defense of all human rights such as freedom and justice. There are other relevant questions also, such as whether the faith in *tawhīd* is or is not a part of human rights, and whether *jihād* is or is not basically opposed to the right of freedom. The discussion of these questions can be both interesting and instructive, but in its proper place.[3] For the present, suffice it to say that Islam is not a religion directing that should one slap your right cheek, you should offer him your left cheek,[4] nor does it say, "Pay unto Ceasar that which is Ceasar's, and unto God that which is God's."[5] Likewise, Islam is not a religion which is not permitted to have a sacred social ideal, which it may consider it necessary to defend.

The noble Qur'an, in many *ayāt,* has mentioned three sacred concepts, side by side: *imān, hijrat* and *jihād.*[6] The man of the Qur'an is a being attached to faith and detached from everything else. To save his own faith, he migrates, and to save society he carries out *jihād.* It would take too long to reproduce all the *ayāt* and *hadīths* on this subject. We will therefore content ourselves by quoting a few sentences from the *Nahj ul-Balāgha:* "Certainly, *jihād* is an entrance to Paradise, which God has opened for His chosen friends. It is a garment of piety, God's impenetrable armor and trust-worthy shield.

God will clothe those who refrain from it because they find it distatesful in a garment of humiliation and a cloak of disaster."[7]

Jihād is a door to paradise, but it is not open to all and sundry. Not everyone is worthy of it; not everyone is elected to become a *mujāhid*. God has opened this door for his chosen friends only. A position of *mujāhid* is so high that we cannot call him simply God's friend. He is God's chosen friend. The Qur'an says that paradise has eight doors. Obviously, the purpose of this number of doors is not to avoid overcrowding; there is no question of this in the next world! As God can check the accounts of people instantly (the Qur'an says, "He is quick at reckoning"),[8] he can also arrange their entry into paradise through one door. There is no question of entering in turn or of forming a queue there. Similarly, these doors cannot be for different classes of people, for there are no class distinctions in the next world. There, people will not be classified according to their social status or profession. There, people will be graded and grouped together only on the basis of the degree of their faith, good deeds and piety. A door analogous to their spiritual development in this world will be opened for each group, for the next world is only a heavenly embodiment of this world. The door through which the *mujahidun* and the *shuhada* will enter, and the portion of paradise set aside for them, is the one which is reserved for God's chosen friends, who will be graced with his special favor.

Jihād is the garment of piety. The expression, "garment of piety" *(libās al-taqwā),* is used in the Qur'an in *sūra* al-A'raf.[9] Imam Ali says that *jihād* is the garment of piety. Piety consists of true purity, that is, freedom from spiritual and moral pollution which is rooted in selfishness, vanity and avarice. On this basis, a real *mujāhid* is most pious. He is pure because he is free from jealousy, free from vanity, free from avarice and stinginess. A *mujāhid* is the purest of all the pure. He exercises complete self-negation and self-sacrifice. The door which is opened to him is different from the doors opened to others morally undefiled. That piety has various grades can be deduced from the Qur'an itself, which says:

> There shall be no sin (imputed) to those who believe and
> do good works for what they may have eaten (in the past).
> So be mindful of your duty (to God), and do good works;
> and again: be mindful of your duty, and believe; and once

again: be mindful of your duty, and do right. God loves
the good. (5:93)

This *āyah* yields two valuable points of Qur'anic knowledge. The
first point is that there various degrees of faith and piety. This is the
point under discussion at present. The other point concerns the
philosophy of life and human rights. The noble Qur'an wants to say
that all good things have been created for the people of faith, piety
and good deeds. Man is entitled to utilize the bounties of God only
when he marches forward on the path of evolution prescribed for him
by nature. That is the path of faith, piety and good deeds.

Muslim scholars inspired by this *āyah,* and by what has been
explicitly or implicitly stated in other Islamic texts, have classified
piety into three degrees: (a) average piety; (b) above average piety;
and (c) outstanding piety. The piety of *mujāhidīn* is that of supreme
self-sacrifice. They sincerely renounce all they possess, and surrender
themselves to God. Thus, they put on a garment of piety.

Jihād is the impenetrable armor of God. A Muslim community
equipped with the spirit of *jihād* is not vulnerable to enemy assaults.
Jihād is the reliable shield of God. The armor is the defensive
covering worn during fighting, but the shield is a tool taken in hand
to foil the enemy's strokes and thrusts. A shield is meant to prevent a
blow, and armor is meant to neutralize its effect. Apparently, Imam
Ali has compared *jihād* both to armor and to a shield because some
forms of it have a preventive nature and prevent the onslaught of the
enemy, while other forms of *jihād* have a resistive nature and render
enemy attacks ineffective.

God will clothe with a garment of humiliation a person who
refrains from *jihād* because he dislikes it. The people who lose the
spirit of fighting and resisting the forces of evil are doomed to
humiliation, disgrace, bad-luck and helplessness. The noble Prophet
has said, "All good lies in the sword and under the shadow of the
sword."[10] He has also said, "God has honored my followers because
of the hoofs of their horses and the position of their arrows." This
means that the Muslim community is a community of power and
force. Islam is a religion of power. It produces *mujāhidīn.* Will
Durant, in his book, *The Story of Civilization,* says that no religion
has called its followers to power to the extent that Islam has.[11]
According to another *hadīth,* the noble Prophet has been quoted as

having said, "He who did not fight and did not even think of fighting will die the death of a sort of hypocrite." *Jihād,* or at least a desire to take part in it, is an integral part of the doctrine of Islam. One's fidelity to Islam is judged by it. Another *hadīth* reports the Prophet as having said that a *shahīd* would not be interrogated in his grave.[12] The Prophet said that the flash of the sword over his head was enough of a test. The fidelity of a *shahīd,* having once been proved, need not be questioned further.

In the early days of Islam, many Muslims had a special spirit, which may be called the spirit of longing for *shahādat.* Imam Ali was the most prominent of such people. He himself says, "When the *āyah* was revealed: 'Do men think that they will be let off, because they say, We believe, and will not be tested with affliction?' (29:2), I asked the Prophet about it. I knew that as long as he was alive the Muslims would not be subject to an ordeal. The Prophet said that after him, a civil strife would break out among the Muslims. Then I reminded him that on the occasion of the battle of Uhud, when I was dejected because a number of Muslims had been killed and I had been deprived of *shahādat,* he consoled me, saying that I would attain *shahādat* in the future. The Prophet affirmed it, and asked me whether I would observe patience at that time. I said that that would be an occasion for being thankful to God, not for merely being patient. Then the Prophet gave me some details of the events to come.[13] This is what we mean by the longing for *shahādat.* Had Imam Ali lost the hope of attaining *shahādat,* life would have become meaningless for him. We always have Imam Ali's name on our lips, and claim to be devoted to him. If, mere verbal professions could do, no one would be better Shi'a than we are. But true Shi'aism requires us to follow in his footsteps, too. We have given just one example of his conduct above.

Apart from Imam Ali, we know of many other people who longed for *shahādat.* In the days of Islam, every Muslim prayed to God for it, as is evident from the supplications which have come down to us from the Imams. In the supplication which is offered during the nights of the noble month of Ramadan, we say, "Oh God! Let us be killed in your way, in the company of your friend (Imam), and attain *shahādat.*"[14] We find that during the early days of Islam everyone, whether young or old, high or low, had this longing. Sometimes the people came to the Prophet and expressed this desire. Islam does not allow suicide. They wanted to take part in *jihad*, and to be killed while doing their duty. They requested the Prophet to pray to God to grant them *shahādat*.

In the book, *Safīnat al-Bihār*,¹⁵ there is a story of a man named Khaythumah (or Khathimah). At the time of the battle of Badr,¹⁶ he and his son were both keen to take part in the fighting and to get killed. They argued with each other. In the end they drew lots. The son won, and accordingly went to the battlefield where he laid down his life. Some time later, the father had a dream in which he saw his son living a very happy life, who told him that God's promise had come true. The old father came to the Prophet and narrated the dream. He told the Prophet that though he was too old and too weak to fight, he was desirous of taking part in the fighting and falling a *shāhid*. He requested the Prophet to pray to God to grant him his desire. The Prophet prayed accordingly. Within less than a year the old man not only had the good fortune of taking part in the battle of Uhud, but also of achieving *shahādat*.

There was another man, whose name was Amr ibn Jamuh. He had several sons. He was lame in one leg and so according to Islamic law, exempt from taking part in the fighting. The Qur'an says that the lame are not under constraint (to take part in *jihād*) (48:17). On the occasion of the battle of Uhud all his sons equipped themselves with arms. He said that he must also go into battle and lay down his life. His sons objected to his decision and asked him to stay behind, since he was not under any obligation to go to battle. But still he insisted. His sons brought the senior members of their family to exert pressure on him, but the old man would not change his mind. He went instead to the Prophet and said, "Prophet of God, why don't the children let me become a *shahīd*? If *shahādat* is good for others, it is good for me, too." The Prophet then asked his sons not to restrain him. He said, "this man longs for *shahādat*. If he is under no obligation to fight, neither is he forbidden from it. You should have no objection." The old man was pleased. He immediately armed himself. On the battlefield, one of his sons was watching him. He saw his father, in spite of being aged and weak, fought recklessly and zealously. At last he was killed. One of his sons was also killed.

Uhud is situated near Medina. There, the Muslims suffered heavy losses and their position became critical. In the meantime, a report reached Medina that the Muslims had been defeated. The men and women of Medina hurried to Uhud. One of the women was the wife of Amr ibn Jamuh. She went to Uhud and found the corpses of her husband, son and brother. She loaded them onto a strong camel, and set out for Medina with the intention of burying them in the cemetery of Baqi. On the way, she noticed that her camel moved very haltingly and slowly towards Medina and turned constantly toward Uhud. Meanwhile, other women including some of the wives of the Prophet were going toward Uhud. One of the wives of the Prophet asked her where she was coming from. She replied that she was coming from Uhud.

"What are you carrying on your camel?"

"Nothing. Only the corpses of my husband, son and brother. I want to take them to Medina."

"How is the Prophet?"

"Thank God! Everything is all right. The Prophet is safe. The designs of the infidels have been frustrated by God. As long as the Prophet is safe, everything else is immaterial."

Then the woman said that there was something queer about her camel. It appeared that it did not want to go to Medina. It should have been going to its manger eagerly, but it wanted to go back to Uhud. The Prophet's wife proposed that they should go together to the Prophet to tell him about it. When they met the Prophet, the woman said, "I have a strange story. This animal goes on to Medina with difficulty, but comes to Uhud easily." The Prophet said, "Did you husband say anything when he came out of his house?" Yes, when he came out of the house, he raised his hands in prayer and said, 'Oh God, grant me that I don't come back to this house,'" said the woman. "That's it. Your husband's prayer has been granted. Now let him be buried at Uhud along with the other *shuhāda,*" advised the Prophet.

The Commander of the Faithful, Imam Ali, used to say, "I prefer a thousand strokes of the sword to dying in bed."[17] Imam Husayn on his way to Karbala, used to recite certain lines of poetry. His father is also reported to have recited these verses occasionally. We give a translation of them here:

> Though worldly things are fine and charming,
> The recompense of the hereafter is far better.
> If all possessions and wealth are to be left behind,
> Why should one be stingy about them?
> If our bodies are meant to die and decay,
> Is it not better that they are cut to pieces in the way of
> God?

The motivation of a *shahīd* is different from that of ordinary people. His logic is the blind logic of a reformer; it is the logic of a gnostic lover. If the two logics, that of the earnest reformer and that of the zealous and gnostic lover are put together, the result will be the motivation of a *shahīd*. Let us elucidate this point further.

When Imam Husayn decided to leave for Kufa, some prudent members of his family tried to dissuade him. Their argument was that his action was not logical. They were right in their own way. It was not in conformity with their logic, which was the logic of the worldly wise. But Imam Husayn had a higher logic. His logic was that of a *shahīd*, which is beyond the comprehension of ordinary people. Abdullah ibn Abbas[18] was no small person. Muhammad ibn Hanafiyyah[19] was not an ordinary man. But their logic was based on the consideration of personal interests and political gains. From their point of view, Imam Husayn's action was not discreet at all. Ibn Abbas made a proposal which was politically very sound. It is the usual practice of clever people to use others as their tools. They push others forward and remain behind themselves. If others succeed, they take full advantage of their success. Otherwise, they lose nothing. Ibn Abbas said to Imam Husayn, "The people of Kufa have written to tell you that they are ready to fight for your cause. You should write back asking them to expel Yazid's officials from there. They will either do what you suggest or they won't. If they do, you can go there safely. If they are unable to do so, your position is not affected." The Imam did not listen to this advice. He made it plain that he was determined to proceed. Ibn Abbas said:

"You will be killed."

"So what?" replied the Imam.

"A man who goes somewhere knowing that he may be killed does not take his wife and children along with him."

"But I must."

The logic of a *shahīd* is unique. It is beyond the comprehension of ordinary people. That is why the word *"shahīd"* is encircled with a halo of sanctity. It occupies a remarkable position in the vocabulary of sacred and highly glorious words. It connotes something higher than the sense of a hero and a reformer. It cannot be replaced by any other word.

What does a *shahīd* do? His function is not confined to resiting the enemy, and in the process, either striking a blow or receiving one. Had that been the case, we could say that when his blood is shed it is wasted. But at no time is the blood of a *shahīd* wasted. It does not flow into the ground. Every drop of it is turned into hundreds of thousands of drops, nay into tons of blood, and is transfused into the body of his society. That is why the noble Prophet has said, "God does not like any drop more than the drop of blood shed in his way." *Shahādat* means the transfusion of blood into a society, especially into a society suffering from anemia. It is the *shahīd* who infuses fresh blood into the veins of the society.[20]

The distinctive characteristic of a *shahīd* is that he charges the atmosphere with courage and zeal. He revives the spirit of valor and fortitude, courage and zeal, especially divine zeal, among the people who have lost it. That is why Islam is always in need of *shuhadā*. The revival of courage and zeal is essential for the revival of a nation.

A scholar serves the society only through his knowledge. It is on account of his knowledge that his personality is amalgamated with the society, just as a drop of water is amalgamated with the sea. As a result of this amalgamation, a part of his personality, his thoughts and ideas become immortal. An inventor is amalgamated with the society through his inventions. He serves the society by making himself immortal by virtue of his skill and invetions. A poet makes himself immortal through his poetic act, and a moral teacher through his wise sayings. Similarly, a *shahīd* immortalizes himself in his own way. He gives invaluable fresh blood to the society. In other words, a scholar immortalizes his thoughts, an artist his art, an inventor his inventions, and a moral teacher, his teachings. But a *shahīd* immortalizes all his faculties. That is why the Prophet said, "Above every virtue there is another virtue, but there is no virtue higher than being killed in the way of God."[21]

There is a *hadith* which says that there are three classes of people who will be allowed to intercede with God on the day of judgement. They are the prophets, the *'ulama* and the *shuhada*.[22] In this *hadith,* the Imams have not been mentioned explicitly, but as the report comes down from the Imams it is obvious that the term, "*'ulama,*" stands for the true divines, who par excellence include the Imams themselves. The intercession of the prophets is quite apparent. It is the intercession of the *shuhada* which we have yet to comprehend. The *shuhada* secure this privilege of intercession because they lead the people onto the right path. Their intercession will be the portrayal of the events which took place in this world. The Commander of the Faithful, Imam Ali, says, "God will bring forward the *shuhada* on the day of judgement with such pomp and splendor that even the prophets, if mounted, will dismount to show respect for them. With such grandeur will a *shahid* appear on the day of judgement."

Among the *shuhada* of the early days of Islam, the name of the most brilliant *shahid* was "Hamzah ibn Abd ul-Muttalib." He was given the epithet, *"Sayyid al-Shuhada."* He was an uncle of the Prophet and was present at the battle of Uhud. Those who have had the good luck of visiting Medina may have paid a visit to his grave. When Hamzah migrated from Mecca, he was alone, for nobody lived with him in his house. When the Prophet returned from Uhud, he found women weeping in the houses of all the *shuhada,* except that of Hamzah. He uttered just one sentence: "Hamzah has no one to weep for him." The companions of the Prophet went to their houses and told their womenfolk that the Prophet had said that Hamzah had nobody to weep for him. All the women who were weeping for their sons, husbands and brothers immediately set out for the house of Hamzah and wept there, out of respect for the wishes of the Prophet. Thereafter, it became a tradition that whenever anybody wanted to weep for any *shahid,* he or she first went to the house of Hamzah and wept there. This incident shows that although Islam does not encourage lamenting the death of an ordinary man, it tends to want people to weep for a *shahid.* A *shahid* creates the spirit of valor, and by weeping for a *shahid* one participates in that valor in conformity with the longing for *shahadat.*

The title, *"Sayyid al-Shuhadā"* was first applied to Hamzah. After the tragedy of the tenth of Muharram, the *shahādat* of Imam Husayn overshadowed all other cases of *shahādat,* and the title was transferred to him.[23] No doubt this epithet is still applied to Hamzah, but he was the *Sayyid al-Shuhadā* of his time, whereas Imam Husayn is the *Sayyid al-Shuhadā* of all time, just as the virgin Mary was the exemplar of the women in her time, and the lady of light, Fatimah, is the exemplar of women of all time.

We deem it necessary at this juncture to refer briefly to the philosophy of lamentation over a *shahīd.* Nowadays, many people object to the weeping for Imam Husayn. Some of them assert that this custom is the result of incorrect thinking and a wrong conception of *shahādat.*[24] Moreover, it has had bad repercussions, and is responsible for the backwardness and decline of the people who have adopted it. The present writer remembers that when he was a student of Qum, he read a book by Muhammad Masud,[25] a well-known writer of those days. In it he drew a comparison between the Shi'a custom of weeping for Imam Husayn and the Christian practice of celebrating the crucifixion (according to their own belief) of Jesus Christ with festivities. The author wrote along these lines:

> It is to be noticed that one nation weeps for its *shahīd* because it regards *shahādat* as something undesirable and regrettable, whereas another nation rejoices at the death of its *shahīd* because it regards his *shahādat* as a great achievement and a matter of pride. A nation which weeps and mourns for a thousand years naturally loses its vitality and becomes weak and cowardly, whereas the nation which celebrates the *shahādat* of its hero becomes powerful, courageous and self-sacrificing. For one nation *shahādat* means failure. Its reaction is weeping and lamenting which leads to weakness, helplessness and submissiveness. But for the other nation, *shahādat* means triumph, and hence, its reaction is joy and rejoicing, which bolsters up its morale.

This is the gist of the criticism made by this author. The same arguments are advanced by other critics also. We would like to analyse this question and prove that the festive celebration of *shahādat* by the Christians stems from their individualistic approach, and the weeping for the *shuhadā* by the Muslims stems from their social approach.[26]

Of course, we cannot justify the attitude of those of our masses who look at Imam Husayn only as a person to whom a great injustice was done, and who was killed just for nothing. They express profound regret at his death, but pay little attention to his heroic and praise-worthy performance. We have already denounced this attitude. We intend to explain why the Imams have exhorted weeping for a *shahīd,* and what the real philosophy of this exhortation is.

We do not know when and by whom the festive celebration of the *shahādat* of Jesus Christ was initiated. But we know that weeping for the *shuhāda* has been recommended by Islam, and it is an indisputable doctrine of the Shi'ite school of Islam. Now to analyse the main point, let us first discuss the individual aspect of death and *shahādat.* Is death an achievement on the part of the individual, or is it something undesirable? Should others regard it as a heroic deed on the part of the individual concerned?

We know that in this world there have been schools of thought, which may still exist, according to which the relationship between a man and the world, or between the soul and the body, is similar to the relationship between a prisoner and a prison, or the relationship between one who falls into a well and the well, or between a bird and its cage. Naturally, according to these schools death is equivalent to liberation and emancipation. Therefore, they allow suicide. It is said that the famous false prophet, Manichaeus,[27] held this view. According to this theory, death has a positive value and is desirable for everyone. No one's death is regrettable. A release from prison, getting out of a well, and breaking out of a cage is a cause for joy, not sorrow.

Another theory holds that death means nonexistence, complete annihilation and utter destruction, whereas life means to be and to persevere. Obviously, existence is better than nonexistence. It is a matter of instinct of life, whatever its form may be, is preferable to death. The famous mystic poet, Mawlawi,[27] quotes the Greek physician Galen,[29] as having said that in all circumstances he preferred to live rather than die, no matter what form life took. He preferred life, even if it meant living in the belly of a mule, with only the head protruding out for breathing. According to this theory, death has only negative value.

There is another theory, according to which death does not mean annihilation. It means only shifting from one world to another. The relationship between man and the world, and between the soul and the body, is not like that between a prisoner and the prison, the fellow in the well and the well, the bird and the cage. It is like the relationship between a student and his school, or between a farmer and his farm. It is true that occasionally a student has to live away from his home, where he misses the company of his friends and has to pursue his studies within the limited atmosphere of the school, but the only way to lead a happy life in society is to successfully complete one's course of studies. It is also true that a farmer has to leave his house and family life to work on his farm, but that provides him with a good means of livelihood, and enables him to enjoy his family life throughout the year. The relationship between this world and the next, and between the soul and the body is of this very nature. To those who have this outlook on the world, but who fail in practical life because of their lethargy and malpractices, the idea of death naturally appears to be dreadful and terrible. In fact, they are afraid of death because they fear the consequences of their own deeds. But the attitude of those who are successful in their practical life is naturally that of the student who has paid his whole-hearted attention to his studies, or the farmer who has worked hard. Such a student or farmer yearn for their return home, but would not think of leaving their task incomplete.

The noble men are like the successful students. They long for death, which means going to the next world. At every moment they impatiently await death. Imam Ali has said about them, "If God had not fixed the time of death, their souls would not have remained in their bodies for a moment, because of their desire for recompense and fear of retribution." At the same time, they do not run after death, for they know that it is only this life which gives them the opportunity to work and attain spiritual development. They know that the longer they live, the greater is the perfection they achieve. Hence they resist death and always ask God to grant them long life. Addressing the Jews who claimed to be the friends of God, the

Qur'an says, "If you claim to be friends of God to the exclusion of (other) men, then express your desire for death."(62:6) It further says that they will never wish for death, because they know what deeds they have committed, and what retribution they are to receive in the hereafter. These people belong to the third category mentioned above.

There are two conditions in which the noble men refrain from praying for a long life. First, when they are not attaining continuous success in doing virtuous deeds, and they fear that instead of progressing, they may retrogress. Imam Ali ibn al Husayn used to say, "O God, prolong my life only as long as it is spent in obeying you, but if it becomes the grazing field of the devil, carry me to yourself."[30] Secondly, the noble men pray for *shahādat* unconditionally, for it constitutes a virtuous deed as well as spiritual progress. We have already quoted a prophetic saying to the effect that *shahādat* is the highest virtue. Further, *shahādat* means going to the next world, for which the noble men have such yearning. That is why we find that Imam Ali's joy knew no bounds when he felt that he was going to die as a *shahīd*.

Many statements uttered by Imam Ali during the interval between his being wounded and his demise are recorded in such texts as the *Nahj ul-Balāgha*. One such statement which bears on the point of our discussion is the following:

> By God, nothing unexpected and undesirable has occurred. What has occurred is what I wanted. I have achieved *shahādat*, which I desired. I am like a man who was in search of water, and has suddenly struck upon a well or spring. I am like a man who was actively looking for something, and got it.

In the early morning of the nineteenth of Ramadan, when his assassin struck him on the head, the first or second sentence heard from him was, "By the Lord of the Ka'ba, I have succeeded." So, from the Islamic point of view, *shahādat* is a great, nay the greatest achievement of the *shahīd*.

Imam Husayn said, "My grandfather told me that I was destined to attain a very high spiritual position, but that could not be attained except through *shahādat*."

So far, we have analysed the individual aspect of death and

shahādat, and have arrived at the conclusion that death in the form of *shahādat* is really an achievement as far as the *shahid* is concerned. From this angle, no doubt death is a happy event, and that is why the great scholar Ibn Tawus[30] has said, "Had we not been given instructions about mourning, I would have preferred to celebrate the days of the *shahādat* of the Imams with festivities." On this ground, it may be said that Christianity is right to celebrate the *shahādat* of Christ as a festive event. Islam also fully recognizes that *shahādat* is an achievement of the *shahīd.* But, from the Islamic perspective there is another side of the picture to be seen. From the social point of view, *shahādat* is a phenomenon which takes place in specific circumstances, and is proceeded and followed by events which have to be duly assessed. Similarly, it creates a reaction in society which does not only depend on the success or defeat of the *shahīd,* but which is primarily based on the opinion held by the people, and on the respective positions of the *shahīd* and his opponents.

One more aspect of *shahādat* is important. It is the two-fold relationship between the *shahīd* and society: (a) his relationship with those who have been deprived of his presence among them; and (b) his relationship with those who by their depravity created an atmosphere in which he had to stand against them and lay down his life. It is obvious that from the perspective of his followers, the death of a *shahīd* is a great loss. When they express their emotions, they really cry over their bad luck. *Shahādat* is desirable, if we consider the situation in which it takes place. It is necessitated by an undesirable and ugly situation. In this respect, it is comparable to a surgical operation which becomes necessary, as in the case of appendicitis, duodenal or gastric ulcer, and the like. In the absence of such circumstances, the operation would clearly be a mistake.

The moral which people should draw from *shahādat* is that they should not allow similar situations to develop in the future. The idea of mourning is to project the tragedy as an event which should not have happened. Emotions are expressed and the oppressors and killers of the *shahīd* are condemned in order to dissuade the members of society from following the example of such criminals. Accordingly, we find that none of those trained in the school of the mourning of Imam Husayn would like to have the least resemblance to Yazid, Ibn Ziyad, and the like.[31]

Another moral which the society should draw is that whenever a situation demanding sacrifice arises, the people should have the feelings of a *shahīd* and should willingly follow such a heroic example. Weeping for the *shahīd* means association with his fervor, harmony with his spirit, and conformity with his longing. Now let us see whether festivity, rejoicing, dance and sometimes even joking, drinking and revelry, as witnessed during the religious feasts of the Christians are more in keeping with the spirit of *shahādat* than weeping and mourning are.

A common misconception about weeping prevails, for it is thought that weeping is caused by pain and distress, and hence that it is bad. Weeping and laughter are two peculiar activities of human beings. Other animals feel pleasure and pain and get happy and sad, but they neither laugh nor weep. Laughter and weeping are the manifestations of intense emotions peculiar only to human beings. Laughter has many varieties which we do not intend to discuss at present. Weeping also has varieties, but it is always accompanied by a sort of sensitivity and excitement. We are all aware of tears of love and longing. When one weeps because of the excitement of love, he feels closer to his beloved. Joy and laughter, on the other hand, have an introvertive quality, whereas weeping has an extrovertive quality, for it signifies self-negation and unification with the object of love.

Because of his noble personality and heroic death, Imam Husayn evokes the deepest emotions of hundreds of millions of people. The whole world could be reformed if our preachers could utilize this enormous fund of emotions to bring the spirit of the common man into harmony with the spirit of Imam Husayn. The secret of Imam Husayn's immortality lies in the fact that on the one hand, his activity was logical and rational, and on the other hand, it evoked deep emotions. The Imams gave the most judicious direction when they resorted to weeping for him, for it is weeping that has firmly rooted his movement in the hearts of the people. We again wish that our preachers knew how to utilize this emotional treasure.

When her father gave Fatimah al-Zahrā the well-known liturgical formula (which we, also, usually repeat after prayers, or at bedtime),[32] she went to the grave of her great-uncle, Hamzah ibn Abd al-Muttalib, and collected earth from there to make a *tasbih* (rosary).

What is the significance of her action? The grave of a *shahīd* is sacred. The earth of its vicinity is sacred. She required a *tasbīh* for counting the liturgical formula. Actually it made no difference whether the *tasbīh* was made of stone, wood or clay. The earth could be taken from anywhere. But she preferred to take it from the vicinity of the grave of the *shahīd*. Her action signified respect for him. After the *shahādat* of Imam Husayn, the epithet, *"Sayyid al-Shuhada,"* was taken from Hamzah and conferred upon the grandson of his brother. Now, if anyone seeks the blessings of the grave of a *shahīd*, he should make a *tasbīh* from the earth of Imam Husayn's mausoleum.

We have to offer our prayers. At the same time, we do not regard it as permissible to perform prostration on rugs, or anything which is edible or which may be worn. Therefore, we keep a piece of clay with us.[33] The Imams have said that it is better to prostrate oneself on the earth of the grave of a *shahīd*. If possible, the earth of Karbala should be obtained, for it emits the smell of the *shuhāda*. While offering your prayers, you can put your head on any earth, but if for this purpose you use the earth which has had some sort of contact with the *shuhāda*, your reward will be enhanced a hundred times. An Imam has said, "Perform prostration on the grave of my grandfather, Husayn ibn Ali. When a person offering prayers performs prostration on that sacred earth, he pierces seven veils." The idea is to urge people to realize the importance of the *shahīd*, and to caress the earth of his grave.

It is the usual practice, in the modern world, to dedicate a day every year to a certain group or class of people, to pay homage to them. Mothers' Day and Teachers' Day are examples of such days. But we do not find any day being dedicated to the *shuhāda* by any people, except the Muslims. It is the day of Ashura. Its night may also be regarded as *Shahīd's* Night.

We have already said that the logic of a *shahīd* is a combination of the logic of a lover and that of a reformer. If the personalities of a reformer and of a gnostic lover are combined, a *shahīd* comes into existence. A Muslim ibn Awsajah, a Habib ibn Muzahir, and a Zuhayr ibn Qayn come into being.[34] Anyhow, it must be remembered that not all *shuhāda* hold the same status.

Imam Husayn has offered a testimony concerning the *shuhāda* of

Ashura which indicates their high status. It is known that the *shuhāda* hold a prominent position among the pious and the virtuous. And the companions of Imam Husayn hold a prominent position among the *shuhāda*. do you know what Imam Husayn's testimony was? Though his companions had been screened previously and those found unfit had been asked to leave, he gave them their final test on the night of Ashura. This time, not a single person was rejected. There are two versions of the report. According to the first version, Imam Husayn had a tent where the water was placed. He is reported to have assembled all his companions there. The second version just says that he assembled all his companions in the evening. Why he chose that tent, we do not know exactly. Probably he did so because that night there were no water-skins there. The only water which might have been available was that which was brought by Imam Husayn's son, Ali Akbar, from the watering place at the Euphrates. It is reported by the authentic chroniclers of the battle of Karbala that on the night of the tenth of Muharram Imam Husayn sent his son with a small contingent to fetch water. The mission was successfully accomplished. All drank from the water he brought. Later, Imam Husayn asked them to take a bath and wash themselves. He told them that it was the last supply of water in the world that they were getting. Whatever might be the case, he assembled together all his companions and permitted anyone to leave who so wished. He then delivered an eloquent and forceful sermon to them, in which he referred to the developments of that afternoon.

You must have heard that the enemy had delivered his last ultimatum on the evening of the ninth of Muharram, according to which the Imam had to make his final decision by the morning of the tenth of Muharram. Imam Zayn al Abidin,[30] who was present on that occasion, related that Imam Husayn assembled his companions in a tent, adjacent to the tent in which he (Imam Zayn al-Abidin) was confined to bed, and delivered a sermon. He began by saying, "I praise God with the best praise. I am thankful to him in all circumstances, whether pleasant or otherwise."

For a person who takes a step in the pursuit of truth and righteousness, all that happens is good. A righteous man, consciously performs his duty in all circumstances, irrespective of the consequences. In this connection, Imam Husayn gave a very interesting reply to the celebrated poet, Farazdaq,[35] who met him on his way to Karbala. Farazdaq explained the dangerous situatin of Iraq. In reply the Imam said, "If things develop as we want, we will praise God and seek his help in being thankful to him; but if anything untoward happens, we won't be the losers, because our intentions are good and our consciences are clear. Hence whatever comes about is good, not bad. I am thankful to him in all circumstances, whether pleasant or otherwise." What he meant to say, was that he had seen good days and bad days in his life. The good days were when, in childhood, he sat on the lap of the Prophet, and when he rode on his shoulder. There was a time when he was the most favorite child in the Muslim world. He was grateful to God for those days. He was thankful to God for the present hardships also, for all that came about was good to him. He was thankful to God, who chose his family for prophethood and who enabled his family to understand the Qur'an fully and to have a true insight into the religion.

After stating this, the Imam produced his historic testimony in respect to his companions and the members of his family, and he said, "I do not know of any companions better and more faithful than my own companions, nor do I know of any kinsmen more virtuous and more dutiful than my own." Thus, he accorded to his own companions a status higher than that of the companions of the Prophet who were killed fighting in his company, and higher than the status of the companions of his own father, Imam Ali, who were killed in the battles of Jamal, Siffin and Nahrawan.[36] He said that he did not know of any kinsmen more virtuous and more dutiful than his own. Thus, he accorded recognition to their high position and expressed his gratitude to them. Then he went on to say, "Gentlemen! I would like to tell you all, my companions and my kinsmen both, that these people are not concerned with anybody but me. They regard me to be their sole adversary. They want me to take the oath of allegience. If they could eliminate me, they would have nothing to do with you. The enemy is not concerned with you. You have pledged your allegience to me. Now I release you from your commitment. You are under no obligation to stay here. You are compelled by no friend or foe. You are absolutely free. Whosoever wants to go, may go." Then addressing his companions, he said, "Let each one of you take hold of the hand of one of my kinsmen and leave." The members of Imam Husayn's family included both adults and minors. Moreover, they were all strangers there. The Imam did not want them all to leave together, so he asked each of his companions to hold the hand of one of them and to leave the battlefield.

This incident throws light on the high character of Imam Husayn's companions. They were not compelled by anyone. The enemy was not concerned with them. The Imam has set them free from their obligations. In these circumstances, the heart warming reply given by each of the companions and relatives of the Imam, was remarkable. On the tenth of Muharram, and during the night preceding it, it was a matter of great satisfaction for the Imam to see that all his relatives from the smallest child to the most aged person, were following in his footsteps. Another matter of satisfaction for him was that none of his companions showed the slightest sign of weakness. None of them joined the enemy. On the contrary, they brought a number of hostile personnel over to their side. Such people joined them both on the day of Ashura and on the night preceding it. Hurr ibn Yazid was one of them.[37] In all, thirty people joined him during the night of Ashura. These were the gratifying events for the Imam. One by one, Imam Husayn's companioins said to him, "Sir! Do you permit us to go away and leave you alone? That cannot be. Life has no value in comparison with you." One of them said, "I wish that I were killed, that my body were burnt and my ashes scattered. I wish that process were repeated seventy times. To be killed only once means nothing." Another said, "I wish I were killed a thousand times consecutively. I wish I had a thousand lives, all to be sacrificed for you." The first one to speak was his conscientious brother, Abu al Fadl al-'Abbās.[38] Others repeated what he said.

This was their last test. After they had all pronounced their decision Imam Husayn disclosed what was going to happen the next day. He said, "I tell you, that you will all be killed tomorrow." They all thanked God for being given an opportunity to sacrifice their lives for the sake of their noble Prophet's descendant. Here there is much food for thought. Had it not been a question of the logic of a *shahīd*, it could have been argued that the stay of those people was useless. If Imam Husayn was to be killed in any case, why should they sacrifice their lives? But still they stayed. Imam Husayn did not compel them to depart. He did not tell anyone that their stay was useless, or that they would only lose their lives in vain and that their stay was therefore forbidden. Imam Husayn did not say any of this. On the contrary, he hailed their willingness to make the supreme sacrifice. This shows that the logic of a *shahīd* is different from that of other people. A *shahīd* often sacrifices his life to create fervor, to enlighten society, to revive it and to infuse fresh blood into its body. This was one such occasion.

The defeat of the enemy is not the only object of *shahādat*. It aims at creating fervor, too. If Imam Husayn's companions had not laid down their lives that day, how could so much fervor have been created? Though Imam Husayn was the central figure in this event of *shahādat,* his companions added to its lustre, grandure and dignity. Without their contribution, the *shahādat* of Imam Husayn might not have assumed significance sufficient to move, educate and encourage people for hundreds, nay thousands of years.

NOTES

1. For a discussion of the term *"shahīd"* (martyr), see the introduction. This piece was published in English as an anonymous translation in pamphlet form entitled *The Martyr* by Morteza Motah-hary (Houston: FILINC, 1980). It was originally delivered as a speech in the Grand Mosque of Narmak, Tehran, on the night before Ashura, in 1973.

2. For the significance of *"mujahid,"* see the introduction to the volume. *"Walī"* has the sense of a guardian or a friend or a master. The term is very important in the Shi'ite context because according to the jurists, only one whose actions are guided by a *walī* are acceptable to God. Also Ali is considered the *walī* of God, in the sense of a friend of God or a guardian appointed by God. The terms *"walī,"* "truthful one" *(siddiq),* "pious one" *(zahid),* and a host of others, are used as nicknames or titles in Muslim society after a person becomes recognized for such attributes. For example, the famous jurist, Ahmad Ardabili (c. 910/1505-993/1585) became famous in his own lifetime as *Muqaddas,* the saint.

3. Cf. Mutahhari's *"Jihad* in the Qur'an" in this volume.

4. Cf. Matt. 5:39, Luke 6:29.

5. Cf. Matt. 22:21, Mark 12:17, Luke 20:25.

6. Cf. (2:118), (8:72), (8:74), (9:20).

7. *Nahjul Balagha* is a collection of sermons, letters, commandments, and words of wisdom attributed to Imam Ali ibn Abitalib, compiled by Sharif Abul Hasan Muhammad al-Radi in the fifth century A.H. (11th c. C.E.). Many early scholars, such as al-Madayini, Yusuf ibn Hasan, who was the judge in Baghdad, al-Hijrani, and most famous of all, Ibn Abi al-Hadid, have written commentaries on it. The first modern publication appeared in 1885 in Beirut, with a commentary by Muhammad Abduh. Several English translations have appeared, including S. M. Askari Jafery, *Nahjul Balagha* (Elmhurst, New York: Tahrike Tarsile Quran, n.d.). The passage cited by Mutahhari may be found in the Jafery translation on p. 24. Other English editions are: Dr. Muhammad Ali al-Hajj Salmin, (Lahore: Accurate Printers, n.d.); Sayed Ali Reza, (New York: Tahrike Tarsile Quran, 1984).

8. Cf. (2:202), (3:19), (3:199), (5:4), (6:62), (13:41), (14:51), (24:39), (40:17).

9. (5:93), cf. also (7:26).

10. See al-Tusi (d. 1067 C.E.), *Tahdhīb al-Ahkām,* Vol. II, p. 42; al-Kulayni (d. 940 C.E.), *Al-Kafī,* Vol. III, p. 327, 329; al-Sadūq (d. 991 C.E.), *Thawab al-A'māl,* p. 103; id., *Al-Majālis,* p. 344.

11. Will Durant, *The Story of Civilization* Vol. IV, (New York: Simon and Schuster, 1950) pp. 155-346.

12. See al-Hurr al-Amili (d. 1692 C.E.), *Wasa'il al-Shī'a,* Vol. XI, p. 6; *Al-Kafi,* Vol. III, p. 342. According to Shi'ite belief two angels called *Nakīr* and *Munkir* come to the grave of a person as soon as he is buried and question him about his God, his prophet,

his Noble Book, and his Imams. If he answers well it is assured that he will enter paradise, otherwise the matter is undecided, and he is tortured in his grave. There are many popular stories of the horrors and difficulties of such an ordeal.

13. See Tabatabai, *Al-Mizan fi Tafsir al-Qur'an,* Vol. XVI, p. 110, which is abbreviated from *Nahj al-Balagha.* For the exact narration, see *Sharh Nahj al-Balagha,* by Ibn Abi al-Hadid, Vol. IX, sermon 157, p. 205; sermon 155 in the edition of Fayd al-Islam; sermon 157 in that of al-Haj Salmin; or sermon 159 in the trans. of Askari Jafery.

14. See Shaykh Abbas al-Qummi, *Mafatih al-Jinan,* p. 177.

15. Compiled by Shaykh Abbas al-Qummi, this is a supplementary index to *Bihar al-Anwar,* which is an encyclopedic collection of Shi'ite sources, compiled by M. B. al-Majlisi (d. 1700 C.E.).

16. The battle of Badr was the first major military engagement of the Prophet with the Meccans. In Ramadan 2/March 624, roughly one thousand Meccans were routed by about one third that number of Muslims. At the battle of Uhud (3/625) the Muslims suffered a setback against the Meccans.

17. Cf. al-Tusi, *Tahdhib al-Ahkam,* Vol. II, p. 42; *Al-Kafi,* Vol. III, p. 342; *Wasa'il,* Vol. XI, p. 10.

18. Abdullah ibn Abbas (-3/619-68/687), son of the paternal uncle of the Prophet, who is known as the father of *tafsir* (Qur'anic exegisis). He was a pupil of Ali ibn Abi-Talib, for whom the prophet of Islam is reported to have prayed: "Oh God, make him deeply knowledgeable in religion and teach him interpretation." He trained many later experts of *tafsir.*

19. Muhammad ibn Hanafiyyah is the son of Ali by his wife Khawlah Hanafiyyah. He was known for both his courage and piety. After the martyrdom of his half-brothers Hasan and Husayn, he was nominated to succeed them as Imam. He declined, but nevertheless there emerged a sect known as *Kaysaniyah* who took him as imam and believed that he was the Messiah of Islam who would return to avenge the blood of Husayn. See A. A. Sachedina, *Islamic Messianism,* pp. 9, 11, 141-8, 165.

20. This image is also used by Shari'ati in his "After *Shahadat*" in this volume.

21. See *Al-Kafi,* Vol. III, p. 342; *Wasa'il,* Vol. IX, p. 8.

22. See *Tahdhib,* Vol. II, p. 41; al-Saduq, *Al-Khisal,* Vol. I, p. 8; *Al-Kafi,* Vol. III, p. 342; *Wasa'il,* Vol. XI, p. 10.

23. A paralled discussion may be found in Shari'ati's "Discussion of *Shahadat*" in this volume.

24. Cf. Shari'ati's "After *Shahadat*" and Taleqani's "*Jihad* and *Shahadat*" in this volume.

25. Muhummad Mas'ūd was a popular Iranian writer and social critic of the first half of the twentieth century. He was executed under the Pahlavi dictatorship.

26. Both Masud and Mutahhari appear to be unaware that according to Christian belief it is not the crucifixion of Jesus which is to be celebrated, but the resurrection.

27. Mani (c. 216-276 C.E.) was an Iranian of noble Parthian blood whose father had joined an ascetic community in Babylonia. Mani's religion combined elements of the Judeo-Christian and Gnostic traditions. However, he saw the world as almost wholly evil, to be renounced as much as possible in favor of a celibate, ascetic life. He was protected by the Sasanian court at Ctesiphon until the high priest of the Zoroastrians, Kirder, prevailed upon Vahram I to have Mani tried and executed. Cf. Mary Boyce, *Zorastrians: Their Religious Beliefs and Practices* (London: Routledge and Kegan Paul, 1985) pp. 110-114. Also see Sayyid Hasan Taqizadeh, *Mānī va Dīn-e 'Ū (Mani and His Religion*, in Persian).

28. Mawlawi is known in the west as Runi. Cf fn. 59 to Taleqani's "*Jihād* and *Shahādat*" in this volume.

29. Galen (c. 130-200 C.E.) was a Greek physician and philosopher whose works were tremendously influential west of the Indus until past the sixteenth century. He was extensively studied and commented on by Muslim scholars. To this day, a significant number of his writings exist only in Arabic translations.

30. Ali ibn al-Husayn (38/658-95/713), known as Zayn al-Abidin ("the ornament of the worshippers") was the fourth Imam and the only male survivor among Husayn's forces at the Battle of Karbala. The collection of his prayers, a masterpiece of eloquence and devotion, is known as *Al-Sahīfah al-Sajjādiyah*, or "The Psalms of the Family of Muhammad," compiled by Sayyid ibn Tawus al-Hasani (d. 1265 C.E.).

31. Ibn Ziyad was Yazid's governor of Kufah at the time of the battle of Karbala.

32. According to tradition, Muhammad told his daughter Fatimah to recite the litany of thirty-four repititions of "*Allāhu akbar*"⁹God is greatest⁰, thirty-three "*Al hamdu li Allah*"⁹Praise be to God⁰, and thirty-three "*Subhān Allāh*"⁹God is sublime⁰. This litany is counted on a rosary, called a *tasbīh* or *sabha*.

33. According to Shi'ite jurisprudence, during the prostrations which occur as part of the five ritual daily prayers, the forehead must rest on either earth or something which grows from the earth, such as a leaf, which is neither edible nor used as clothing. This is a sign of humility. For this purpose small clay tablets are commonly used, called "*muhr.*" It is considered especially pious to use a *muhr* which is made from the clay of Karbala.

34. These three were nobles of Kufah and companions of Husayn who, as old men, were martyred at Karbala. Zuhayr ibn Qayn was at first attached to Uthman until once, when returning from *hajj*, he met Husayn and became a devoted Shi'ite.

35. Farazdaq (641-732 C.E.) was perhaps the most eloquent poet of the Umayyad period. A collection of his poetry is translated into French, published in 1870-5, and again in Munich (1900-1). Al-Farazdaq is famous among the Shi'ites for his astounding homage to the fourth Imam in the presence of the caliph Hisham ibn Abd al-Malik, resulting in his imprisonment and eventual death.

36. Jamal, Siffin, and Nahrawān are three major battles of the 'first *fitnah*,' the time of civil war in which Ali's caliphate was disputed. Ali was victorious at the battle of Jamal (656), *("jamal"* means camel), which was named after 'Āyishah's camel, 'Āyishah, a widow of the Prophet, sided with the forces opposed to Ali. It was only after her camel was killed that Ali won this battle. The battle of Siffin ended in a stalemate in 657. Ali's forces were victorious over those of the rebel Kharijites at Nahrawan in 658.

37. Al-Hurr ibn Yazid al-Tamimi was a leader of the Kufan cavalry who first confronted but later joined Husayn and was killed with him. In Shi'ite culture, he is the symbol of the sudden realization of truth and repentence.

38. Abbas ibn Ali ibn Abitalib was a brother of Husayn and is considered a symbol of bravery, loyalty, and self-sacrifice. He was martyred at the Battle of Karbala.

Dr. Ali Shari'ati $5.$

Shahadat

It is difficult for me to speak today about *shahādat* since today marks the Shi'ite anniversary of the *shahādat* of Imam Husayn. There has been much written and said and much continues to be written and said about Imam Husayn and the role he played in history. The medievals have described him one way and the innovating intellectuals describe him another way. Recently, however, I have come to the realization that we cannot know what Imam Husayn has done without understanding what the meaning of *shahādat* really is.

The greatness of Husayn and some of the views of him which have been expounded have combined to cause that which is greater than Husayn to be concealed by the radiance of his own charisma. That which is greater than Husayn is that for which Husayn was sacrificed. We have always spoken about Husayn, but rarely have we spoken about the purpose for which Husayn so generously sacrificed himself. Today I intend to speak about the concept of the sacrifice which Husayn and others like him have made in the history of mankind and of our religion. And so, in the presence of the people, in the presence of the created and of the Creator, I would like to cite that idea and say something of its meaning as it has been demonstrated by the sum total of their lives and deaths, that idea called *'shahādat.'*

It is a difficult task. To begin with, my knowledge and intellectual capacities are inadequate for such a difficult task. The contradictory pattern which this issue follows (at least with respect to me) makes my position even more difficult. On the one hand, I must present *shahadat* from an intellectual scientific and philosophical point of view. I can use only my head. Only science and logic can assist me. On the other hand, the story of *shāhadat* and that which *shahādat* challenges is so sensitive, so belovedly exciting that it pulls the spirit toward the fire. It paralyzes logic. It weakens speech. It even makes thinking difficult. *Shahādat* is a mixture of a refined love and a deep, complex wisdom. One cannot express these two at the same time and so, one cannot do them justice.

The task I have taken up is especially difficult for a person such as myself, since I am emotionally and spiritually weak. But I will try my best and I hope to succeed in communicating some of the things which it is my intention to express.

In order to understanding the meaning of *shahādat,* the ideological school from which it takes its, its expression, and its value should be clarified. The concept of *shahādat* should be studied within the context of the school of thought and action which it is based upon, and in the school of thought of which Husayn is the manifestation *par excellence.* In the flow and struggle of human history, Husayn is the standard bearer of this struggle and his Karbala, a battlefield among battlefields, is the only link uniting the various fronts, the various generations and the various ages, throughout history from the beginning until the present moment and flowing on into the future.

Husayn's meaning becomes clear when we understand his relationship to that movement beginning with Abraham, which we have discussed in either lectures. This meaning should be made clear if Husayn's revolution is to be interpreted. To view Husayn and the battle of Karbala as isolated from historical and social circumstances would lead us to view the man and the event purely as an unfortunate, if not tragic, occurrence of the past, and something to cry about (and we certainly do continue to cry)[2] rather than as an eternal and transcendent phenomenon. To separate Karbala and Husayn from their historical and ideological context is to dissect a living body, to remove only a part of it and to examine it in exclusion from the living system of the body.

As I have mentioned in my previous lectures, throughout the whole history of humanity, religious movements may be divided into two classes. Whether these movements are related to the contents of the religion and the conduct of the prophets and founders of the religion, or to the social class connections of the leaders of the religion and to what they were calling the people to do, all the historical prophets, whether true or false, as well as anyone who has begun a religious movement, are divided into two different classes. The first group consists of the links of the religious chain which began with Abraham. This chain of prophets, from the historical point of view, are nearer to us and therefore we know them better. They consist of prophets whose view of society arose from the most deprived social and economic class of society. As Muhammad has said, and history shows us, all of these prophets were either shepherds, or simple hungry artisans or workers. These prophets stand in sharp contrast with the messengers of the other group of founders of intellectual and moral schools of thought, such as those which arose in China, India, and Iran, and the scientific and ethical schools of Athens. This latter group, without exception, was composed of aristocrats. They arose from the noble, powerful, comfortable classes of their society.

Throughout history, the rulers of society have been of one of three groups: the powerful, the wealthy, and the clergy. Together they exercised political and economic power as well as control over the faith of the people. All the non-Abrahamic messengers from Indo-China to Athens were either connected on their mother's side or their father's side or even both sides to emperors, clergymen and aristocrats. This holds true for Confucius, Laotzu, Buddha, Zoroaster, Mani, Mazdak, Socrates, Plato, and Aristotle.[3]

The Qur'an emphasizes, "We appointed among the ordinary people, a Prophet from themselves." (3:164). They were ordinary people from the masses and among the community. Thus the Abrahamic prophets arose from the mass of the people. This means that the prophets were only human beings, not angels or supernatural beings with fantastic powers. They were appointed from among the ordinary mass of people rather than from a special, noble, and selective class of society. Some people believe that because the Prophet of Islam arose from among the Arabs, he should speak Arabic, or Moses, who was appointed to the Jewish people, should speak Hebrew. It is obvious that a Prophet appointed from among the Arabs could not speak a language other than Arabic! The important thing is to speak in the language of ordinary people, to speak the tongue and use the idioms which the mass of that community understands.[4] In order to speak about their needs or troubles in a language which is understandable to them, the prophets must use a language and idioms with which the people are familiar. Philosophers, poets, intellectuals, scholars and educated people neither understand the thoughts and emotions of the ordinary people nor are they understood by the ordinary people. This is still noticeable in discussions regarding the Abrahamic prophets! When we discuss these prophets, we are talking about the people, for the mission of these prophets differs from that of all other leaders.

The mission of the non-Abrahamic messenger is always founded on the existing power structure so that power supports these messengers' ideas. The Abrahamic prophets, on the other hand, were always supported by the ordinary people against the powerful rulers of their time. Look at Abraham. As soon as God appointed him, he wielded his mace to destroy the idols. Moses took up his shepherd's staff and stormed Pharaoh's palace.[5] He brought down the wealthy and powerful Korah,[6] buried him in the earth and drowned Pharaoh in the sea. And the prophet of Islam first went through a stage of individual development, then began his struggle. Within a period of ten years, he fought sixty-five battles, that is, every fifty days, a battle, a military encounter. The miracles of the Abrahamic prophets are also in accordance with their mission. The turning of the staff into a serpent was used to destroy wizardry and to attack the Pharaoh's throne.[7]

The Qur'an clearly announces the principle that Islam is not a new religion because, in fact, throughout history, there has only been one religion.[8] Every prophet was appointed to establish this religion in accordance with the circumstances of the time and in compliance with the needs of that era. There is only one religion and its name is Submission, "Islam." With this announcement the Prophet gives the idea of Submission a universal, historical perspective. He relates the Islamic movement to other movements which have, throughout history, been fought to free people. The prophets stood up against the powerful, the wealthy, and the deceivers. In this way they demonstrated their unity of vision: one spiritual struggle, one religion, one spirit, and one slogan throughout the whole of human history in all domains, for all times and for all generations!

Let's take a look at an *ayāh* of the Qur'an and consider its context and choice of words, and let's see how the historical perspective is expressed in the Qur'an, how movements are placed one after another.

> As to those who deny the Signs of Allah, and in defiance
> of right slay the prophets, and slay those who enjoin
> justice, announce to them a grievous penalty. (3:21)

We see that in this *ayāh* three points are connected to each other. First, the signs of Allah, second, the Prophets, and third, men who call for equality in opposing the disbelievers. The Prophets and men of justice are put on one level. A kind of social encounter and philosophy of human history along with a description of previous movements is thus seen to be expressed in the Qur'an.

The Prophet of Islam is the last messenger of this religion of Submission, which throughout history, as the Qur'an has repeatedly shown, the Prophets came to bring.[9] Their message consisted of wisdom, the Book, and justice for the world. The Prophet of Islam is the last messenger of this world movement, this human movement, who in the name of Submission *(islām)* called the people to serve God, the One, so that they would be freed from obeying and serving any other than Him.

The Prophet of Islam came to confirm the universal doctrine of *tawḥīd,*[9] and to bring that unity into human history, to all races, nations, groups, families and social classes, and to eliminate the discord brought by polytheistic religions. The slogan of Islamic *tawḥīd* was a slogan which brought freedom. Slaves, the tortured, hungry and belittled were sensitive and aware of this before the intellectuals, scholars, and philosophers were. It is because of this that the group which gathered around Muhammad in Mecca were among the most debased elements of society.[10] The Prophet of Islam was scorned by his enemies because only the dregs of humanity surrounded him. In fact, this constitutes the greatest honor of this movement, while in contrast we see that the leaders of the Buddhist religion were nobles and aristocrats of China and India. Values have certainly changed!

The Prophet of Islam marked the turning point for the slaves who throughout history were certain that their fate was slavery. The slaves and other debased members of society were convinced by the tongues of religion, science, and philosophy, or by poetry and art, that their fate was to serve their masters. They believed that they existed solely to experience suffering, to carry heavy loads, and to go hungry so that others might enjoy themselves. They were born and created for this. This deprived class which was convinced that God or the gods were their enemies, believed that they were created as porters to carry the loads which enabled others to do their jobs, which made possible the functioning of the world. As the prophet Mani had said speaking of light and darkness, "The wretched and defeated are of the essence of darkness and the conquerors are of the essence of light."[11] Aristotle and Plato, intellectual geniuses though they were, had said, "God or nature has created some as slaves and others as free in order that the slaves may perform the ordinary jobs and the free may be left to attend the higher affairs, such as morals, poetry, music and civilization."[12]

The Prophet of Islam was appointed to complete the movement which has existed throughout history in opposition to deception, falsehood, polytheism, discord, hypocrisy, aristocracy, and class differences. This was made a goal of the struggle by the announcement that all humanity is of one race, one source, one nature, and of one God. Equality was declared for all; and with philosophical disputation as well as fighting against the economically powerful regime, social equity was upheld. Madinah was the ideal city, and a model for every Islamic community.[13] There Bilal, a debased slave, was recognized as more noble and of greater value, and was treated with greater respect than the aristocrats of Arab society.[14] Everyone accepted his position. Suddenly the inhabitants of Madinah, the Arabs, Jews, and Quraysh[15] found themselves greeting the young slave of Hudhayfah as an equal. He who had once gone about in the narrow streets as a debased and deprived slave, now, in the Quba Mosque,[16] stood for prayer in frontof the noble *Muhajirūn*[17] of the Quraysh as one of their dearest and most radiant figures. The most distinguished personages of the pre-Islamic era prayed behind Bilal, as indeed do those of the present era as well.

All values were shattered when the Prophet himself began his efforts to destroy all of the values of aristocratic thinking and of the *jāhiliya*[19]. He instructed the people to shorten their long flowing robes and to trim their beards, since these were signs of aristocracy. He ordered people not to strut with pride through the streets.[20] He instructed people to ride two at a time on horseback, one behind the other. Sometimes, in order to break down the values of the aristocracy in the eyes of the people, he would ride a donkey bareback.

One day an old woman came before the Prophet. She had for many years heard of his greatness and magnificence. She stood tongue tied, in awe before him. The Prophet, softly, kindly, and simply took her by the shoulder and said, "Why are you afraid? I am the son of that Quraysh woman who milked sheep. Who are you afraid of?"

When this shepherd, who was the last appointed prophet, the last messenger for those who suddenly arose out of the silent deserts and assaulted the lords of power, wealth and deceit in the cities — when this shepherd died, everything was different. Immediately there were disruptions. At first the path of historical events did not deviate from the truth by more than a centimeter. The angel which appeared between the School of Islam and the History of Islam, between the truth and the reality, was narrow at the beginning. But after the Prophet died, the gap between them grew wider and wider. It was like the angle between two lines which are at first close together (no more than a thousandth of a centimeter apart) but gradually the angle widens as history moves forward. The two lines separate so that in an eternity there are kilometers of space between them. With various factors and causes, the line of history deviates from the line of truth, as the two lines extending from an angle move apart.

After the death of the Prophet, the deviation which was so very slight at first, developed generation after generation. The distance between honesty, rectitude, truth and justice progressed so far in fourteen or fifteen years that by that time Uthman, like a magnetic pole, attracted all the counter-revolutionary agents who were scattered about.[21] He gathered them at the center of Islamic power and Islamic movement. Uthman served as a link between the mentality of the *jahiliya* and the Islamic revolutionary period. His link was the Caliphate which served as a bridge for the most despicable members of the rejected aristocracy who still lingered on.

They usurped the positions which had been gained through the struggle of the *Muhājirūn* and the *Ansār*.²² Uthman bridged the gap, and across his bridge of the Uthman Caliphate passed the dirtiest, half-dead, rejected agents of aristocracy. They took the positions which had been gained through the *jihād* of the *Muhajirūn* and of the Companions of the Prophet. Uthman acted as the instrument of the Umayyids, the base enemies of Islam, and through him, they not only made up for the blows they had received at the time of the Prophet, but they appropriated the successes of the revolution as well.

This kind of setback has repeated itself over and over again throughout the course of Islamic history, to the point of becoming a rule — I do not mean to say a necessary rule — that a revolution must devour its children. But Uthman allowed the faithful children of the revolution to be devoured. Those who wielded their swords and pursued their *jihād* with faith, self-sacrifice, devotion and endurance were destroyed by the oppressors and usurpers of power, government, the rights of the people, and the heritage of the revolution. The founder of the movement and the first sacrifice of Uthman and the Umayyids who dominated him was Ali, a victim of the revival of the *jāhiliya* by the surviving counter-revolutionaries. The political, social and international make-up of the group which supported Ali was eminently representative of a new struggle, a struggle between the leaders and loyalists of the new set of values, of the new faith, who rose up with the new and genuine slogans of Islam and found themselves confronting greed and the worst elements of the revival of the *jāhiliya* which was imposed with a new fervor. These usurpers, with new vigor, both openly and undercover, launched their struggle against the noblest figures of the Islamic revolution.

The Prophet is the manifestation of the struggle of an age in which, on the one hand, true, believing Muslims confronted foreign enemies who were known to be anti-Muslims, while Ali is the manifestation of an age in which an internecine struggle took place between those who remained loyal and faithful and retrogressive elements who had donned the mask of faith. The struggle between the Prophet and Abu Sufyan²³ was an external struggle, a battle purely and simply between friend and foe. Whereas in contrast the struggle between Ali and

Mu'awiyah,[24] the son of Abu Sufyan, was an internal affair between friend and pseudo-friend, or should we say, 'an internal enemy,' who paid mere lip service to the movement. The battle on the foreign field, the struggle with the external foe, resulted in victory, whereas the struggle with the internal foe ended in defeat. These foes, described in Islamic terminology, in the language of the Qur'an, as 'hypocrites' *(munāfiqūn)*[25] are considered more base and more dangerous than the *kāfir*,[26] or even the polytheist. The Prophet is thus the manifestation of Islamic victory on the foreign front, over *kufr* and polytheism, whereas Ali is the manifestation of Islamic defeat within the ranks, at the hands of hypocrisy.

Confronting the 'neo-*jāhiliyah*' and 'neo-aristocracy,' which comes to life within the context of Islam under the cover of Truth and the very heart of the justice-seeking revolution of Islam, Ali is the base of resistance. For many years Ali struggles and strives against polytheism within his ranks, a polytheism which has cloaked itself in the dress of *tawḥīd*. He has to grapple with the *kāfir* who has assumed the mantle of Islam and who has positioned the Qur'an on the point of a lance.[27] In the end Ali is killed by the pious but unconscious people who always become tools in the hands of a cunning enemy.[28]

As we move forward in time the true base of the Islamic revolution becomes increasingly weakened, while in contrast, the base of neo-*jāhiliya* and the internal enemies grow ever stronger until we reach the age of Imam Hasan,[29] the eldest son of Ali and Fatimah. Imam Hasan is the inheritor of Ali's administration and he becomes the commander of an army riddled with hypocrisy which spreads even among his closest friends. His best commanding officers are involved in intrigue with the Umayyids who negotiate with the tender of money, power, and promises. Those officers barter their souls in a bargain with Mu awiyah and his court, who buy off humanity and honor in Damascus. From the administrative point of view, Hasan has no authority over one of the most powerful, dangerous and sensitive sections of the Islamic domain (the province of Syria) which has entirely fallen into the hands of the enemy. In Iraq, the various factions are in dissention. The aristocrats can not remain loyal to the government of Ali. The masses are neglected and indifferent. The Khawārij,[30] who are the most fanatic, dangerous zealots in the populace, confront Imam Hasan who is the personification of the last struggle of the dearest, most aware and most progressive companions of the new Islamic movement. The ranks of hypocrisy, the internal enemy, grow stronger day by day, until the agonizing and catastrophic moment of the last struggle to defend the Islam of justice against the Islam of aristocracy. The only alternative open to Hasan is to make peace. He is defeated. A defeated party does not specify the terms of a peace treaty. Just as his defeat is imposed on him, likewise is the peace.

Thus Hasan, the leader and exemplar of the spirit of the struggle of the revolution, sits in resistance to a reawakened neo-*jāhiliya*. Disarmed like an ordinary soldier, the Imam and leader of the people is among turncoats and Umayyid spies even within his own household. Those who had broken bread with him now turn against him. Even his wife is bought off, and through her Hasan is poisoned.[31] We can see to what extent justice, freedom and the people themselves have weakened. The power of Imam Hasan, the leader of a force which is still resisting today and defending the name of Islam, has so dwindled that when he dies, he cannot be buried next to the Prophet of Islam, his grandfather, in Madinah, the city of his grandfather, father and mother, the city of the *Muhājirun* and *Anṣār* of the Prophet of Islam. Imam Hasan is buried in the public cemetary of Baqi'.[32]

Imam Hasan, as the model of loneliness and isolation in Islamic society, even in the Madinah of the Prophet, clearly shows that the Truth-seeking party in Islam is utterly shattered. The new face of the revolution completely overwhelms everyone and everything and conquers in every domain. Now it is Husayn's turn.

Husayn inherits the Islamic movement. He is the inheritor of the movement launched by Muhammad, continued by Ali, and in whose defense Hasan makes the last effort. There is nothing left for Husayn to inherit, no army, no weapons, no wealth, no power, no force, not even an organized following. Nothing at all. It is now about the year 60 A.H. (679 C.E.), fifty years after the death of the Prophet. Each Imam chooses the form his struggle will take. (Please pay special attention from here on to what I am trying to say. This is where I am getting to my main point.)

The form of the struggle of each Imam and each leader is not based upon his own personal tastes, but is shaped to fit the circumstances, through the evaluation of the strength of the various factions, and estimation of the enemy's forces and position. Thus the form of the struggle which Husayn chooses cannot be understood without taking into account the nature of the circumstances in which his struggle is launched. When Husayn's turn comes, the times and the people are ready for someone. How difficult it is when such a situation arises — sometimes the fate of a nation, the fate of a faith, an idea, a society, a generation is looking to an individual or several individuals in anticipation. The responsibility of safe-guarding the revolution has fallen upon Husayn's shoulders at a time when the last bastions of rsistance have been lost. Nothing has remained for him from the power of his grandfather, his father, his brother, the Islamic government or the party of Truth and justice, not a sword, not a single soldier.

The Umayyids occupy every base of society. For years the Quraysh, in their neo-*jāhiliya,* dominated the values and misappropriated the fruits of the Islamic revolution. It has been years since the convergence of the Islamic revolution has been pulled apart and the companions and the early strugglers of the revolution, the disciples of Muhammad, have fallen into three groups.

The first group, the one which refused to tolerate the perversion of the movement, which stood up and died for the cause, disappeared by the year 60 A.H. Abu Dhar is no more. 'Ammar, 'Abdullah ibn Mas'ūd, Maytham, and Hujr ibn 'Adī have all passed away.[33]

The second group consists of those who in these difficult times when the love of truth requires self-sacrifice and when remaining a true Muslim results neither in conquest nor in the acquisition of booty but rather in torture and imprisonment — in such times as these another alternative occurs to the members of this second group. Instead of seeking paradise in the battlefields of *jihad,* they seek paradise in the secure solitude of the cloisters of gnostic meditation, in long fasts and supererogatory prayers. The prime example of this group is Abdullah ibn Umar.[34] At the very moment when the Muslim masses are being lashed by the whips and slain by the swords of the Umayyids, when they look toward those who were fostered in the Islamic revolution and had struggled shoulder to shoulder with the Prophet to rise up and resist, and at the moment when they should have taken a stand on the field of *jihād,* they retreat to the corners of the mosques in the silence of self-mortification. The best Muslim figures are sacrificed while the devout retreat from the agents of oppression and disbelief. The hands of those who at such times have left the field of combat and have crawled off into the niche of the mosque, away from society are polluted with crime, polluted with the blood of the pure-hearted heroes and even with their own blood.

The conscious person feels his responsibility and recognizes the difference between right and wrong; if he retires in solitary devotion, it is as if had directly sacrificed a free and conscious *mujāhid*[35] to the oppressor. This sacrifice may even be himself. He is a criminal who commits a crime even if it be without pay or through blackmail. He sacrifices the best elements of faith in favor of disbelief. These are the worst elements. They commit suicide at the feet of the oppressor.

The third group consists of those Companions who had honorably left the battlefield. They are from the contingent that fought at Badr, Uhud and Hunayn[36] and at the Madinah of *jihad* and *hijrat*[37] side by side with the prophet of Islam. They sold off the honors they had gathered directly to Mu'awiyah in his Green Palace.[38] They collected their money by selling their accounts of what the Prophet said and did at the rate of one dinar per *hadīth.*[39] These people included Abu Darda, Abu Hurayrah, and Abu Musa.[40] Abu Hurayrah, being a companion who was always beside the Prophet of Islam, was known as the companion who specialized in the science of *hadīth.* He had attained such eminence in the Umayyid court that Yazid (the son and successor of Mu awiyah to the Caliphate) had employed him as a go-between to propose marriage to Uraynab, the wife of 'Abdullāh ibn Salam.[41]

Now, what do you suppose the young people thought when presented with such a situation? This is the time of Husayn. It is only the second generation after the revolution. A generation has grown up which did not experience that glorious time, those precious victories, the zeal and love as the Companions had. To hear such things from the tongue of one of these Companions drew love from the hearts of the youth. All of their hopes, faith, and thoughts had rested with the Companions who had been trained in the revolution. When everyday they see one of their heroes fall, what disappointment, what loss of faith they must have experienced in that thing they call Islam.

This is the fate of the Companions, yesterday's generation, the generation of the age of the Prophet, the age of the revolution.

The second generation which comes to the fore, full of excitement, zeal and spirit — whether experienced or not — ready for the struggle against the order of neo-*jāhiliyah,* is nevertheless aware of what is going on. The model and leader of the second generation of the revolution is Hujr ibn Adi. Hujr had been a youngster at the time of the Prophet. He had grown to be a youth at the time of Ali and then entered the adult arena at the time of Hasan. He has the qualities of a statesman. He is a responsible and an aware *mujāhid.* At the time of the peace treaty between Imam Hasan and Mu awiyah, he had been one of the most vigorous and radical opponents of Imam Hasan's signing of the treaty. He had even gone so far as to chide the Imam, saying, "You have really humiliated the people by doing this!" He is a zealous and fiery revolutionary, but Imam Hasan takes him aside at Madinah and quietly convinces him and even makes him hopeful of the future of the struggle.

There is no clear account of this conversation in history. All we know is that Hujr comes away reassured. Hujr is not a credulous person, nor is he somebody to accept a conservative approach involving compromise or the logic of dissimulation,[42] passive endurance, or a non-dangerous approach to the struggle. Nor is he such an idolizer of leadership that he simply accepts Imam Hasan's opinion without question.

Taha Husayn[43] writes about this meeting of Hujr and Imam Hasan as well as another encounter with Sulayman ibn Surad al Khazai[43] and the Imam. Both Hujr and Sulayman were bitterly critical of and angry about the peace treaty, yet both were later supporters of the treaty. After explaining that overt military action would be useless in their situation and that it would only result in the dissipation of their forces, Hasan lays the foundation for an underground organization and establishes a clandestine resistance movement in opposition to the regime. This same organization established a vast network throughout the Muslim countries during the two centures of the Imamate until the time of the last Imam, and which continued the covert struggle of the Shi'ite resistance movement during the reign of both the Umayyid and Abbasid Caliphates.[45]

Hujr, and his companions, like 'Adi ibn Hatim,[46] are zealous men who cannot tolerate this age of suppression and dark dictatorship of ever-increasing oppression, autocracy, and exploitation in which the rights of the people are violated and the human aims of the Islamic movement are undermined. They insist on defying this perverted rule over the people which is growing stronger day by day at the expense of right, justice and Islam. The struggles, under the leadership of Hujr, increased and became ever more vigorous until the Umayyids, through a nefarious plot, issued a decree against Hujr condemning him as a *murtadd*[47] (and this coming from the likes of the Umayyids!). Then these young paragons of resistance of the second generation of the movement, these disciples of the school of Ali, who loyally persevered in their resistance, are seized and executed in Syria for their revolt against the establishment of Damascus.[48]

Now Husayn appears, but the central base of the power of the revolution has been lost. The Companions of the resistance struggle have either been killed off or silenced. The faithful Companions who had not sold themselves sought the security of devotion in out of the way corners rather than be bothered with the battling for that which is right, rather than take the risks involved in social and political struggle, to liberate the people and free them from their oppressive lot. They slipped into the shell of respectability, piousness, self-centeredness and silence. A group of the most notable Companions of the Prophet, have been passing their time in the Green Palace of Mu awiyah, helping themselves to the public treasury, while the second generation, which did strive and struggle against the Umayyids, has been defeated. The power of the tyrant, enforced with sword or with money or with position or with deception, bring a pall of stifled silence upon everyone. The mechanism of neo-mystification goes into operation along with the pressure of fear, money and fraud, while the freedom of license and corruption comes with the repression of ideas and faith and responsibility — we might say there is 'freedom of repression' and the 'repression of freedom.' In this way the regime brings about the decay of the moral fiber of society. They bombard and obliterate the real fundamentals, the truth of faith, the revolution, the bases of the movement and Islam. They paralyze hearts and minds by making sly appeals to quietism.

The regime of neo-*jāhiliya* knows well that the danger of revolution will not be vanquished by destroying the family of Muhammad, or by murdering Ali, or by defeating the army of Hasan, or by the secret and unmanly destruction of Hasan himself. It knows that the uprooting of every base of resistance or the scattering of all uncertain forces, the ruthless massacre of the fiery figures of the revolt of the younger generation of Kufah, including Hujr, is pointless. Pointless too, is exile, murder, impoverishment, and the denial of the rights for which the Companions such as Abu Dhar struggled through the glorious power of faith. The regime senses that the breadth, the fine sensitivity of awareness, the keen edge of faith in the Truth, the profound understanding of the spirit of Islam, the true knowledge of the path of the call, the real meaning of the mission of the Prophet could not be repressed by brute force, aggression, underhandedness and the travesty of justice which the Umayyid establishment stood for. Even the killing of brave souls like Abdullah ibn Masud, who stood up in protest against injustice and was tortured, is useless, as is the leveling of every barricade in the fight for justice, the eradication of every potential of resistance against the system of the ruler, and, altogether, the martyring of the true leaders of the movement and the forcing aside of the deserving participants in the struggle. The most important men are taken into Umayyid service, while the strivings of the greatest talents are crushed until the total hegemony of the Umayyid monarchy is established in all the lands of Islam, from Syria to Khurrasan. In spite of all this, there is no way of rooting out the resistance. However much they want to guarantee the stability of their regime and rule with a free hand, the fact is that all of these efforts: conquest, domination, seizure of the reins of leadership, destruction of the people's liberation front, the scattering and crushing of all defenders of the faith, lovers of freedom, seekers of rights, the disarming of justice, and finally the inheriting of the arms, shields, armor and steeds of Islam, the bringing of the people under the lashes of their dominance — all these efforts come to nothing.

The intelligent, aware politicians among the Umayyids know themselves well. They know their people and the spirit of the times. This society is only one generation away from the birth of the great intellectual, social, political, and spiritual revolution which is Islam. From one point of view this regime is one generatin away from *jāhiliya* and polytheism, from the battles of Badr, Uhud and Khandaq, the age of from the time when all these leaders of the *kāfir*, idolatrous, slave-dealing and capitalistic faction fought the Prophet.

The Umayyids know that under the black ashes of defeat smolders the red threat of a potential explosion. The army may have been defeated but Islam is still very much alive. The party of faith has been dispersed but faith itself lives on. The leaders of justice and supporters of the Truth, the arms and shields of freedom and humanity all have been destroyed. The barricade of liberty has been razed and the base of resistance has been destroyed.

But what about the cause of justice, the worship of the Truth, the taste for freedom and the love of humanity? Ali is slain at prayer, but what of the fire of Ali? Abu Dhar is exiled, then silenced by death at Rabadhah,[49] but what about the rallying cry of Abu Dhar? Hujr is executed in Syria, yet what of the rebellion of Hujr?

The true heart of these dangers, the well-spring of these revolts is not in Madinah where people are massacred, nor at the Ka bah where people are stoned, nor at Kufah which has been seized through a coup d'etat, nor at the Mosque of the Prophet where people are trampled under the feet of horses and chopped down by their riders, nor even in the house of the Prophet which lies in ruins, nor in the house of Fatimah which is now ashes, nor in the Qur'an which they pierce with spears. Then where indeed, is the heart of the fire, where is the constant well-spring of danger? It is in the people's hearts and minds! If these two sources are not destroyed, all the Umayyid victories remain without effect and all their forces are endangered. If these two remain alive, all the people like Abū Dhar, Ḥujr, 'Ammār, and Mālik[50] will also remain alive in their *shahādat* and will send new people to the battlefield. Every "Ali" will achieve *shahādat* before death and will die in life. But if the fire of his school of thought is not destroyed, no immunity, neither black nor red, can be maintained by mass executions.[51] They will not remain immune for a moment in the sea of blood and the cemetery of death.

The mission of divine revolution is not in the Qur'an, it is here. Although Ali is murdered in the Kufah Mosque, he still exists. All of those who are killed, all of the places which are conquered, all of the forces which are defeated, all of the arms and fortresses which are taken and occupied belonged to truth, freedom, and justice. The struggle for securing truth, freedom and justice still exists; and the enemies of this struggle are busy working to undermine the hearts and minds of the people. If these two fire-giving, luminous powers, these movement-creating centers are destroyed, the enemy can remain and make a nest. Attacks begin. Arms are gathered to destroy the two sources of danger, the two real sources of explosion and fire: hearts and minds.

But this battle required weapons, shields bows and arrows of a different type than had been used before; it also required a different type of army, policy, design, plan, ruler and conqueror. In the leading of this army and attack, bribes of gold and of *wilāyat*[52] offered to Rey or Iraq would not be effective, nor would trickery, nor the genius of Amrw, nor the murders and other misdeeds of Bars ibn Artat, Yazid ibn Muhallib and Hajjaj ibn Yasuf.[53] In this surprise attack, the Qur'an is the weapon, the sunnah of the Prophet[54] are the shields. Thought and science are the equipment, faith is the fortification, Islam is the flag, and the army consists of exegetes, reciters, theosophists, jurisprudents, sages, judges and *imāms*. The *imāms* are the great Companions of the Prophet, the important clergymen and the great *muftis*.[55]

The attack begins. The army of religion progresses smoothly and successfully in the land where a worldly, earthly army had already progressed and had eliminated any obstacles and resistance. Thus they enter, develop and progress in the two main centers of fire, gradually conquer them, and without any noticeable resistance, they ruin them from the inside with a terrible poison. They use an elixir, the making of which formal clergymen of all religions know well. This recipe has been passed down from one generation to another throughout history. It is the same inauspicious elixir from which Moses is given the power to destroy the Pharaoh, Korah, and to make the Jews, who were more murderous than the Pharaoh, greater worshippers of wealth than Korah, and more deceitful than Bal'am,[56] and from which the lover and founder of peace, Jesus Christ, is made a Caesar with satanic actions and disdain for religion.

The intellectual sells out and the clergy support the powerful. In Islam the fate of everything changes. All values are annihilated. The spirit of the Islamic revolution is killed, its direction is changed, and finally, the people are sacrificed in the name of religion.

It is the first time that Islam, with the assistance of religious scholars, testifies on behalf of the regime. The religious authorities compulsively believe that everything should be related to God. Two horrible cancers fall upon the people — "in the Name of God" and "the religion of God."[57]

The first one is the cancer of the *Murjiah,*[58] who are pseudo-Islamic scholars and clergymen. They are theologians of Islam, religious scholars and prayer leaders. They have no official position. They are not murderers. They study in the corners of the schools, learn, and teach. Who are the *Murjiah?* The thesis of the *Murjiah* is that anyone, sinful or pure, anyone who has done a wrong, a deceitful thing, created a conspiracy, or committed a crime, must have hope for the mercy and forgiveness of God. He must have hope because God has said, "There are people who are hopeful in God's command."[59] It is having hope that allows God's forgiveness, mercy and compassion. God forgives, and there is hope that he will forgive any crime. Therefore, it is forbidden for anyone, who may himself be sinful, to call such criminals bad names. You cannot call them bad names or fight against them. On the other hand, when you call a criminal an oppressor and traitor and condemn him, and call another person oppressed, a slave, it is as if you claim to be God, because God is the chief commander and it is on this basis that God takes everyone's actions into account and judges the procedure and behavior of everyone against the balance of justice. So you do not have the right to judge the oppressor and traitor. You want to establish the balance of the scales of justice here. Are you God? Do you want to accuse people and clear their accounts before God does so? No. It is not our duty to judge between a traitor and a servant of God. We are not allowed to condemn the criminal. We are not permitted to stand against this or that group. We should accept all of them. We must be patient and leave the punishment of everyone to God. This is the problem which arises from saying of the *Murjiah,* "Leave everything to God."

This disease of 'hope' or cancer of the *Murjiah* paralyzes the second generation of Islam, who have not had sufficient training in the school of Islam and who have not received the language of the Qur'an and Islam from the tongues of the Prophet, Ali, the *Muhājirūn* and the *Anṣār*. Thus they are obliged to receive their Islamic teachings second hand from those who have sold their thoughts and ideas. It is for this reason that their awareness, understanding and religious spirits are permanently poisoned with the propaganda of the *Murjiàh* who are backed by the ruling regime. The strict, responsible fundamentalist Muslims, sense their responsibility every moment to "enjoin the good and forbid evil,"[60] while thick-headed people who extend themselves by imbibing in both God and the devil exist side by side, one having nothing to do with the other.

The second cancer is the cancer of *jabr*[61] which also grows in this period. The first religious school of thought which is created during the time of the Umayyids is the school of the *Murjiah*. They use the Qur'an as a means to paralyze and destroy all ideas and beliefs, not just *jihād*. The school of *jabr* is the first school of philosophy that comes into being during the Umayyid times as a divine philosophy.

We are going to see what corruption is hidden behind saintly and sacred faces. Divine Fate means, as the Qur'an tells us, "God is the Absolute Commander."[62] The religious authorities extend this to mean that whatever suffering occurs in the universe takes place in accordance with His Will. Whatever one does is done according to the Will of God. Whatever position one has, whatever the situation, whatever choice one makes, whatever action one takes, whether corrupt or pure, criminal or non-criminal, whether one is executed or is the executioner — all are determined by God's Will. Whether one is a slave or master, the ruled and the ruler belong to God. It is God who gives power and takes it away. It is God who kills and brings into being. It is God who bestows honor and disgrace. No one has any rights whatsoever.

The attraction of *jabr* had a powerful influence upon the faithful Muslims who interpreted the words of the Qur'an with the aid of *hadīth* which were automatically produced by people like Abu Hurayrah in 'hadīth-making-machines' until they reached forty thousand different *hadīth* in the name of the Prophet. The Prophet would have had to have lived a thousand years to have said all these things!

These teachings of the scholars had a paralyzing effect upon the thoughts of Muslims living in obedience to God's Will. It was explained to them that the Umayyids ruled because God gave them this power. If Ali was defeated it is because God willed him to be defeated. Whether or not one is bad or good, if the good are destroyed and the bad rule, it is all based on a higher wisdom that is not clear to us, but depends upon the Will of God. It is out of our hands. Therefore any protest against any person in any position, against any crime or exploitation is considered to be a protest and criticism of the Will, Power and Determination of God.

Sixty years have passed since the *hijrah* of the Prophet. Everything won by the revolution has been destroyed. All of the successes earned half a century before have been abolished. The Book brought by the Prophet is placed on the spears of the Umayyids. The culture and ideas which Islam had developed through *jihād,* through struggles and efforts in the hearts and thoughts of the people, became a means for justifying the Umayyid rule. All the mosques are turned into support systems for polytheism, oppression, deceit, and for making fools out of the people. All the swords of the *mujāhids* are put to use by the executioners. All the income from *zakāt* and other religious taxes is used to run the Green Palace of Mu awiyah. All the words relating to reality, unity, the Prophet, the *sunnah,* the Qur'an, and revelation are in the possession of Mu awiya and his regime. All of the leaders of the community, judges, exegetes of the Qur'an, reciters of the Qur'an, scholars and theologians either have been killed, or like mice have crept into their corners, or have become like radio transmitters which broadcast propaganda for the Umayyid regime in Damascus.

The principles of Muhammad no longer have a spokesman nor an altar nor a pulpit. Throughout the whole of this wide territory which included Rome, Iran and the Arabia, no one remains who is related to the Prophet's family or who was of the generation of those faithful to the revolution. The results of all the sufferings of the *Muhājirūn* and the Companions went with the wind. The palace of Mu awiyah gained a treasure, easily won.

The revolutionaries of the past have either died in the remote desert of Rabadhah, or have been killed in the fields of Maraj al 'Adhra.[63] The second generation of the revolution, which created a

movement, fought and struggled, is executed *en masse.* The others
are either engaged in a pessimistic philosophy of *jabr* or surrender to
the side of the religious leaders. They realize that any effort to change
the present situation is useless. Through experience they have
learned that any struggle to guard Islam and to establish truth and
justice, and to fight against the ever increasing neo-*jāhiliya,* has been
defeated.

So, now, sixty years after the *hijrah,* all of the powers are in the
possession of the oppressive ruler. Values are determined solely by
the regime. Ideas and thoughts are developed by agents of the regime.
Brains are washed, filled and poisoned with material presented in the
name of religion. Faiths are altered, bought, paralyzed. If none of
these efforts prove successful, faith is cut off with the sword. It is this
power which Husayn must now face, a power which controls
thought and religion, and which has at its disposal the Qur'an,
wealth, weaponry, armies, the tools of propaganda, and the
inheritance of the Prophet. Husayn appears with empty hands. He
has nothing. What can he do? Should he become an ascetic and run
away to a corner to worship? Should he keep quiet, rationalizing that
since he is the grandson of the Prophet, the son of Ali and Fatimah,
therefore Paradise has been guaranteed to him? These arguments
hold no sway over him. The other believers accept them, but Husayn
is responsible, committed. Can he exchange his responsibiltiy to
perform the *jihād* for the attainment of nearness to God through
reading and reciting prayers, which is certainly easier? He cannot
choose this solution because it is just sixty years after the *hijrah* and
no prayer books have as yet been printed!

Husayn has two ways open before him — he could say "No. I
cannot start a political fight against the Umayyid tribe because a
combat like that needs an army and I have no power so I have to just
sit down and perform an intellectual, a mental *jihād.*" But Imam
Husayn cannot choose this solution.

If we see later on that Imam Jafar al Sadiq,[64] establishes an
intellectual school, it is because of two facts. During the last days of
the Umayyid government and the early days of the Abbasid
Caliphate,[65] on the one hand Greek philosophy enters the thoughts
of the Muslims,[66] and on the other hand, Indian and Iranian Sufism

as well as Christianity have become very dear to the hearts of the Muslims. Because of these, the Muslim intellectuals at the time of the Abassids intend to become sensible about politics. They begin thinking about right and wrong, truth and falsehood. They begin to wonder why Ali went and Mu'awiyah came. They begin to wonder who should rule the community and who should not. They are concerned with the "Seven Cities of Love.'[67] They are occupied with the relationship between prime matter and the other matter which seemed to have come about *ex nihilo*.[68] They are concerned with the identity of the original or basic material from which God had created the world. It is for answers to these philosophical questions that they turn to the Qur'an, or they search the Qur'an for answers to some particular gnostic questions. But even if they succeed in discovering answers to these questions, their answers are not worth a penny.

Gradually questions concerning the soul, the body, matter, essence, attribution, emanation, etc., develop among them, but the problems of responsibility, commitment, to society, the community, justice, equality, leadership, etc., have been entirely forgotten.

The regime has begun to create its own schools of thought, and it supplies these schools with theosophies, rationalizations, philosophies and ideologies, so that the roots of Islam can be changed and the regime can then justify its position. In such a situation, an intellectual struggle is obligatory especially for a person like Imam al Sadiq who has no possibility of engaging in a political struggle, who has said, "If I only had seven faithful men, I would rebel."

But in the time of Imam Husayn, the situation is different. Sixty years after the *hijrah* there is still no sign of Western philosophy.[68] The sciences which convert the reality and truth of Islam have not as yet entered into it. Islam still has its original roots and the people still have a clear recollection of it.

Mu awiyah wants Imam Husayn to sit in the Damascus mosque and teach theology, explain the $\bar{a}y\bar{a}t$ of the Qur'an, Islamic culture, *tawḥīd*, the history of Islam, or the biography of the Prophet, or anything else that he wishes. He is even prepared to provide a budget for him, provided that Imam Husayn does not engage in political activity which Mu awiyah considers to be an inferior activity for an Imam! But the Imam knows that the 'value of any action in society is equal to how much it hurts the enemy!' What must he do? He must rebel. Armed revolution? An armed revolution needs power and Imam Husayn has no power.

A book has recently been published which has become very popular — and has been very much attacked.[70] Its contents inadvertently show it to be a worthwhile book. I noted in studying it that it is the only book among the books written by our scholars which is based upon the studies of the author himself. All of the relevent documents have been studied and views on both sides of the issue have been presented, analyzed, explained and criticized. The author has even shown great courage by rejecting some of these views. In other words, he undertakes an extensive study with a wide range of references to perform scientific research in order to be able to announce a new theory. These are the values of this book, and I admire the author, although I do not know him personally. I respect him as a scientist who has undertaken serious research, explanation and analysis, as an independent thinker who announces a new thesis: "Imam Husayn left Madinah in order to undertake a political or military revolt against the ruling government, and by destroying the oppressive regime, to obtain his own rights and the rights of the people."

Despite the merits of this thesis, I have come to a different opinion through my research, for the author's thesis does not conform to the particular realities of the situation. One person, in rejecting this theory, said, "Imam Husayn was not a politician in order to be able to revolt against the ruling power." This is surprising. For what purpose then, were the Prophet and Ali fighting? For what purpose was Imam Husayn fighting? Is it not the question of politics? Is it not the fact that criminals are ruling over people? Therefore, a person who is responsible should abolish oppression and by taking rule, give the people their rights. It is not the right of the leader to do so, rather it is his obligation.

Therefore, the Imam must certainly, either militarily or politically rise up against the usurping government and destroy the powerful *jāhiliya,* govern the revolutionary power, and establish the truth in the community, keeping leadership in his own possession. I would like to propose that this military or political revolution is the very mission of Imam Husayn, but that he does not actually possess the ability to carry out this mission.

Those who believe that Imam Husayn undertook a political and military revolt use the argument that Kufah was a center which supported and protected Imam Husayn, his family, and the family of the Prophet and Ali. It is true that Iran is behind Kufah and that the Iranians supported Ali and his family and that they even believe that all of Kufah is in the possession of Imam Husayn, and that the people of Kufah are faithful and loyal to Imam Husayn's agent, Muslim ibn Aqil.[71]

I suppose that if Kufah were so powerful, then if Imam Husayn had been able to reach there, he could have transformed it into a strong Islamic base and could even have defeated Damascus and have established a free Islamic government under his leadership. Nevertheless, I believe that the movement of Imam Husayn was not a political and military one. Let me add — not for the reason that, as some people say, it is beneath Imam Husayn to attend to politics and undertake a political revolution. No. This is the duty of an Imam. What I say is that he did not have the opportunity to make such a revolution.

You may argue, "How is it possible that if Imam Husayn had reached Kufah, you yourself admit that Kufah could have defeated Damascus, and thereby could have given the leadership of the government to Husayn? Why then do you not believe the revolt of Imam Husayn to have been a political and military revolution against the Umayyid regime?" In order to clear up this point we should look at the start and the form of the Imam's movement from Madinah.

Imam Husayn leaves Madinah and goes to Mecca. In Madinah he receives the invitation of the people of Kufah, "We believe in you and expect you to accept leadership. We need your leadership. We will give power to you. We will stand with you against usurpation and oppression. We will defend you. Please release us from this exploitative government." In Madinah, Imam Husayn announces, "Following in the traditions of my grandfather and my father, I am leaving Madinah to 'invite people to the good and to forbid evil.'" Then he travels six hundred kilometers and arrives openly in Mecca, accompanied by his family. In Mecca, he announces to the pilgrims who had come for the *hajj*, "I am going to my death." A person who is planning a political rebellion does not speak in these terms, but would say, "I am going to fight to kill. I will conquer. I will destroy the enemy." But Imam Husayn addresses the people saying, "Death, for the sons of Adam, is as beautiful as a necklace around the neck of a young and beautiful girl. Death is an ornament for mankind." He then leaves Mecca to go towards death.

Is it possible that a politician living in the center of power of the Umayyids, in the midst of a district of the ruling government, in reply to an invitation sent to him from one of the remote cities which had rebelled against the central government, would go to them to accept revolutionary leadership and formally announce, "I am coming," take his wife, children and all the members of his family, his nephews and all the men and women of his family in an open caravan — not secretly — move very naturally from one town to another, all of which are occupied by the enemy which supports the central government? Husayn crosses six hundred kilometers in this manner, and enters Mecca. There, all those who are ruled by the Damascus government, all of the powers, fronts and Islamic nationalists are gathered. Here he announces once more that he intends to go to Kufah. He leaves by the western side of the Arabian peninsula and passing the whole east-west diameter, in the same manner, goes to Iraq and arrives near Kufah, the center of rebellion and revolution. It is obvious that the central government would not permit such a movement.

If a well-known political personality, or even an ordinary opposing politician intends to leave a country to join the revolutionaries who are out of the country, to participate in their activities against the regime, it is clear under what conditions and in what manner he should leave the country and approach them. Certainly he should not announce it. He should not make the invitation known. He should keep his goal and his journey quite secret. It is obvious that if he formally announces to the government, "I am a revolutionary who opposes the regime. I will not give my allegiance to the regime. I intend to leave the country in order to join the revolutionary group outside of the country and fight with them against the present regime. The revolutionaries have asked me to become their leader. Because of this I am leaving the country. Please issue my passport!" they will not issue him a passport, but will seize and destroy him. But what does Imam Husayn do? He formally, clearly and distinctly announces to the government, to the ruling power, to the military governor, to the people, "I do not give my allegiance. I am leaving Mecca. I am migrating to Kufah. I am migrating to death. I am making my move!"

If the people suddenly realized that Imam Husayn had left the city, if Imam Husayn had left the city secretly, if he had quietly migrated and through the help of the tribes, reached Kufah in the same way that the Prophet migrated from Mecca to Madinah, then after a time the central government would realize that he was in Kufah and among the revolutionaries. It would then be obvious that Imam Husayn had rebelled against the government. But the form of his movement, his moving with the caravan shows that Imam Husayn has moved for another purpose. His purpose is neither to run nor to seek seclusion. He is neither surrendering nor putting aside politics and a political rebellion for intellectual, scientific, theological and moral affairs, nor for a military revolution. Then what?

It has reached the point where thoughts have become paralyzed. Personalities have sold out. The faithful have been left alone. Virtues have been isolated. Young people are either in a state of hopelessness or they have sold themselves out. The important pioneers of Islam have either been martyred or silenced and choked or made to sell out. It is time when no sounds are heard from the community. Pens have been broken. Tongues have been cut off. Lips have been sealed shut. All of the pillars of truth have been knocked down, and have fallen on top of the faithful followers.

Imam Husayn, as a responsible leader, sees that if he remains silent, Islam will change into a mere civil religion. Islam will be changed into a military-economic power and nothing more. Islam will become as other regimes and powers. When their power diminishes, when their army and government are destroyed, nothing will remain. It will be nothing more than a memory in history, an accident which occurred in the past and has ended. It is for this reason that Imam Husayn now stands between two inabilities. He can neither remain silent nor can he fight. He cannot remain silent because time and opportunity are passing. Everything is being destroyed, abolished in the minds and deep consciences of the people

— feelings, thoughts, aspirations, meanings, ideals — everything brought by the message of Muhammad, everything about Islam that he brought and developed through *jihād*. All of the others are obeying the ruling power. They are being deceived. The present atmosphere is one of complete silence, quivering and surrender. He cannot remain silent because he has a duty to fight against oppression.

On the other hand, he cannot fight because he has no army. He is surrounded by the ruling, oppressive regime. He can neither shout out nor surrender nor attack. He remains with empty hands, yet the heavy burden of all of these responsibilities rests on his shoulders. He inherited nothing of the power and the results of the struggles and efforts of his grandfather, the Prophet, his father, Ali, and his brother, Imam Hasan, except honor, misery, and a very heavy responsibility. He is alone, unarmed. Opposing him is one of the most savage empires of the world which is disguised by the fairest and most deceiving cloak of piety, sacredness, and unity which the ruling power possesses. He is alone. He is a lonely man who is responsible to a school of thought. In this school of thought, it is the responsibility of this lonely man to oppose the power of fate because responsibility springs from awareness and faith, not from power. Whoever is more aware is more responsible, and who is more aware than Husayn?

What is his responsibility? It is his responsibility to fight against the elimination of truth, the destruction of the rights of the people, annihilation of all of the values, abolition of all of the memories of the revolution, destruction of the message of the revolution, and to protect the most beloved culture and faith of the people, for their destruction is the aim of the most filthy enemies of the people. They want, once again, to bring about unknown mysterious deaths, exiles, to put people in chains, worship pleasure, discriminate, gather wealth, sell human values, faith and honor, create a new religious foolishness, racism, a new aristocracy, a new *jāhiliyah* and a new polytheism.

The responsibility of resisting, struggling and fighting against all of these treacheries and crimes against the people, the responsibility of *jihād* against the new conservatism, the responsibility of guarding that great divine revolution, are all placed upon the shoulders of one man alone. No one else has remained in the ranks of truth, justice, awareness, in the ranks of the people and God. All fronts have been given up. All the defenders have either been killed or have run away. He has remained alone, empty handed, without any possibility, surrounded by the enemy who caused others to surrender to the silence, to become indifferent and fall into public *jāhiliyah*. He can neither keep silent nor cry out. He cannot remain silent because everything depends on the actions of this lonely man. He cannot cry out because the sound of his voice has been cut off. His cry will not reach the terrible silence of the sacrificing people; it will not reach the threat of immunity, the negligence of *jāhiliya*, the stupefication of the ruling religion; it cannot effect the skirmishes, the false and savage wars of the Caliphate which are performed in the name of *jihād* for victory and booty with rituals and rites, congregational prayer, *hajj*, the Qur'an, and Islam. In the meantime, dance, music and art progress; power, pleasure and corrupt liberties drown out the voice of Husayn.

Husayn must fight, but he cannot. How strange! He must and yet is unable. This responsibility is the burden of his conscience. It results from 'being Husayn' not from his 'ability.' He is still Husayn — alone, unable, unarmed and helpless. What should he do? 'Being Husayn' calls him to fight but he has no arms to fight with, and yet he still has the duty to fight. All of the supporters of wisdom and religion, advisors of tradition and common law, those who recommend goodness and logic, all unanimously say, "No!" But Husayn wants to say, "Yes."

He leaves Madinah for this purpose. He has come to Mecca to announce his unique answer to all Muslims who have gathered there for the *hajj*. He leaves Mecca to reply to the question, "What is to be done?" The question exists in this important moment of history in which the fate of the people and of Islam are to be determined. At this moment, everything has collapsed. All of the intellectuals and aware people and those who are faithful to the truth, justice, freedom of Islam and revolution, all those who can see, feel, understand and thus suffer and feel themselves responsible, who are thus looking for a revolution, are then asking, "What is to be done?"[72]

Everyone has an answer. The fatalists say, "Nothing." Whatever has occurred will continue to occur in accordance with divine wisdom and divine profundity. God wishes it to be this way. You must be satisfied with what has been given to you and be grateful for it, because you are not allowed to freely decide your fate. They say that it is true that there is crime, oppression and the usurpation of rights. The claims made about *zakāt, jihād, sunnat,* the Caliphate, and the victory of Islam, claims that the temples of idols have been turned into mosques, claims about the propogation of Islam and the increase in the number of Muslims — all of these are lies. But what can be done? A leaf does not fall from a tree unless God so wills. God has so wished. This is how his wisdom rules. No one can protest, criticize, or even say why it is so. Everyone is subject to his or her fate. Everything that occurs, good or bad, is determined by eternal fate and is in accordance with the Qur'an.[73] If Ali is defeated and remains alone, if Mu awiyah conquers and attains power, these are all in accordance with God's will. The Qur'an says: "God causes whomever He wishes to arise." "God brings down whomever He wishes." "God gives power to whomever he wishes."[74] So, what can one say? What can one do? One can only be patient and remain silent. Other than remaining content and surrendering, what can a person who is bound in the chains of fate and destiny do? Nothing.

It is not accidental that Umar Khayyam is being revived in our culture.[75] After the Second World War he met the desires of all of the people of the world. Not the scientist Khayyam, mind you, but the poet! Not the genius Khayyam with his miraculous arithmetic thoughts, but the cunning Khayyam who composed a few repetitive quatrains. It is not without purpose that the majority of orientalists, Islamologists and Iranologists write such huge tomes on the various aspects of cultures and civilizations and show such interest in the revival of Sufism. While over seventy percent of our scientific, literary, Islamic, historical, philosophical and artistic works remain in manuscript form in the storerooms of public or private libraries, works on Sufism are printed in several forms and editions. It is true that everything which happens has a purpose which is unknown to us, and that everything is ruled by fate, but not by the destiny of divine wisdom, rather by a fate and destiny of gods, not in heaven, but upon the earth!

We see that with such a philosophy, the questions of ability, inability, and *jihād* are not even important. All sense of responsibility is lost because there is no way to choose the right way. The *murji'ah* reply, "What must we do? Against whom? In opposition to what? God asks all of the people to hope and to seek salvation and paradise. How can we condemn a person and say that he will go to hell and then fight him? It is as if you performed a godless act by arising before the day of doom to condemn someone prior to the day of judgement. What will happen if this condemned person, this criminal Mu awiyah is forgiven by God on the day of doom? You may not forgive him, but what if God forgives him? If tomorrow God should bless him, what will your reply be? What will your duty be? What is to be done? Whom should you ask? Who must reply? Who must act? No one. Nothing. We must wait and see what God does."

The *murji'ah* also argue that Abu Bakr, Umar, Uthman, Ali, Talhah, Zubayr, Mu awiyah, and Yazid were all Companions of the Prophet. They were al *mujāhids*. Each of them acted according to his own findings and religious discernment. There is no discrepancy between *dīn* and *kufr* the oppressor and the oppressed, friend and enemy. Experts are not obliged to consider the views of the public. The sheep-like people should not interfere with religious experts and theologians. God is the final Judge. God is most merciful. You and I are not allowed to ask what is to be done. The holy ones reply: "There are as many ways to God as there are people. Is *jihād* the only answer? The ritual prayer is one of the pillars of the religion while *jihād* is one of the branches related to encouraging good deeds and prohibiting evil deeds. Do you yourself perform and follow all of the formalities, performances, rules, commandments, duties, and stipulations which relate to the daily ritual prayer?[75] Do you remember all of the regulations regarding doubts in the ritual prayers which are like complicated logarithmic tables?[76] Have you learned the rules of the pure and the impure, and of the importance and obligatory rules of the prayer?

"Have those of you who are thinking about the people and who are intending to guide and direct them, rectified yourselves? Have you reached the position of never stumbling — not being selfish, not having any desires, being completely pure and innocent? Are all of your thoughts and deeds, even the slightest ones, for the sake of the satisfaction of God? Only and purely for God? Have you corrected all of the principles and the various branches of your religion? Have you been purified, are you pious? Do you now consider yourself as innocent and rectified so that you are now trying to rectify the community?

"On the other hand, paradise has eight doors.[77] You are not obliged to enter only through the door of *jihād*. *Jihād* is simply one of the keys which opens the doors to Paradise. Prayer, other forms of worship, and incantation are safer keys and you can use them without harm, loss, danger or risk! There are a lot of charitable affairs that will take you to the same point, such as feeding the needy, looking after poor families, visiting the holy places, praying, asceticism, piety, making vows, dedication, helping your neighbor, incantation, prayer ceremonies, lamentation, and intercession. You will reach the same goal as the person who chooses *jihād*, so why cause yourself suffering and pain by choosing the much more difficult action of *jihād*? It has been mentioned in some of the prayer books that simply by reading some of the prayers in that book, a person is given more rewards and benefits than seventy martyrs at the Battle of Badr! So is it not clear what is to be done?"

Another issues concerns the belief that the entrance of a holy personality or a religious clergyman into political affairs is a deviation from true religion. It means selling religion to the materialists and instead of attending to ethics and religious affairs it means to seek after wealth and the gathering of earthly things. These cannot be mixed with each other.

"Did the Prophet not say, returning from *jihād*, "We are now returning from the lesser *jihād* but we are confronted by a greater *jihād*' They asked him what the greater kind of *jihōd* was. He answered, 'The *jihad* against carnal desires!'[78] Therefo. , one must put aside the lesser *jihād* and only attend to the greater one. One should confront one's carnal desires, not an external enemy."

The Companions, outstanding personalities, theologians and religious scholars, dependent upon the regime, declare, "Ali's type of thinking is not practical and contains too much hardship. It is too strict. One must consider realities. One must be a realist, not an idealist. Ali ruled over the greater part of the known world, but he still mends his own shoes himself! He works like a common laborer. Today people judge by what they see. This is particularly true since Iran and Rome have been defeated and Muslims have seen the glory and magnificence of the huge, fantastic palaces and the greatness and majesty of the King of Kings of Iran and the Caesars of Rome. No, Ali's kind of living is not acceptable! It is not good for the reputation and prestige of an Islamic Government!

"On the other hand, can Ali's regime be tolerated in the aristocratic societies of Iran and Rome? When Ali was appointed Caliph, he changed all of the wage scales of the salaries, making everyone equal. He gave the same salary of three dirhams monthly to Uthman ibn Hanyf, the great and important politician and close friend and outstanding officer in Ali's government, as he gave to a slave!"[79]

According to this view, Ali's economic system is impractical. It is argued, "We saw and still remember that in Iran, which is now occupied by the Arabs and is part of the Islamic Empire ruled by Ali, when Chosroes[81] was coming to fight the Muslims — realizing that due to the conditions of war he should leave aside as many ceremonies as possible — yet he had seven thousand women, slaves, servants and musicians with him! We do not want to argue as to whether or not this was right. We are saying that if Ali failed, it was because his school of thought was not practical in such society. He could not adapt himself to the current situation and social realities. He was not a politician! He was not a sociologist! He offended everyone! He was too strict! He never humbled himself before the outstanding personalities, the heads of the tribes, the powerful, the aristocrats or the noble families! You must not compare the Caliphate with the Imamate and Prohecy! You must not compare Mu awiyah and Yazid with the Prophet and Ali! You should compare them to the Caesars and Kings. The present court of Damascus which you have announced to be a Green Palace, in which public funds have been invested and the rights of the people have been destroyed is the place from which the Islamic Empire of the world rules over Iran, Rome, etc. But it is still more humble than the palace of a Roman Consul or of an officer who was appointed as the governor of Syria."

Abu Dhar attacks Mu awiyah with these words, "Why is your bread made of bleached wheat and you only eat the center of the bread? Why do you wear a different dress during the day and another at night?"

The followers of Ali seem to believe that we are still living in

Madinah as it was at the time of the Prophet and that the 'civilized' Romans and Iranians who have joined the Islamic world are *Muhājirūn* and *Anṣār*! They argue, "We should consider the relativity of the issues. Love of Truth and absolutism are idealistic. You must see the realities. It is not possible to convince the poor, backward Muslims who are ruling an important part of the world with both an Eastern and a Western Empire, that one should live like they did at the time of the Prophet or behave as Ali is behaving. Standards of living have progressed. The traditions, rules, etiquette of society, economic and aristocratic systems, thoughts, ideas, tastes, literature, poetry, music, dance, amusements, social relations, ethics and manners of 'civilized' Rome and Iran, the social class system and aristocratic regime, the political system of the Caesars and Kings, the type and form of the monastic and clerical traditions which are hierarchial, bureaucratic, official and classical systems of rule, and finally, the progressive Iranian and Roman civilizations — certainly had an influence upon the simple Islamic communities.

The wealth, power, position and countless 'spoils' which had been earned in the Muslim victories make the people grow fat and it is because of this that they are no longer listening to Ali's advice, his aspirations and his sufferings. The majority of the people are quite happy with the situation. They are no longer fond of such problems as good and evil, right and wrong. They show no sensitivity whatsoever to them. These people have now changed into being the servants of wealth and power. Those few who did not obey have been tried by the sword!

Do you remember what happened to Ali and Fatimah in their own town of Madinah, in their own time, at the hands of their own friends and companions, and those who fought in the same rank as they did? You saw that the Umayyid tribe had not been present in either Madinah or Saqifah.[81] None of them had been part of the *shūrā*.[82] Do you recall the outstanding officers of Imam Ali and Imam Hasan with their glorious backgrounds? How they sold themselves to Muawiyah at the peak of the battle? How they dealt a good hand to themselves, their religion, their past self-respect and all of the soldiers under their command with Muawiyah?

The Khawarij[84] had been neither from the Umayyid tribe nor had they been related to the Umayyid regime. They had even been the blood enemies of the Umayyids and their regime. They had all come from the mass of the people, ordinary tradesmen from the countryside. They had even been symbols of the sacred, pious devotees who underwent ascetic practices. They had been outstanding and well-known examples of the strict religious types. You noted how they unconsciously had become tools in the hands of the Umayyids. They had been indirectly agitated from Damascus and thus had opposed Ali. In the crisis of the battle, they had argued with Ali and had left him alone. So they became unpaid servants of the enemy; they are used to defeat Ali. They are good, religious people who weakened Ali by accusing, insulting and even excommunicating and debasing him. Those like Amr Aas,[85] who had been infamous among the people, could not hurt Ali's spiritual and religious reputation, but the "pious" Khawarij could destroy him through excommunication. We saw how they finally manage to kill him with their fanaticism. Through these experiences one may think the answer to "What is to be done?" is "Nothing."

Mu awiyah suits these people, not Ali. On the other hand, Muawiyah, taking all of his weak points and deviations into consideration, is much more of a modern thinker and is more realistic than Ali. Ali intends to have the people live with a piety and simplicity which is impossible! But Mu awiyah's regime, even though it is oppressive, corrupt and discriminating, rapidly develops the community! With its free and careless spirit, it easily imitates all of the forms and types of Iranian and Roman civilizations. During the twenty years in which he had held power, after the settling of internal difficulties and discrepancies, after dealing with such personalities as Abu Dhar, Ali, Hasan, Hujr, etc., Muawiyah turns the capital of Islam into a modern and progressive western-like town. He establishes an armed marine force in the Mediterranean, occupies Cyprus, and holds a permanent offensive line against the king of the Byzantine Empire.

In the construction of the Green Palace of Mu awiyah, a Roman style of architecture is followed and it is decorated in a Sassanian style. Instead of a few bedouin Arab slaves, he manages an orchestra full of the best Iranian musicians together with Roman dancers. He imitates the traditions and the customs of the courts of the Caesars and the Kings of Iran. Their clothes, food, entertainment, decoration, music, poetry, literature, manner of living, city-plans, palaces, and socio-political systems have all been altered from the original simple Arabian styles to modern civilized and 'Revolutionary' Roman styles. So, putting aside arguments of truth and falsehood, oppression and justice, whether Ali is right or Muʿawiyah is right, from the apparent progress and point of view of civilization a lot had been done and would continue to be done. Anyway, renewing the construction of the capital, the respectful manner of living of the Caliph, and his palaces all bring honor and respect to Islam in the eyes of the foreigners, the Christians and Magians!

On the other hand, comparing the previous regime, that of Ali, with the Roman and Iranian regimes, they say that one has to admit that the new Caliphate of the Umayyids is better serving the people and is more useful to them. They make the people behave better; things are smoother and freer. They are also creating respect, power, spoils, victories, expansion, a good reputation and a sense of importance for Islam. Many temples and churches have been replaced by mosques. There are many cities and towns in the profane lands where the cries of *Allāhu Akbar, Lā ilāha illā Allāh,* and *Muḥammadun rasūl Allāh* can now be heard.[85] There are many treasures and spoils running into the public treasury. Even though these funds may not have been obtained properly (that is, justly and in accord with Islamic principles), they are being used in Islamic countries. Some of the Muslims take advantage of this. Furthermore, these victories create new professions and income for the young people, positions for the nobles and jobs for some of the Muslims.

Therefore, in reply to "What is to be done?", the answer is given, "The idealistic revolutionary standards of Islam at the time of the Prophet should be reviewed. Times have changed and Islam today no longer revolves around Mecca and Madinah. It stretches from the Byzantine Empire to Iran. It therefore ought not come under the influence of Ali's idealistic aspirations and his strict and difficult ways of striving towards complete justice." Even Ali's own brother ran to Mu'awiyah. How can one expect the people, who are being ruled by a Caesar or a King, to tolerate anything but this.

"You must look at the present situation realistically. You must admit that the Umayyid's power, politics, intelligence, wealth and force are being used in the name of Islam for the purpose of establishing the rituals of Islam in the world, the development and growth of Islam. It is undertaking a struggle with polytheism, enhancing the reputation of Islam, taking the Qur'an and the Prophet forward. It is trying to promote the civilization of the Islamic community, to develop cities, raise the standard of living, create social welfare, gain wealth, and borrow from the great civilizations of the East and West.

"Therefore in response to the question 'What is to be done?', we say one should do as we have done: join with the Umayyid regime. We have seen that interference, internal fighting, political struggles, intellectual and mental debates of right, justice, Imamate, selection, election, virtue, piety, chastity, traditions, innovation, heresy, are all useless and its results are defeat. Furthermore, it is not advisable when the Umayyid Caliph is fighting a *jihād* against Rome and Iran, with Christianity and the Magians, with unbelieving external enimies, that a combat on the internal front be undertaken which will cause official Islamic power to be weakened. This will only inhibit its progress.

"All of us with a realistic spirit must discontinue political struggles, choose seclusion, Sufism and piety by accepting the present reality, and try to support the Umayyid regime in its services to the people of Islam. As to its deviations — we should try to correct and amend them. How can we play our parts? It is obvious — by adhering to the ruling system. On the one hand, we can serve the poor people, earn rights for the oppressed ones, undertake social affairs, help the needy, even be religiously active and propogate religion, promote ideas, reform society, and combat any future corruption when we are part of the ruling system and have an important and high position and profession. On the other hand, scholars and men of letters say: 'It is sixty years since the *hijrah*. Ali's revolution has been defeated. Hasan, the last leader who opposed oppression and the old inhuman anti-god reactionary forces, had to make peace with Muawiyah, and was poisoned by him. Therefore nothing can be done. It is useless. We should only attend to religious problems, divine knowledge, religious jurisprudence, research, gnostic discoveries and observations and through these means, acquaint the people with Islamic thoughts, ideas and realities and discover the spiritual aspects and scientific secrets of the Qur'an. We should only undertake research that allows us to sink into divine knowledge and wisdom, theosophy, secrets of the Qur'an, rhetoric, eloquence, semantics, poetic techniques, the collection of *hadīth,* the study of the biography of the Prophet, jurisprudence, philosophy, theology, etc. We should concern ourselves with research, training, the propogation of religious knowledge, rituals and roles, promotion of Islamic culture, serving Islam and the Islamic community mentally and scientifically and nothing else!"

It is so wonderful that it is so clear to intellectuals, that is, the followers of Ali's, even Ali's family and those who are close to the Prophet's family and the Bani Hashim, [87] that the response to the question, 'What is to be done?' is 'Nothing!,' because the result of any action is defeat. Nothing can be done. It would be like trying to drive a nail with one's fist. It is not lawful to stand bare-headed before the sword. It is not permitted. And yet, you are still responsible and will be punished. Has it not been said, "Do not place yourself before death with your own hands?" [88] A *jihād* in which one's destiny and death are fixed is certainly suicide. It is to the advantage of disbelief and oppression. It is useless.

So we see that all classes, including those who were in power, religious men, scholars, even Shi'ites, intellectuals who sought out the truth and knew that the truth, that their social, mental and political policy was clear and distinct — all of them at this time, sixty years after the *hijrah,* in reply to the question of the times, without any exception, say "No!"

There is only one man, a lonely man, who says "Yes." And what is that 'yes'? It is a response behind which lies total inability, total weakness in a time of darkness and silence, against oppression and tyranny, an aware and faithful man who still has the responsibility of the *jihād.* It is Imam Husayn's command: "Yes!" There is also a necessity despite his inability. For him it is a living idea and *jihād.*

If he is alive, then to continue living he must bear a responsibility to fight for an idea. The *living* man is responsible, not just the able man, and who is more alive than Husayn? Who in our history has more right to live and is more worthy to be alive than Husayn? The soul of humanity, being aware, having faith, being alive, creates the responsibility of *jihād* in man, and Husayn is the highest example of being alive, loving and aware of humanity. Ability or inability, weakness or strength, loneliness or crowds only determine the form of the mission and the manner of approaching the responsibility, not its necessity. He must fight. But he has no arms. Nevertheless it is his duty to fight. Husayn answers his command and he is the only one whose opinion is "Yes." He is the only man who in answer to this question in such a condition says "Yes!" He is a lonely man. He has left his home in Madinah. He has gone from Madinah to Mecca as it is the season of the *Hajj* beside the Ka'ba, where the people have gathered to say, *"Labbayk."*[89]And now he is leaving Mecca. He is in a hurry. His *Hajj* goes half finished in order to show the world, 'how'.

It is sixty years after the *hijrah,* fifty years after the death of the Prophet. All are missing. Ali is missing. Hasan is missing. Abu Dhar is missing. Ammar is missing. In the second generation, Hujr is missing, and his companions have been massacred. The gallows have been dismantled and the blood washed away. Thoughts have turned to despair, obscurity, deterioration, deviation, silence, fear. Darkness has spread everywhere. Persons like Abu Hurayrah, Abu Musa, Shurayh, Abu Darda and those similar to them, those who during the revolution of Islam, in that glorious period, had boasted and gained such respect, had become disgraced and had evidently made allegiance with profanity and oppression.[90]

Those warriors, the Companions and *Muhajirūn,* were sticking their heads into the stables of the public treasury. Their stomachs were bloated with food. They had given the hands and arms of *jihād* to the hands and arms of the executioners, and with the excuse of abject poverty, they had gathered around Yazid. The shadow of the red sword of security had spread itself all over from Khurrasan to Damascus. The massacres, defeats, treacheries, conspiracies, escapes, desertions and black disappointments had spread death all over the empire, had imprisoned breath within the ribcage.

> In the bloodless cemetery of a town,
> Even the owl's hoot has become silent.
> Those with a cause worth fighting for are silent.
> Water has stopped driving the millwheel round.

The blood's been washed away and the gallows taken
down.
Where labor, anger and revolt were planted, now only
dung-weeds are found.
Where devastating clenched fists once beat the sky, those
hands are open now and empty.
They have only opened to slap someone down, or to turn
themselves into empty beggars' bowls.

We, the shameless, have remained.[91]

Now, time awaits one man. Everything is in expectation of a man
who embodies the values which are being destroyed, who embodies
the symbols of all of the ideals which have remained friendless and
abandoned. The supporters of the manifestation of these ideals and
this faith have joined the enemy. Yes. Time is awaiting a man's
action. It is sometimes so in history. Sixty years after the *hijrah,* fifty
years after the death of the Prophet of liberty, justice and the people,
the time has come when everything drops away. All of the fruits of
the revolution have been destroyed and disappointment becomes the
faith of the people.

In these dark times the *jāhiliyya* aristocracy is being revived.
Power is being dressed in piety and sacredness. The desire for liberty
and equality created by Islam is vanishing from the hearts of those
who have been sacrificed for power and policy. Tribal ignorance has
replaced the humanitarian revolution. The Book of Truth has been
placed upon the spears of deceit.[92] From the minarets the sound of
the call to polytheism is heard. The golden calf is calling for *Tawḥīd.*
Nimrod[93] replaces Abraham. Caesar wears the turban of the Prophet
of God. The executioner takes the sword of *jihād.* Religion becomes
the opiate of the people. The labor of the *mujāhidian* is gone with the
wind; indeed, it has become the windfall treasure of the *munāfiqīn.*[94]
Jihād is transformed into massacre. *Zakāt* becomes public plunder.
Prayer is public deception. *Tawḥīd* is a mask for polytheism. Islam
has become a shackle of submission. *Sunnat* has become the base of
government. The Qur'an is the means to ignorance. *Ḥadīth* has
become the facility of deception. The flash of the sword and the
sweep of the whip are once more above the shoulders of the people.

Nations are being taken into slavery as before. Freedom is bound by a permanent chain. Thoughts are imprisoned in jails and remain silent. The masses have surrendered. The free have been captured. The foxes are agile. Wolves are being fed. Tongues are either sold for gold, shut off by force, or cut off by the blade.

The respect and honor which the Companions had won at a costly price during the period of faith and *jihād,* during the revolution, have been sold at cheap rates and have been exchanged for civil governorship. They had avoided the risks of revolt by refusing to shoulder their responsibility. They escaped into secure corners and pure, restful asceticism, thereby earning their health and safety in a respectful way, maintaining silence in the face of oppression, submitting to *kufr.* Or they have been killed in the Rabadhah desert or the Maraj al-'Adhrā.

Now religion and the world are running in favor of *kufr* and oppression. Swords are broken. Throats are cut. Gallows have been dismantled. The blood has been washed away.

The waves of revolution, the shouts of protest, the flames of rebellion have all been calmed. Excitement and enthusiasm have diminished. Shadows of fear and strangulation have spread over the cemeteries of martyrs as well as on the cold and silent cemetery of the living. There is not even the hoot of an owl to be heard in the ruined place of the faith and hope of the Muslims. New *jāhiliya* darkens the heavens. It is more savage than the previous *jāhiliya.* The enemy is more intelligent, more victorious and more aware than the former enemy. Intellectuals have tasted the bitter experiences of rebellion which resulted in their defeat and martyrdom.

Suddenly a spark appears in the darkness and bursts into flame! The radiant visage of a 'martyr who walks alive upon the earth'. From the depths of darkness, the immense corruptions and obscure nights of despair, the light and powerful feature of 'a hope' is seen.

Once more, from the silent and sorrowful home of Fatimah, the little house which is greater than the whole of history, a man emerges — angry, determined, in a state of rebellion against all of the palaces of cruelty and fronts of power. He is as a mountain which holds a volcano within it, or as a hurricane, like the one God sent to the tribe of 'Ad.[94]

A man emerges from Fatimah's house. He looks at Madinah and the mosque of the Prophet, at Mecca and Abraham, at the Ka'ba which is enchained by Nimrod, at Islam and the message of Muhammad, at the Green Palace of Damascus, the hungry people, the slaves, and ...

A man emerges from Fatimah's house. The load of all of the responsibilities has been placed upon his shoulders. He is the heir of the great suffering of humanity. He is the only heir to Adam, Abraham, Muhammad ... a lonely man.

But no! A woman has come out of Fatimah's house with him, walking side by side with him. She bears half of the heavy mandate of her brother upon her shoulders.[95]

A man emerges from Fatimah's house. Alone, friendless, with empty hands he confronts the terror of the darkness and the sword. He has only one weapon — death. But he is the son of the family which has learned the art of dying well in the school of life. There is no one in the whole world who knows better 'how to die' than he does. His powerful enemy who is ruling the world is deprived of this knowledge. It is because of this that this lonely hero is so confident of his victory over the immense army of his enemy and is so determined. He welcomes his victory without doubt.

The great teacher of *shahādat* has now arisen in order to teach those who consider the *jihād* to pertain only to those who have ability and who think that victory lies only in conquest that *Shahādat* is not a loss, it is a choice, a choice whereby the warrior sacrifices himself on the threshold of the temple of freedom and the alter of love and is victorious.

Husayn, the heir of Adam, who gives life to the children of mankind, the successor of the great prophets, who taught mankind 'how to live,' has now come to teach mankind 'how to die'.

Husayn teaches that 'black death' is the miserable fate of a debased people who accept scorn in order to remain alive. For death chooses those who are not brave enough to choose *shahādat*. Death chooses them!

The word *shahīd* has the heaviest load of meaning for what we want and for what I have to say. In the lexicon, *'shahīd'* signifies one who is present, an overlooker, an observer, a witness and one who bears witness. It also means the truthful and honest informant, and it also means conscience. It is what is sensed and seen, the one toward whom all eyes are directed, and last but not least, it means pattern, exemplar, model.

Shahādat in our culture and in our religion is not a bloody and tragic occurrence. In other religions and tribal histories, *shahādat* refers to the sacrifice of the heroes who are killed in the battles with the enemy. It is considered to be a sorrowful accident full of misery. Those who are killed in this way are called martyrs, and their death is called martyrdom. But in our culture, *shahādat* is not a death which is imposed by an enemy upon our warriors. It is a death which is desired by our warriors, selected with all of the awareness, logic, reasoning, intelligence, understanding, consciousness and alertness that a human being can have.

It is unfortunate that the movement of '*Āshūra!*[97] the most magnificent manifestation of the school of *shahādat*, has been misreprsented. It has been presented as "the school of mourning," and consequently, we remember it and weep for it throughout our lives without knowing, understanding, or considering it.

The most shining dimension of this movement is unfortunately also the darkest dimension, that is to say, the effects that Āshūra has had in the political, social, and intellectual history of Islam. The few scholars, who have more or less investigated these effects, have limited it to the course of Shi'ite history and to the social changes and revolutionary movements of the Shi'ites; whereas Āshūra was actually such a devastating blow that throughout the fourteen centuries of the political and social history of Islam, it exposed the infamy of the ruling system in any guise, under any motto, and with any ideology, in the eyes of Islamic society. Thanks to this exposure, any Islamic and scientific personality who believed in his own faith and virtue was cautious not to get close to the regimes, even though the regimes were "Islamic" regimes, and the ruler considered himself to be "Caliph of the Prophet" and would go to *hajj* one year and *jihād* the next.[98] This is despite the fact that those personalities, scholars, and experts of jurisprudence were of the Sunni sect and considered the Caliphate to be a legitimate regime. But the fatal blow of martyrdom had effected the history of Islam so deeply that the social conscience, option, and ethics of Muslim societies would consciously or unconsciously read the mark of cancellation that Husayn had stamped on the forehead of every government, even though it might call itself "Caliphate." This mark of cancellation not only endangered the base of the deceptive political regimes, separating the people and government as two distinct poles, but it also created a sort of unofficial "negative resistance," which became a magnificent social tradition among the people.

The polarization of the Shi'ites and their leaders and imams is quite familiar. What is significant in terms of the amplitude of the effect of martyrdom on the history of Islam is the considerable extent to which the Sunni imams became uncompromising in their negative resistance to the Umayyid and Abbasid dynasties, despite the support, respect, and glorification that they received from the regime of the Caliphate, which is to be contrasted with the denial of influence, liberty and opportunity according to the Shi'ite imams.

At the end of the Umayyad era, Abu Hanifah (d. 150/767), the greatest Sunni imam,[99] was invited by ibn Hubayrah, the governor of Iraq, to hold the position of *qādī*. He decisively rejected the invitation, and because of this he was severely flogged, despite his religious and scientific status. When the Abbasids took power, Mansur invited Abu Hanifah to accept the position of supreme *qādī* of the entire Islamic empire. This invitation was also rejected, and therefore Abu Hanifah was put in prison, where he died. Malik (97/715-179/795), the imam of the Malikites, who was supported by the Caliphate instead of Imam al-Sadiq, was flogged by Ja'far ibn Muhammad, the governor of Medina, because of his protest against the regime and because of his having said, "One cannot rule over people by force and compulsion."

Buwayti, one of the great experts of jurisprudence, and one of the learned disciples of Imam Shafi'i (150/767-205/820), died in the prison of Baghdad. Sarakhsi,[100] another famous expert of jurisprudence, wrote his well-known book, *Al-Mabsut,* while in prison, Ibn Taymiyah[101] and Ibn Qayyim[102] were imprisoned in the military castle of Damascus, where ibn Taymiyah died.

An Abbasid caliph invited together Abu Hanifah, Qadi Abu Mutī, and another expert of jurisprudence to accept positions as *qādīs*. They all rejected the offer. The Caliph threatened Abu Muti with death, and thus compelled, he accepted the appointment. Several months later he went into hiding.

Ahmad ibn Hanbal (164/780-241/855), the imam of the Hanbalites, was invited by Caliph al-Wathiq (r. 842-847 C.E.) to support the theory of "the creation of the Qur'an."[103] Ahmad refused to support it, so he was tortured and imprisoned. In *Faza'el-e-Balkh*,[104] which was written in the seventh century, I read the following story which indicates the scope of political hatred and the power of the negative popular resistance to the regime, even in the "lowest social strata":

> Salih ibn Ahmad ibn Hanbal (the son of Ahmad ibn Hanbal, the imam of the Hanbalites) was an extremely pious man who fasted every day and said prayers all night. One year he was the *qādī* of Isfahan. He was such a diligent *qādī* that he did not close the gate to his house at night. He slept behind the door, so that if someone needed him in the middle of the night, he would be accessible.
>
> One day, bread was being baked in the house of Imam Ahmad. He asked, "Where did the yeast come from?"
>
> They replied, "It was brought from the house of your son, Salih."
>
> He asked, "Wasn't he the *qādī* of Isfahan for a year?" Then he would not eat from that bread. He told them to leave the bread until a beggar should come to take it. "Don't forget to tell them that its yeast came from Salih, who was the judge of Isfahan for a year." The bread remained for forty days, and no beggar accepted it. It became stale.
>
> One day Ahmad asked the servants what the did with the bread. They replied, "We threw it in the Tigris river." Until the end of his life, Ahmad did not eat fish from the Tigris.

You can see what kind of profound issues are in our history, in Islamic culture, and in Shi'ism. Alas, we think our responsibility to Ashura and the mission of *shahādat* is limited to crying, making others cry, and even pretending to cry. This issue is especially profound. On the one side is the religious regime of the Islamic Caliphate, and on the other side are the greatest Sunni imams and the founders of the original sects of this school of thought, who think of the Caliphate as a legitimate regime. Again on yet another side is the scope of the negative resistance and anti-government polarization, which has gone as far as the basest social type, who, due to poverty and ignorance, are alienated from their human character in every social system, and for whom the issues of faith, zeal, principles, reaction and resistance are not meaningful. The hungry beggar does not take that bread because its yeast came from the house of Salih, the pious son of Imam Ahmad Hanbal. True, Salih is a pious man, but he was *qādi* for one year and received money from the government. The Sunni imam does not eat the fish from the Tigris river because a piece of bread was once thrown into it, the yeast of which perhaps had been purchased with a cent of that money which was received for holding the position of *qādi* in such a system.

Hair-splitting people may express the scientific query at this point, "How does one know that this story relates something which really happened?" I must assert that this truth is above reality. The subject of my speech at present is not historiography, which they call "history." I am talking about the political and sociological investigation of a historical issue, specifically the intellectual and political effect of the school of *shahādat,* caused by the revolutionary impact of Ashura in the relationship of the people to the regime of the Caliphate in the history of Islam and in the Sunni Muslim society, including the evaluation of the bases of these religious regimes among the religious masses and in the view of well-known religious personalities. In this context, if this story is not factual, it is demonstrated even more clearly that it embodies truth. If it had actually happened, it would only be a minor and unique event, indicating a particular outlook. On the other hand, if such did not actually happen, it symbolizes a general reality. It symbolizes the public feeling which manifests itself in such stories, which are fabricated by the collective spirit and social conscience of the people.

These powerful and influential caliphs — whether of the Umayyad dynasty, who were of the Quraysh tribe and thus thought of themselves as the superior Arab race, or of the Abbasids, who were of the Bani Hashim, and thus of the family of the Prophet — who were all great conquerors of countries and victors for the Arab and Muslim forces and who created so much glory, wealth, and power, are despised and condemned in the eyes of the people, particularly among the religious masses and the Islamic scientific circles, whose criteria are piety, knowledge, and faith! Why should only some charlatans, such as executioners, clowns, astrologers, panegyrists eunuchs of harems, Turkish slaves, enslaved Persian aristocrats, etc. be clients of the court of the "Caliph of Islam" and the "Commander of the Believers?" The Sunni experts of jurisprudence, scholars, and narrators of *ḥadith* are supported by the regime of the Caliphate, which seeks to make them an institution of official clergy and scientific, intellectual, and jurisprudential authority, in order to weaken the position of the *Ahl al-Bayt*[105] and the Shi'ite revolutionary movement, which is in fundamental and uncompromising antagonism with the regime. Yet, these Sunni scholars, despite the Shi'ites and their leadership, take a more or less popular and anti-regime position, either for the pleasure of God and loyalty to the general trend, spirit, and mission of the fundamentals of Islam, or for the sake of the people and guarding the scientific and Islamic prestige of their own morality and virtue. It is worthy of consideration that they, despite close ties to the government on the point of socio-religious affinity and common interest, and despite their social, political, and religious disputes with the Shi'ites, are in accord with and cooperate with the Shi'ite movement. With regard to their "political behavior" and "social spirit" vis-a-vis the Caliphate's political apparatus, they are under the influence of Shi'ism, and therefore are against the government. This contradiction is worthy of our meditation.

The Sunni religious community has juridically recognized the regime of the Caliphate. The Sunni schools of thought are heavily supported by the caliphs. Even some of the imams, such as Malik, are invited to compile their jurisprudence in a book, in order that it might be made the official jurisprudence of the grand community of Islam by the government, to be published as the source of juridical and penal law in public and private affairs in the entire territory of the Caliphate and to be announced to all the *qāḍis* of the land. The majority of the Sunni zealots, preachers, and experts of jurisprudence considered the caliph to be "the shelter of Islam," and "the guardian of the Qur'an and *sunnah*." They appeal to the caliph to save the true religion from the sedition of the *rawāfiḍ*,[106] by employing the devastating force of the "sword of Allah." They appeal to the caliph, saying,

> The disgraces of the *rawāfiḍ* are innumerable. The blood of this group must be shed, for they are polytheists, despisers of the companions of the Apostle, seekers of rebellion and the disunity of Muslims, and are at war with the government of Islam. It is the duty of the experts of jurisprudence, narrators of *ḥadīth, qāḍis,* imams of religion, and the guardians of the religion of the best of the apostles to decree the apostasy of this group, not to accept their testimony, and to warn other Muslims of their evil and corruption.

Taking such a relationship into consideration, the issue is worthy of thought. Why then is the acceptance of a position of *qāḍi,* ministry, governorship, and in short, any official position or close cooperation with the government considered sacreligious and contrary to piety, honor, and the Islamic values of the Sunni imams, scholars, and men of religion, contrary to the religious outlook of the Sunni people themselves, and contrary even to the views of the anti-Shi'ite scholars and great experts of jurisprudence, who possess intellectual character, scientific originality, and independence of thought?

What factor except the eternal impact of *shahādat* — particularly its most excellent, most perfect, most severe, most developed, and most proper instance, that designed and executed by Husayn at the most sensitive moment — could have condemned the Islamic government so absolutely, even from within the regime of the Caliphate itself, declaring politics to be contrary to truth, the Caliphate to be incongruous with imamate, and government to be polluted with worldliness, corruption, transgression of divine law and ordinance? What factor except the eternal impact of *shahādat* could declare the political apparatus to be synonymous with injustice, hunger for power, mammonism, charlatanism, and corruption, contrary to the spirit of religion, the truth of Islam, the pleasure of God, virtue, honor, scholarship, and morality?

When did Husayn do that? Sixty years after *hijrah;* that is to say, precisely when the political regime of Islamic society is in transition from "elected caliphate" to "hereditary government"; and when both the Apostle's *wiṣāyat* as well as *bayat, shūrā,* and *ijmā,* [107] are abolished as criteria for choosing the caliph or leader of the community. For the first time, a new foundation, which is the most extreme innovation, that is, inheritance, becomes the official base of the Islamic regime. Muawiyah officially installs his son as "future" caliph. The installation takes place after the truce is imposed on Imam Hasan, and after the imam, the obstacle in the way of such a transition, is poisoned and martyred. It is when all the bases of resistance have been demolished and the opposition personalities are gone. *Jihād,* that is to say, "armed struggle," cannot possibly bring about the downfall of the regime in Damascus. With sound political calculation, Muawiyah determines that the new regime is not confronted with imminent rebellion and revolt of the *mujahīdīn.* Thus amidst public silence and submission the political foundations of hereditary monarchy would become official. It is precisely in such circumstances that Husayn introduces *shahādat* as a principle above *jihād* and as a duty when *jihād* is not a feasable alternative. With all his careful prognostications, this had not been foreseen by Muawiyah. He had imagined that if the *mujāhid* is defeated and *jihād* is fruitless, the defeated and the disarmed front of the truthful would have no alternative other than silence in the face of the powerful oppressors, and their silence would be a virtual submission, a kind of agreement and approval.

Imam Husayn had learned from Ali that *shahādat,* in the particular and supreme sense of the word, is not merely the occasion of the death of a *mujāhid* at the hands of the enemy, but it is an independent "rule," distinct from *jihād.* It is an alternative which remains after *jihād.*

Ali, the human crystalization of Islam, who from his childhood has been educated by the Apostle and has grown by the light of revelation, in his elaboration on the philosophy of Islamic beliefs and rules, presents the principles of Islam one by one and explains the philosophy and goal of each by a simple, short, and profound interpretation.

God has required belief as purification from polytheism, prayer as abjuration from arrogance, *zakāt* as a source of daily bread, fasting as an examination of sincerity, *hajj* as the fortification of religion, *jihād* as glory for Islam, "enjoining the good" as public reform, "proscription of evil" as curtailment of ignorance . . . *wa al-shahādat istizhāran 'alā al-mujāhadāt* [. . . and *shahādat* as exposure of that which is denied].

Ali's power of expression and depth of thought is astonishing. All I have been trying so hard, but unsuccessfully, to express of the meaning and philosophy of *shahādat* as an independent principle and of its social function, role, and special mission, in contrast with *jihād*, has been expressed by Ali precisely, perfectly, clearly and simply.

What is it that had been denied and covered from the public mind, causing the Muslims to be negligent? What secret conspiracy and anti-human catastrophe had been designed which the people did not suspect? What was being deceptively fabricated and installed, such that public opinion would gradually accept it as Islamic tradition, thanks to the cooperation, seclusion, verbal support, or silence of the Companions and influential personalities and thanks to money, force, politics, propaganda, *hadīth* fabrication, exegetism, philosophism, abuse of religion, sham justification of beliefs and rules, exploitation of the weakness of great Islamic personalities through political position, money, lust, selfishness, hypocrisy, jealousy, personal complexes and short-sightedness, the ignorance of the public, the use of all pulpits for setting the intellectual and psychological foundation of excommunicating the opposition and baptising the status quo, tampering with the Qur'an and changing the spirit and mission of Islam. . .

Islam had hitherto been both a religion and a mission: a religion consisting of belief in the unseen, resurrection, revelation, and prophethood, performance of the commandments and acts of worship, reliance on moral virtues, purification of self, etc.; and at the same time, it was a mission of establishing an *'ummah* [community], which suggests the negation of aristocracy, class antagonism, and exploitation of labor by money, with a super-structure of the imamate, which suggests the negation of despotism, of individual

202 JIHAD AND SHAHADAT

rule, of aristocracy, of oligarchy, and of the dictatorship of an individual family, class, or race.

In short, the Apostle of Islam embodied both prophethood and imamate. His invitation was addressed to the people and was concerned both with this world and with the hereafter. "Better life" means both God and bread, both worship and justice.

The first deviation was the detachment of Islam as a religion from its social base, from its socio-political and philanthropic dimension - to the extent that it could become merely one religion like other religions, whose goal and mission could be summarized as, "the sum of beliefs and actions which purify and individual for the salvation of the Hereafter" - so that Islam might not be in contradiction to the return of the political regime, the class tradition, the pre-Islamic racist aristocracy, or the following of the Iranian and Roman social systems. Such religion would not only be in agreement with the interests of the Quraysh, but also it would be the most suitable new base of political power for looting the nation and suppressing the people. And so it became.

In order to reach that goal, the background for the achievement of "political power" had to be prepared, because, if the political control of the Islamic community was to fall into the hands of the old anti-revolutionaries, the road would have to be paved for a change in the content of Islam and in Muslim society. But from the "Imamate of Muhammad" to the "Sultanate of the Quraysh," there is too much distance to be travelled in one jump; Muslims, particularly those of the first generation, would not tolerate it. There had to be a transitional period to make the change possible. After the Prophet, Muawiyah could not immediately succeed, but Ali could be pushed aside. After the Imamate of the Prophet, the government of law (since even the Prophet himself, despite his exceptional authority, had the duty to confer with people and to be ruled by law, rather than ruling), the hereditary sultanate of the Quraysh could not immediately succeed. First *wisāyat* must be negated. But how? By substituting the principle of the "general will."

Bay'at and *shūrā,* and thus the election of governors by public vote, is a legitimate and acceptable principle. It has a traditional precedent in Arab society. It can be explained with reference to the Qur'an and the *sunnah* of the Prophet, and it accords with the general spirit of Islam, which relies on freedom and respect for public opinion and need, and the principle of *shūrā*. It is in this context that the event of Saqifah[108] takes place: "electing the caliph by a public vote" — a principle intended for the negation of another principle, a right for trampling upon another right. And "public allegiance" is thus intended for the negation of the "testament of the Prophet"[109] — the main goal being to put Ali aside. And so indeed he was. As much as the danger of Ali for the internal power is weakened, reliance upon "free elections" is weakened. The first caliph, as we know, was elected; the second was appointed; and the third was "appoint-elected"! In the fourth caliphate, when Ali comes to power following an egalitarian revolt and is appointed over the internal powers, the background features necessary for implementing the policy that he called "my policy" had already changed. Instead, every factor for the emergence of a despotic political power and hereditary rule had been prepared.

And now, in the year 60 A.H., the new regime, that is to say, a "hereditary" regime rather than the "caliphate," has officially replaced *wiṣāyat*. Allegiance has been received from all Islamic countries, not allegiance signifying appointment, but mere support and submission. Fifty years of political preparation, conspiracy, and treachery was aimed at achieving this goal. Now the foundation is so well prepared that not only ordinary people, but also such great, pious, and influential people as Abdullah ibn Umar,[109] who is so piously cautious not to commit sacrilege by voting for Ali that he openly votes for this regime and even threatens his slaves, in case they doubt whether they should follow suit. The one who has foreseen the future (Muawiyah) knows precisely that, since there is no possibility for *jihād* to oppose Yazid's regime, it will stand as an Islamic regime. He tells Yazid:

> I have prepared the foundation for you. Abdullah ibn Zubayr (whose parents were Zubayr, the great Companion, and the paternal aunt of the Prophet) will sit like a lion in a foxhole and will trick you like a fox. He will be waiting for the opportunity to rebel. If he does so, and if you should overcome him, triumph over him, and arrest him, tear him to pieces. And Abdullah ibn Umar has made piety his profession, such that if all the people

swear allegiance, he will be the last to do so. And Husayn
ibn Ali is a nimble man, and the people of Iraq will not let
him be until they convince him to rise and revolt against
you. If he rebels and you should become victorious over
him, forgive him, because he is our kin and he has a great
right. Besides, he is a relative of the Prophet.

From this advice, it is evident that Muawiyah had considered the
role of *shahādat* to be more or less devastating and he had foreseen
the danger. Is it clear now what it means to be a fighter of *jihād?*

It is evident now that there was no possibility for *jihād*. This
weakness is asserted by Muawiyah, and Husayn also confesses it. As
Muawiyah correctly predicts, the inability of the lovers of truth to
wage *jihād* causes them to remain silent. The agents of the regime
prepare the foundation and the environment for strengthening the
power of the new hereditary regime and removing the obstacles; and
the people, either due to ignorance, fear, or indifference, submit to
profess their allegiance. Then there is the program of changing
wisayat to Caliphate and Caliphate to hereditary government. Then
it would become a religious tradition and an Islamic system,
legitimate and acceptable to the people, and it would even be
founded in the depth of public faith.

In these fifty years, step by step, Islam has changed from a
revolutionary movement that was opposed to aristocracy, class,
tribe, race, despotism, and exploitation, and which called the people
to liberty, equality, glory, and justice, and introduced the "mission of
the prophets and divine books throughout history for the sake of the
people's struggle for equity,"[111] and counted ignorance, oppression,
and hunger as manifestations of polytheism and the causes of
unbelief, a religion declaring that "for worship there are ten gates,
eight of which are seeking lawful daily bread," and whose Prophet
declares, "Anyone who has no worldly prosperity has no prosperity
in the hereafter," and whose God gives the glad tidings that "the
oppressed shall inherit the earth" ... But it has now become merely a
collection of rituals, personal feelings, subjective beliefs, and empty
forms, of which the religious goal is reward in the hereafter for
individuals and the worldly goals are the conquest of countries,
suppression of nations, booty, pole-tax, and power. These are those

things that have been changed, replaced, negated, rejected, denied, erased from people's minds, and driven away from the Qur'an, tradition, prophethood, monotheism, *jihād, 'ummat, 'imāmat, 'itrat,*[112] *ḥajj,* assembly, *zakāt,* worship, and ... Islam has become "the opiate of the masses," a means of justification for the prosperous class, and a base of power and looting for the government.

On the other hand, during these fifty years, people have been engaged in personal treacheries, political conspiracies, and internal struggles. It is half a century since people like Ali and Abu Dhar have been allowed to speak. So people simply tolerate this "tragic transmutation." They have become mere bystanders instead of people who manifest sensitivity to what is happening to them. The major characters, including the leaders, conquerors, warriors, and Companions, who would normally say what is right and what is wrong, did not stand for two things: first, the issue of *imāmat,* that is to say, government, and second, the issue of economics, that is, class position. We know what they did with Ali. We know that even during the reign of the grand caliphs, when, at least superficially, the tradition was guarded, Abu Dhar recited the ayah of *kanz*[113] and consequently Muawiyah wrote to Uthman, "If you desire to maintain possession of Syria, neutralize Abu Dhar." And Uthman wrote back to him, "Do not let this wound open; do not let the fire flame from under the ashes." We know that Abu Dhar was exiled to an empty desert, where his voice could not reach the people, and where he was kept until he died of hunger.

Leadership and equality — these two must be uprooted from Islam. Islam minus leadership of the people and equality of classes, a version of Islam which is harmonious with the power and wealth of the Quraysh, is better for that tribe than polytheism. Now the fifty year plan of the Quraysh has reached the pinnacle of success: the official transformation of the regime — hereditary government instead of *wiṣāyat* and Caliphate. The fate of the people under the Umayyad dynasty is guaranteed generation after generation. The heritage of Muhammad, which was taken away from Ali by election, is now being given through appointment to the children of Abu Sufyan. But in order for the new regime to stick and remain stuck, the transformation of the Caliphate to a hereditary institution must be religiously justified, just as the transformation of *wiṣāyat* to

Caliphate was. But how? By the allegiance of all provinces, all Companions, followers, descendants of the Companions, and great men of religion.

This conspiracy must be annihilated.

It can't be done.

Toward the fall of this new regime, one must wage *jihād*.

One cannot!

The tragedy must be publicized. The treason of "silence regarding the transformation of the regime," which legitimizes the regime must be smashed. Whatever has been hitherto concealed from the people, whatever has been omitted from the mission of Muhammad, the "evil" which is disguised as "good" and the "good" which has been presented as "evil" in the eyes of the masses must be exposed naked and announced to the people.

With what?

With *shahādat*, for the "exposure of what is being denied."

It is for this reason that when Walid gives Husayn the news of Muawiyah's death — the news which signifies the annulment of the agreement of truce — and wants him to swear allegiance to the hereditary status of the Caliphate of Yazid, Husayn immediately delivers his will to his brother, Muhammad ibn al-Hanafiyah, saying, "I have made my decision to enjoin the good, prohibit evil, and revive the tradition of my grandfather, the Apostle of God." Then at night, he and his whole household go out of Medina toward Mecca, so that, in the season of *ḥajj*, when Muslims from all over the great Islamic land have assembled, he may declare that he shall not accept the regime. Then he leaves *ḥajj* unfinished and sets out toward the land of his martyrdom, in order — with the most glorious, perfect, severe, revolutionary, and devastating manifestation possible, and with all the facilities at his disposal, by preparation of all his power and possessions under the sun, at the most sensitive and precise moment, being exactly at the beginning of this conspiracy, and against the first link in this chain[114] against the Green Palace of Damascus, against this fake Bardia[115] who disguised himself with the Caliphate of the Apostle and the Imamate of Islam — to deliver the strongest and most disgracing assault of *shahādat*, in which everything would be presented. All the anti-Islamic characteristics and anti-human traits of the ruling power would be exposed.

Istizhār (exposure)!

The victims of the ruling regime's pseudo-religious propaganda and political rumor mongering were conditioned to know nothing of the human values and Islamic morality of the *'itrat,* yet in this *hijrah* from Medina to Karbala led by Husayn, and in the *hijrah* from Karbala to Damascus led by Zaynab, there were astonishing manifestations of faith, love, patience, sincerity, and purity, and much unknown greatness and hidden originality which was presented from the corner of the deserted and locked house of Fatimah, then passed over the Kabah and exhibited itself in the open gallery of the desert in the field of the universe, in the consciousness of history. The event of Husayn's martyrdom made manifest to all unconscious, unaware generations and all dormant and dark ages, what had been locked up in this house and concealed in the midst of a storm of conspiracies and propaganda, a storm of drunken brawls of the power seekers and traitors. Everyone who had been denied, one by one, was reintroduced on the banks of the Euphrates as a "martyr of the people," either at the murder scene of *shahādat* or on the caravan of captivity.

Istizhār!

It was this blow which not only exposed, disgraced and condemned the regime of Yazid in the eyes of the Shi'ites, faithful to the family of Husayn and informed of his way, but it also exposed, disgraced and condemned forever the power of government throughout the history of Islam, even for those who believed in the Caliphate and not in Imamate, to such an extent that a Muslim beggar would prefer to go to bed with an empty stomach rather than eat bread the yeast of which might possibly be polluted by the scent of the money of the Caliph of Islam. And the Sunni imam refuses to eat fish from the Tigris as long as he shall live after hearing that a piece of this bread has been thrown in this river!

Some have expressed doubt concerning the efficacy of Husayn's martyrdom, calling it a defeated revolt. This is incredible! Which successful *jihād* or war has achieved such a vast victory in society, penetrating minds and feelings throughout history with so much depth? At this point, the real issue is whether the efficacy and the resonance of *shahādat* is not broader, deeper, and more continuous than that of *jihād,* even one that is victorious.

These various caliphs waged countless wars, had hundreds of thousands of armed warriors with enormous military equipment, and won tremendous victories which brought even great powers to their knees. But, more often than not, as soon as the war stopped, the echo of the war would die as well. Nothing would remain but ruins, unknown corpses, and a few words in the annals of history. It is the martyrdom to the seventy-two[116] "chosen martyrs" which stamped "transgressor" on the foreheads of all of Yazid's heirs to sit on his throne. No *jihād,* no victory over Kafiristan,[117] no takeover of a Sumanat,[118] no change of church or fire temple into a mosque, and no collection, publication or glorification of the Qur'an has been able to erase this label from their foreheads. They are so condemned in public opinion and so disgraced in history that the Sunni imam is willing to be flogged rather than submit to the disgrace of appointment as *qāḍī* in the regime of the Islamic Caliphate, rather than collaborate with the "Caliph of the Prophet"!

In Karbala, the enemies of Husayn conquered only the bodies of the martyrs, but the ideology of the martyrs condemned these enemies and their regime. With their blood, the martyrs cancelled the grand conspiracy forever. Their martyrdom exposed everything the enemy was trying to hide from the public eye, bury in the depths of history, and take away from humanity, so that it could weave from "faith" a cloak for the stature of transgression by employing thousands of conspiracies and treasons, such as massacres, propaganda, and exegetical, philosophical, scientific and literary activities aimed at power, politics and wealth. The blood of the martyrs removed all the masks and drew all the curtains of deception and made impossible discrimination in the monotheist community, made impossible government of compulsion in the mission of the Prophet, and Pharaohic magic before the eyes of Husayn-loving people. With *shahādat* Husayn did what the miraculous hand of Moses did.[119] From the blood of the martyrs he created something like the breath of Jesus, which gives sight to the blind and life to the dead and stamps the mark of cancellation on the money-worshipping Jews, the deceitful and Christ-killing rabbis, who work hand in hand with the Caesars, and this was not exclusive merely to his own time and land.

Shahādat is not war — it is mission.
It is not a weapon — it is a message.
It is a word pronounced in blood.

It cannot annihilate treason, but it is a shining torch, which amidst the universal darkness, sheds light and illuminates the treason.

An executioner, at midnight, murmuring prayers, approaches in the guise of an imam. People have risen to follow him, to line up behind him. The martyr suddenly lights a candle in the assembly.

That is all.

The popular notion molded under the influence of the Sufi spirit and the Christian world view, exemplified by the martyrdoms of Hallaj[120] and Jesus Christ, says that the martyrs arose to get killed rather than to struggle against the government. Husayn rose to sacrifice himself for the community and for the intercession on the day of judgement on behalf of the lovers of the Ahl al-Bayt (who commit great sins) in order to transform their evil deeds into good deeds on the judgement day.[121] According to this view, Husayn had made a covenant in the world of pre-creation to become a martyr. This is the same as the Christian view, according to which Christ sacrificed himself for humanity, that is to say, he sacrificed his blood so God might forgive and take to heaven the children of Adam, who, after Adam's original sin, had been driven out of paradise.

This view is a most skillful trick which, while preserving the greatness and glory of Husayn, makes his martyrdom meaningless, empty, and without content. It makes it nothing; but at the same time it acquits Husayn's executioners, because the executioners acted not on their own initiative but according to the will of God, because this fate had been determined before creation. Thus they were the means of executing the will of God. It also provides immunity for all the Yazid-like transgressors and Muʿawiyah-like allegiance takers forever from the danger of Ashura and the memory of Husayn. It misrepresents the goal of *shahādat*, which was a struggle against the powers of transgression and usurpation, as a struggle against no one and nothing.

Considering this, the opinion expressed in *Shahīd-e-Jāvīd*,[121] which interprets the mission of Ashura as "revolt and *jihād* for the devastation of the regime of Yazid," is more positive and progressive than the interpretation of *shahādat* by the "Safavid-Sufi-Christian" view, which is the greatest friendly conspiracy against Ashura and against Husayn. In *Shahīd-e-Jāvid* the rise of Husayn is interpreted as a defeated *jihād,* just as the Battle of Uhud[122] under the leadership of the Prophet, or the war against Muawiyah under the leadership of Imam Hasan. But in my opinion, that *shahādat,* in its specific sense in Islam, is itself a rule after *jihād,* and that the martyr, even when he comes to the battlefield, is already a defeated *mujāhid,* is an opinion which is superior to and more progressive and explicable than the opinion of "the defeated revolt of Husayn."

Before Husayn, *shahādat* in this sense, but of course, more simple and on a smaller scale, had precedent in the lives of both the Prophet and Ali. It is interesting that in every epoch there are two examples in every family. Consider the example of the family of Ammar:[123]

Yasir and Summayah, the parents of Ammar, under the torture of Abu Jahl,[124] prefer *shahādat* to denying their faith and dissociating themselves from the Prophet. They die. But Ammar is a young man and when torture is inflicted on him, he bears it until, seeing the torture of his parents, and when his consciousness and will have been crippled, he tells his enemy what he wants to hear. The Prophet gave consolation to Ammar and supported his deed. Therefore, we can conclude that his parents could have survived at the same price, but they chose *shahādat* instead. What they did was not an unskillful and wrong act, nor was it a *jihād* against the enemy, but it was a *shahādat,* one that they had chosen. Ammar continued to live and served Islam for fifty years as a man of the sword. The Prophet loved him and one day predicted, "Ammar, a group of transgressors will kill you." Forty years after *hijrah,* when the war of Siffin was waged, Ammar had become very old. He had no ability for *jihād.* This is a case in which the army of truth was able to wage *jihād,* but one member of that army not able to go to fight and kill the enemy. But if his death in the way of triumph of truth can play a role, he chooses *shahādat.* At Siffin the armies of Ali and Muawiyah face each other. Thousands of Muslims in the army of Muawiyah have drawn their swords against Ali, thinking that they are fighting for the sake of truth, Islam, and the Qur'an, against a power-seeking adventurist who has caused discord in the community and has killed Uthman, the "innocent" caliph of the Prophet.

Mujahadāt.

The trembling hands of Ammar cannot draw his sword. He can do nothing to destroy the power of Muawiyah. But the prediction of the Prophet, that Ammar will be killed by a group of transgressors, is well known. Even the unaware people who have been deceived by the propaganda of the Green Palace have heard this prediction. Ammar thinks, "If I am killed by the army of Muawiyah at Siffin, doesn't my death reveal that this army is that group of transgressors? Doesn't this act lend moral support to Ali's army and shake the spirit of Muawiyah's army? Without doubt!"

Ammar chooses martyrdom. With his white hair and almost blind eyes, and trembling hands. He is a martyr and everyone else a *mujāhid.*

They try to kill.

But he tries to be killed.

With enthusiastic attempts, he presents himself to the swords, and everywhere searches for his own murderer, as if death were something valuable that he has lost in the army of the enemy. This old martyr, who has come out with the *mujāhidīn,* is walking the ground searching for it.

The battle-cry was heard, "Ammar has come to the battlefield." The army of Muawiyah lost its morale. The first influences of *shahādat.* The breezes of martyrdom formed waves on the lagoon of the army of the enemy. There is question, doubt, and protest. The news reaches the ears of Muawiyah. He says, "He is not killed yet, so avoid and run away from him." But the martyr who sought his own death attacked and at last succeeds with an absolute triumph as the pinnacle of victory, honor and success as a martyr. Ammar is killed.

From the heart of the army of Ali, which has now seen the truthfulness of its way and its leader, the battle-cries reach the sky, "The transgressing group has killed Ammar. The Prophet of God told the truth." And in the army of Muawiyah, broken, scattered, fearful, doubtful, and skeptical voices were heard. "Ammar was killed."

"We killed Ammar."

The transgressor group ...

Ammar performed *jihād* for fifty years.

And in one day, he performed *shahādat*.
More interesting than the case of Ammar:
Hurr.[126]
All his life he committed treason, and one day:
Shahadat.

Look at Husayn! He releases his life, leaves his town and rises up in order to die because he has no other means by which to struggle to condemn and disgrace his enemy. He selects this way in order to pull aside the curtains which deceive by covering the ugly faces of the ruling power. If he cannot defeat the enemy in this way, at least he can disgrace them. If he cannot conquer the ruling power, he can at least condemn it by injecting the new blood and the belief of *jihād* into the dead bodies of this second generation after the revolution revealed to the Prophet.

He is an unarmed, powerless and lonely man. But he is still responsible for the *jihād*. He has no other means except to die, having himself chosen a 'red death'. Being Husayn makes it his responsibility to perform the *jihād* against all that is corrupt and cruel. He has no other means at his disposal for his *jihād* but his own death. He leaves his home only to enter the place of execution. We see how well he carried this out with his accurate plans, reasoning, a glorious, accurate and well-planned departure, movement and migration. Stage by stage, he clears the way, explaining the aim which he is moving toward with his unique selection of companions — men who had come to die with him — as well as all of the members of his family. These are all of the things that he possesses in this world and he leads them to be sacrificed at the altar of *shahādat*.

The fate of the faith which is being destroyed, the fate of those people who are awaiting Islamic justice and freedom but have now been captured by an oppression and pressure worse than the period of *jāhiliya*, are now awaiting his action. He who has no arms and no means has come with all of his existence, his family, his dearest companions, so that his *shahādat* and that of his whole family will bear witness to the fact that he carried out his responsibility at a time when truth was defenseless and unarmed. He bears witness that nothing more than this could be done.

You have heard that at the battle of Ashura, on the tenth day of the month of Muharram, Imam Husayn takes the blood flowing from the throat of his child, Ali Asghar, in his hands and throws it up to the heavens saying, "Witness and accept this sacrifice from me! Be my witness, my God!"

It is in this way that the dying of a human being guarantees the life of a nation. His *shahādat* is a means whereby faith can remain. It bears witness to the fact that great crimes, deception, oppression and tyranny rule. It proves that truth is being denied. It reveals the existence of values which are destroyed and forgotten. It is a red protest against a black sovereignty. It is a shout of anger in the silence which has cut off tongues.

Shahādat bears witness to that which some would rather let remain hidden in history. It is a symbol of that which must exist. It is bearing witness to what is taking place in this silent and secret time, and finally, *shahādat* is the only reason for existence, the only sign of being present, the only means of attack and defense and the only manner of resistance so that truth, right and justice can remain alive at a time and under a regime in which uselessness, falsity and oppression rule. All of the bases have been defeated. All of the defenders and faithful followers have been massacred. To be human is to stand at the threshold of decline in the face of the danger of dying forever. All of these miracles are performed by *shahādat:* arising and bearing witness.

Sixty years after the *hijrat,* a savior would appear and arise upon this black and silent graveyard. And Husayn, aware of his mandate which human destiny has placed upon his shoulders, leaves Mecca without hesitation and moves toward his place of *shahādat.* He knows that history is waiting for him. Time, which is held in the hands of reactionaries and polytheists watches for him to take a step forward.

People who are captured, motionless and in silence, in slavery, badly need his movement and his cries. Finally, the message of God which is now in the hands of devils, commands his death so that with it he can bear witness to the disaster. It is said that the Prophet had said to him, "God wishes to see you killed."

Shahādat also has a special meaning in our philosophical anthropology. The creation of a mankind, a blend of God and the devil, a mixture of the spirit and clay, and the combination of the lowest and the highest peaks, in the composition of religion and its recitals, devotions, prayers, jurisprudence, good-deeds, services, science — all of these are only struggles and exercises made by man in order to weaken his inferior being in favor of his superior being, his devil clay part in favor of his divine spiritual part. But *shahādat* is the action which a man performs suddenly and in a revolutionary way. He throws his inferior being into the fire of love and faith and turns it into a light and divine being.

It is for this reason that a martyr does not require the ritual bath, has no need of a shroud, and is not required to give an account of himself on the Day of Judgement. A martyr has already sacrificed the being of error and sin prior to death and now has arisen to bear witness. It is for this reason that on the evening before Ashura, Imam Husayn washes himself carefully, grooms himself so well, puts on his best clothes, and uses the best perfumes. Amidst the destruction of all of his belongings and on the threshold of his departure, seeing the number of martyrs increase as they fall upon each other, his face turns rosy as his excitement mounts. His heart beats faster with enthusiasm. He knows that the distance to his 'presence' is shortening and that *shahādat* itself is presence.

Shahādat, in summary, in our culture, contrary to other schools where it is considered to be an accident, an involvement, a death imposed upon a hero, a tragedy, is a grade, a level, a rank. It is not a means but it is a goal itself. It is originality. It is a completion. It is a lift. It itself is mid-way to the highest peak of humanity and it is a culture.

In all ages and centuries, when the followers of a faith and an idea have power, they guarantee their honor and lives with *jihād.* But when they are weakened and have no means whereby to struggle, they guarantee their lives, movement, faith, respect, honor, future and history with *shahādat. Shahādat* is an invitation to all generations, in all ages, if you cannot kill your oppressor, then die.

NOTES

1. This piece was delivered as a lecture at the Husayniyah Irshad (cf. the introduction to this volume) in Theran on the night of Tasua, the ninth of Muharram, 1970. It was one of the most moving speeches delivered by Shari'ati. At the time the speech was given, ten members of the Mujahidin Khalq had been killed by the government. Among the ten were two sons of Tahir Ahmadzadeh, both of whom were students of Shari'ati. Tahir Ahmadzadeh was a friend of the father of Ali Shari'ati, and was appointed governor of Khurasan by Mehdi Bazargan, after the revolution.

2. Public expressions of grief are encouraged at Shi'ite sermons, *rawda,* which recall the martyrdom of Husayn. Cf. Michael Fisher, *Iran: From Religious Dispute to Revolution* (Cambridge: Harvard University Press, 1980), p. 100.

3. This claim cannot be supported even for the personalities cited by Shari'ati, let alone for all the non-Abrahamic saints and philosophers. Nevertheless, the claim should not be casually dismissed. By and large, these philosophers and religious leaders *were* related to the nobility or clergy, and the prophets did tend to come from among the common people. There are exceptions. Solomon succeeded David as the king of Israel in the tenth century B.C. In any case, it seems that blood ties are not as important for Shari'ati's point as support and affiliation. On the whole, among the traditions of the ancient world, the Abrahamic tradition was exceptional in its concern for the plight of the poor.

Confucius (551-479 B.C.), or Kong Zi, came from an impoverished family of the lower nobility, and became a minor government bureaucrat. Very little is known about the family of Lao Tzu. Buddha (c. 563-483 B.C.), born Siddhartha Gautama, was the son of a tribal chief of the Sakya clan, and of the warrior, or ruling caste. Zoroaster (c. 628-551 B.C.), or Zarathustra, was the third of five sons in a poor family of warriors, or he may have been the son of a pagan priest of a pastoral tribe. Sources vary. Mani (216-276 C.E.) was of Persian descent and related on his mother's side to the royal house of Parthia. Mazdak was the leader of a sixth century politico-religious movement to establish a program of popular semi-egalitarian justice against landed privilege. He was initially supported by the shah Kavad, but was finally condemned to death and massacred along with his followers by Kavad's son, Chosro I. Socrates (c. 470-399 B.C.) was born of a stonemason or sculptor and a midwife. Plato (c. 428-347 B.C.) came from an aristocratic and wealthy family, several members of which had been politically prominent among anti-democratic groups. Aristotle (384-322 B.C.) was the son of the court physician to the king of Macedon.

4. "We have sent no messenger save with the tongue of his people ..." (14:4).

5. The title "Pharaoh" is derived from the Egyptian term for "great house."

6. Korah (Qarun) is described in the Qur'an as someone who because of his wealth, knowledge and strength, challenged the authority of Moses and Aaron. God caused the earth to swallow him up! Cf. (28:76-82). The story is also told in the Bible in Numbers XVI:1-35.

7. (20:70-73); (26:46-52).

8. "He hath ordained for you that religion which He commanded unto Noah, and that which We inspire in thee (Muhammad), and that which We commended unto Abraham and Moses and Jesus, saying: Establish the religion, and be not divided therein ..." (42:13).

9. "Muhammad is not the father of any man among you, but he is the messenger of Allah and the Seal of the Prophets; and Allah is Aware of all things." (33:40).

10. *Tawhīd* is the doctrine of the unity and uniqueness of God. It is a central concept in Islamic theology, which has given rise to the question of how the multiplicity of God's attributes is to be reconciled with His unity. For Shari'ati, *tawhīd* becomes the central facet of his Islamic ideology. According to Hamid Enayat (*Modern Islamic Political Thought* Austin: University of Texas Press, 1982), pp. 155-156:

> [Shari'ati] is the first Iranian writer on religion to have turned this hitherto theological doctrine into a 'world-view' *(Jahan-bini),* a term coined originally by Iranian Marxists in the early forties as an equivalent for a secular, political system of beliefs, or *Weltanschauung,* since in classical Persian the compound is more suggestive of a mind which is preoccupied with the material world *(jahan)* rather than spirit or soul *(jan).* In this sense, *tawhīd* means something much more than the 'oneness of God', which is, of course, accepted by all monotheists. 'But', says Shari'ati, 'what I have in mind (when I use this term) is a world-view. So what I intend by "the world-view of *tawhīd*" is perceiving the entire universe as a unity, instead of dividing it into this world and the thereafter, the physical and the metaphysical, substance and meaning, matter and spirit. It means perceiving the whole of existence as a single form, a single, living, and conscious organism, possessing one will, intelligence, feeling and aim ... There are many people who believe in *tawhīd,* but only as a "religious-philosophical" theory: God is one, not more than one — that is all! But I understand *tawhīd* as a world-view, just as I see *shirk* (polytheism) also from the same standpoint, that is, a world-view that regards the universe as an incoherent combination, full of division, contradiction and incongruity, possessing conflicting and independent poles, diverging movements, and disparate and disconnected essences, desires, calculations, criteria, aims and wills. *Tawhīd* sees the world as an empire; *shirk* as a feudal system.' Ali Shari'ati, *Dars-hā-yi Islam-shināsi,* duplicated by the Islamic Students Association of Europe, the United States and Canada (n.d.) pp. 48-50.

Cf. Ali Shari'ati *On the Sociology of Islam,* Hamid Algar, tr., (Berkeley: Mizan Press, 1979), 82-87. Shari'ati's understanding of *tawhīd* is also discussed in Shahrough Akhavi, "Shariati's Social Thought," in *Religion and Politics in Iran,* Nikki R. Keddie, ed. (New Haven: Yale University Press, 1983), pp. 125-144.

11. (11:27); (26:111)

12. Cf. R. C. Zaehner, *The Dawn and Twilight of Zoroastrianism* (London: Weidenfeld and Nicolson, 1961) for a discussion of light and darkness in Zoroastrian and Manichean thought.

13. Karl Popper, in *The Open Society and Its Enemies,* Vol. I, fourth ed. (New York: Routledge and Kegan Paul, 1962) argues that slavery is to be included even in Plato's best city, or ideal state:" ... Plato, and his disciple Aristotle, advanced the theory of the biological and moral inequality of man. Greeks and barbarians are unequal by nature; the opposition between them corresponds to that between natural masters and natural slaves." (p. 70). The question of whether Aristotle recognized the humanity of the slaves is discussed in E. Barker, *The Political Thought of Plato and Aristotle* (London: 1906).

14. Medina (Arabic, *Madīnah*), means "city." Prior to Muhammad's emigration it was called *Yathrib,* and thereafter was called *Madīnat al-Nabī,* the city of the Prophet. For Shari'ati, Madinah at the time of the Prophet is *la cite par excellence,* the model of an Islamic utopian city-state.

15. Bilal was a slave who was tortured for the profession of his Muslim faith until he was purchased and freed by Abu Bakr, after which time he became the first *mu'adhdhin* who calls the faithful to prayer.

16. The Quraysh was the most powerful tribe of Mecca, whose members for the most part rejected Muhammad's claims to prophecy. Muhammad, and the Caliphs belonged to this tribe.

17. Quba is a suburb of Madinah where the Prophet rested for four days before entering Madinah during the hijrah. Later some hypocrites built a mosque at Quba, which is condemned in the Qur'an, (9:107).

18. The *muhajirun* are the Meccan followers of Muhammad who took part in *hijra,* that is, who emigrated from Mecca because of religious persecution, to Ethiopia or to Medina in 622 C.E.

19. The *jahiliya* is the state of ignorance and savagery, or the pagan state in which the Arabs lived prior to the prophecy of Muhammad.

20. (17:37); (31:18).

21. Marwan was the first person to be exiled by the Prophet Muhammad from Madinah. He was brought back from exile by Uthman, who gave him the castle of Khaybar and an important government function.

22. The *ansar* were the people of Medina who helped Muhammad and the *muhajirun.*

23. Abu Sufyan was a leader of the Quraysh and one of the strongest enemies of Muhammad. He was forgiven by Muhammad after the conquest of Mecca (8/629), at which time he became a Muslim. In Shi'ite history, he and his son, Muawiyah, are considered hypocrites and internal enemies of Islam.

24. Muawiyah was the son of Abu Sufyan. He was appointed governor of Syria by Umar in 634, and contested the Caliphate of Ali. He alleged that Ali was responsible for aiding the murderers of Uthman, and he was supported by the widow of Muhammad, Ayishah. His Caliphate was from 40/661 to 60/680.

25. The *munāfiqūn* were those elements in Madinah who outwardly professed allegiance to Muhammad while secretly they tried to undermine him. Abdullah ibn Ubay, prominent among the Medinan hyprocrites, led his forces to desertion at the battle of Uhud. Cf. Surah 63, which is named after the *Munāfiqūn*. The evil of hyprocisy is an often repeated theme of the Qur'an.

26. A *kāfir* is a disbeliever. To be a *kāfir* is not merely to be without belief in God and His prophets, but to reject belief after having been informed of the claims of the prophets.

27. At the battle of Siffin (37/657) between Ali and Mu awiyah. Muawiyah ordered some of his men to fasten copies of the Qur'an to the points of their lances when it seemed that his defeat was at hand. This political maneuver appealed to Muslim unity, and many of Ali's troops stopped fighting and compelled Ali to enter into arbitration, through which, by means of a diplomatic ruse, Muawiyah won the upper hand.

28. Ali was mortally wounded as led the morning prayer in the mosque of Kufa on the nineteenth of Ramadan, 40/660. He was killed by the Kharijite (cf. fn. 31), Abdul Rahman ibn Muljim-i-Muradi, who slew him with a poisoned sword.

For information on Ali's economic policies, see *Was'sil al-Shi'a,* vol. XI, pp. 79-82. According to one *hadīth,* when Ali is explaining his egalitarian economic policies, his brother Aqil asks, "You count me and a black man in Madinah as equal?" Ali tells him to sit down and states that there is no superiority except due to precedence or piety. According to another hadith, Ali is asked by some of his followers to give a greater share to the aristocrats, which Ali refuses to do, claiming that such an act would amount to "seeking help through injustice and oppression." According to another hadith, there are two women, one Arab and the other non-Arab, and Ali gives each of them twenty-five dirham and a meal. The Arab woman exclaims, "Oh Commander of the Faithful, I am an Arab woman, and this is a non-Arab woman." Ali replies that he does not even discriminate between the children of Ishmael and those of Isaac in this respect. Ali divided the people's share from the public treasury equally among all.

29. Hasan (3/625-50/670) is the second Shi'ite Imam, the successor of Ali as Imam and Caliph.

30. The Khawaraj were a group who had supported Ali until the battle of Siffin. After Ali accepted arbitration they formed a group violently opposed to both Ali and Muawiyyah. Cf. W. M. Watt, *Islamic Philosophy and Theology* (Edinburgh: Edinburgh University Press, 1979), pp. 10-19.

31. The circumstances of the death of Imam Hasan are reported in Shaykh al-Mufid, *Kitāb Al-Irshad,* I. K. A. Howard, tr. (London: Muhammadi Trust, 1981), p. 287, where it is stated that Muawiyah promised Hasan's wife, Ju da, that he would arrange for her to marry his son Yazid, on the condition that she poison Hasan. He also sent her a hundred thousand dirhams. She poisoned Hasan but Mu awiyah would not let her marry Yazid, and arranged for her marriage with someone else, instead.

32. Baqī is the public cemetery in Madinah.

33. Abu Dhar al-Ghiffari was a Companion of the Prophet who was loyal to Ali. He died in 32/651 after being exiled by Uthman. Abu Dhar believed that no Muslim should accumulate any wealth, and is seen by Shari'ati as the paradigm of Islamic socialism.

Ammar ibn Yasir was a Companion of the Prophet and great supporter of Ali who was killed at Siffin (cf. fn. 27).

Abdullah ibn Masud was a leading Companion of the Prophet, one of the scribes of the Qur'an, and one of the major masters of its recitation. He was the sixth person to follow Islam. He had previously been a shepherd of Uqbat ibn Abi Muit, and he came to the Prophet's attention when he refused to give the Prophet some milk on account of his desire to be honest to his employer. He was a constant companion of the Prophet both in war and peace and was the first to recite the Qur'an in Mecca, melodiously and loudly. He is known as "double emigrant" because, due to religious persecution, he had to emigrate once to Ethiopia and once to Madinah. He killed Abu Jahl, one of the strongest enemies of the Prophet and of Islam. He was the first teacher of the Qur'an. During the reign of Umar, he was made governor of Kufah. Following a harsh debate with Uthman, two of his ribs were broken, and he died in 32/653, when he was approximately sixty years old, although on another account he was martyred at Siffin.

Al-Maytham al-Tammar, "the date seller," had been a Persian slave belonging to a woman from the tribe of Bani Asad. Ali bought and freed him. He is known in the history of Islam as one of the opponents of *Taqiyah* (dissimulation) because he was lost his life on account of his vocal support of Ali. In order to silence him, he was first bridled like a horse, and then crucified by Ubayd Allah, the governor of Kufah, shortly before the battle of Karbala.

Hujr ibn Adi was a Shi'ite supporter of Ali who led a revolution against Mu awiyah in Kufa and was executed in 50/670.

34. Abdullah ibn Umar ibn Khattab was the son of the second Caliph and an example of extreme piety.

35. *Mujāhid* one who participates in the Islamic struggle, *jihad.*

36. The battle of Badr was the first major military engagement of the Prophet with the Meccans. In Ramadan 2/March 624 roughly one thousand Meccans were routed by about one third that number of Muslims. At the battle of Uhud (3/625) the Muslims suffered a setback against the Meccans. The battle of Hunayn (8/630) pitted the Muslim force of about twelve thousand against hostile tribesmen from Ta'if whose army numbered about twenty thousand. The Muslims were victorious.

37. The *hijra* is the emigration of the Prophet and his followers from Mecca to Madinah.

38. The Green Palace was the palace of Muawiyyah in Damascus which was made of green marble. It was the first royal palace in the history of Islam. Cf. fn. 24.

39. *Hadīth* usually translated as 'tradition' is literally 'news' or a report of a saying or action of Muhammad. Each *hadīth* consists of a narration *(matn)* and the transmissional chain *(isnād)* which consists of the chain of transmission of those who reported the *matn*. Among the scholars of Islam, the study of *hadīth* has become a science in which the probity of the transmitters listed in an *isnād* is evaluated in order to ascertain the reliability of the text. Cf. Fazlur Rahman, *Islam,* second ed. (Chicago: University of Chicago Press, 1979), pp. 53-58.

40. Abu Darda was known for his piety, and in Shari'ati's view, represents those who are lead astray by their over zealous piety.

Abu Hurayrah was a famous but controversial narrator of hadith who is considered a reliable source of tradition by Sunni scholars, while for the Shi'ites he is not only considered unreliable, but is called "the merchant hadith as well as its fabricator."

Abu Musa al Ash'ari was the representative of Ali in the arbitration at Siffin. Cf. fn. 27.

41. Uraynab was encouraged by Yazid to divorce her husband and to marry him. She did divorce, but married Husayn instead of Yazid. Her marriage to Husayn was not consummated and Husayn returned Uraynab to her original husband.

42. Dissimulation or *taqiyah* is the practice of hiding one's Shi'ite belief when there is good reason to believe that it would place one in danger. Cf. "Allamah Sayyid Muhammad Husayn Tabataba'i, *Shi'ite Islam* (Houston: Free Islamic Literatures, 1979), pp. 223-225. For Shari'ati *taqiyah, taqlīd ('imitation', acceptance of the legal decisions of an appropriate religious authority), and shahadāt* are three essential elements to revolutionary strategy, corresponding to secrecy, obedience and readiness to die, respectively.

43. Taha Husayn is a twentieth century scholar and writer of Egypt. The point of reference is to his famous book, *Aliyun wa Banūh (Ali and His Sons).*

44. Sulayman ibn Surad al Khazai was a leading member of the Kufan Shi'a who died leading a revolt to avenge the blood of Husayn in 65/683.

45. The Umayyid Caliphate reigned from Damascus from 661-750 C.E. The Abbasid dynasty ruled from Baghdad from 750-1258 C.E.

46. 'Adi ibn Hatim al-Ta'i was one of the leading Qur'an reciters of Kufah and a leader of the revolt which led to Uthman's murder in 35/655. He was a strong supporter of Ali and Hasan. Cf. S. H. M. Jafri, *The Origins and Early Development of Shi'a Islam* (London: Longman's, 1979), pp. 106, 118-119.

47. A *murtadd* is an apostate who becomes a renegade against Islam, a capital crime according to Islamic law. Cf. (3:85) ff. Some modernists have argued that the mere rejection of belief, after one had accepted Islam is no crime. Most notably in this vein is the work of the Pakistani legist S. A. Rahman, *Punishment of Apostasy in Islam* (Lahore: Institute of Islamic Culture, 1972). However, it has not always been so interpreted. Traditionally, legal scholars distinguish two kinds of apostates: those who reject Islam after having been Muslims, and those whose parents are apostates. The latter will be forgiven if they repent once they reach the age of reason. Otherwise, apostasy is a capital crime, provided it is committed in the absence of coersion by one who is mature and of sound mind. A man who becomes an apostate cannot return to Islam, his property is to be distributed among his heirs, and his wife is to observe the period of seclusion appropriate to a widow. Women who commit apostasy are to receive life imprisonment and are to be beaten at the times of prayer, unless they repent. Cf. al-Muhaqqiq al-Hilli, *Sharāyi' al-Islam.* p. 55; al-Fadil al-Hindi, *Kashf al-Lithām,* Vol. II, p. 185; Imam Khumayni *Tahrir al-Wasīlah,* Vol. II, p. 336. The most extreme misapplication of the law concerning those who become *murtadd* is reported in Marshall Hodgson's *The Venture of Islam* Vol. 2, (Chicago: University of Chicago

Press, 1974), p. 538:

> We hear of a Suhravardi pir in the Panjab whose bigotry was murderous. A Hindu of high position had praised the pir — either genuinely or out of politeness — as being the best of (Muslim) saints as Muhammad had been the best of (non-Hindu) prophets; and to add to the grace of his tribute, he had used a standard Muslim formula in referring to Muhammad. The pir maintained that the latter statement implied the shahadah declaration, uttering which made a man a Muslim, and demanded that the Hindu acknowledge Islam on pain of death as an apostate.

48. Cf. fn. 33.

49. Rabadhah is the desert to which Abu Dhar was exiled and where he died. Cf. fn. 33.

50. Malik al-Ashtar, known in the history of Islam as "the fighting rooster of Ali," was well educated in jurisprudence and in military strategy. He participated in the battles of Irtidad (11/630), Jamal (36/656), and Siffin (37/657). After the martyrdom of Muhammad ibn Abi Bakr, Ali's appointed governor of Egypt, in a battle against Muawiyah's agent Amrw ibn As, in 38/658, he was assigned by Ali to govern Egypt and was given comprehensive and important instructions on how to rule (see *Nahj al-Balaghah*, letter 53). But shortly after reaching Egypt he was poisoned by agents of Muawiyah.
  For the others mentioned here see fn. 33.

51. By 'black immunity' Shari'ati means the situation in which religion becomes an opiate. 'Red immunity' is the terror of bloodshed.

52. *Wilāyat* is divinely designated leadership.

53. Amrw ibn al 'As was an aid to Muawiyyah famous for his cunning. He represented Muawiyyah in the arbitration at Siffin. Cf. fn. 26.
  Yazid ibn Muhallib was the governor of Khurassan.

54. *Sunnah* is literally a trodden path. It is the custom of the Prophet, the manner in which he conducted himself.

55. A *mufti* is a legal specialist who is capable of rendering a legal opinion *(fatwā)*. In the medieval Islamic world the *muftis* could neither judge nor legislate, and their *fatwās* had no binding force in the courts of the judges *(qādīs)* who were appointed by the Caliph. For a discussion of the origins of these institutions, and a comparison with similar structures in Christendom and among the Jews see F. E. Peters, *Children of Abraham* (Princeton: Princeton University Press, 1984), pp. 70-94.

56. For the Biblical account of Bal'am see Numbers 22-23. In the New Testament, Bal'am is condemned as one who used his priestly status for personal gain. Cf. II Peter 2:15-16; Jude 11; Revelation 2:14. For Shari'ati also, Bal'am is a symbol of a corrupt priesthood.

57. The two cancers mentioned here are *Murji'ah* and *Jabr,* which are presented as sanctioned by religion.

58. The *Murjiah* were an eighth century sect whose members held that judgement regarding those who committed grave sins must be suspended. Politically, they held that the Caliph did not cease to be a member of the community because he did things which were thought to be sinful, and that revolt against the Umayyids was therefore unlawful. In contrast with the Kharijite idea that grave sin excluded one from the fold of Islam, the Murjiah held that membership in the community was to be based solely on belief. Cf. Watt *Islamic Philosophy and Theology,* pp. 32-35.

59. "And say (unto them): Act! Allah will behold your actions, and (so will) His messenger and the believers, and ye will be brought back to the Knower of the invisible and the visible, and He will tell you what you used to do.
"And (there are) others who await Allah's decree, whether He will punish them or will forgive them. Allah is Knower, Wise." (9:105-106).

60. The injunction to command the good and to forbid evil is often repeated in the Qur'an: (3:104); (3:110); (3:114); (7:157); (:71); (9:112).

61. One of the names of God used in the Qur'an is *Al Jabbar,* the Compeller (59:23). *Jabr,* then, is the fate ordained by God, or divine compulsion. The Murjiah who held that it is for God alone to judge, came to be called *Jabriya,* and to subscribe to a fatalism according to which not only the judgement of sinners, but everything is strictly determined by God's decree, and therefore that whatever happens, including the misdeeds of the Caliphs, is to be accepted as the will of God. Cf. Rahman, *Islam,* p. 86.

62. (6:57); (12:40); (12:67).

63. Maraj al Adhra is where Mu awiyyah executed his young enemies such as Hujr ibn Adi. Cf. fn. 33.

64. Imam Jafar ibn Muhammad al Sadiq (83/702-148/765) is the sixth Shi'ite Imam.

65. The period mentioned is the early to mid eighth century. Cf. fn. 45.

66. There is uncertain evidence that the translations of several works of Aristotle, Porphyry, Euclid, and Ptolomy were commissioned by the Abbasid Caliph al Mansur (754-775), but a systematic effort to translate Greek science was not begun until the caliphate of al-Ma'mūn (d. 833). C.P. Richard Walzer, *Greek Into Arabic,* Oxford University Press, 1962, and *The Fihrist of al-Nadim,* two volumes, Bayard Dodge, ed. and tr. (New York: Columbia University Press, 1970).
67. "The Seven Cities of Love" alludes to the Sufi belief in seven stages through which the gradations of the Absolute Being are manifest in the universe and the seven levels of relative perfection through which the individual must pass to achieve unity with God. The "law of seven" is often considered to be the *modus opperandi* of all physical as well as spiritual reality in the universe and has been a central doctrine, not only in much of Sufi thought, but in many religious and philosophical cosmologies, from that of the Vedas to that of Pythagoras, and is still important for such schools of esoteric knowledge as Theosophy.

68. There was a controversy among the Mu'tazilites of the ninth century as to whether the world was created *ex nihilo* or from a pre-existent matter like the Aristotelian prime matter. This prime matter was completely uninformed, unlike the atomistic created matter, according to the reconstruction of Harry Austryn Wolfson, *The Philosophy of the Kalam* (Cambridge: Harvard University Press, 1976), pp. 359 ff.

69. Cf. Walzer, *Greek into Arabic.*

70. Shari'ati refers to a very controversial book, *Shahid-e-Javid,* by Salihi Najaafabadi as published in Qum in 1968, with a preface by Ayatullah Hussayn Ali Muntaziri. As Shari'ati explains, this book suggests that Husayn's revolt was an attempt to defeat Yazid, seize power, and establish a true Islamic government, and that this attempt did not succeed. This thesis contradicts the view of traditional scholars who considered Husayn as the symbol of martyrdom, destined by God to his fate, and not a political aspirant. Cf. the introduction to this volume and Hamid Enayat, *Modern Islamic Political Thought* (Austin: University of Texas Press, 1982), p. 190 ff.

71. Muslim ibn Aqil was the cousin of Husayn who was killed by the governor of Kufah, Ubayd Allah ibn Ziyad, before the battle of Karbala.

72. According to Akhavi, the phrase "What is to be done?" *(Cheh bayad kard?)* was significant in Iran not so much because of Lenin's pamphlet of 1903 as because of the essay by Ahmad Kasravi, written at a time of national crisis in August 1941, entitled *"Imruz Cheh Bayad Kard?"* This was a call for the restoration of the Constitution and social, economic and political reforms. Cf. Sharough Akhavi, *Religion and Politics in Contemporary Iran,* (Albany: SUNY Press, 1980), p. 231, fn. 67. Shari'ati also wrote a pamphlet entitled *"Cheh Bayad Kard?"* calling for the establishment of a free university and criticizing the conservative traditionalist elements in the clergy. Cf. Akhavi, *ibid.* pp. 145-146.

73. "With Him are the keys to that which is invisible and no one but He knows them. He knows what is in the land and in the sea. No one leaf falls except that He knows it, and there is not a grain in the darkness of the earth or (anything) wet or dry that is not in a clear record." (6:59). This ayah is sometimes mistaken as indicating that the Qur'an contains everything, not only essentially, but quantitatively. The locution, *kitabin mubin* ("a clear record") refers not to the Qur'an, but to the eternal knowledge of God.

74. "Say: O Allah! Owner of Sovereignty! Thou givest sovereignty unto whom Thou wilt, and Thou withdrawest sovereignty from whom Thou wilt. Thou exaltest whom Thou wilt, and Thou abasest whom Thou wilt. In Thy hand is the good. Lo! Thou art able to do all things."(3:26) It is reported that Yazid ibn Muawiyah recited this ayah to Zaynab, the sister of Husayn. She pointed out that Yazid did not understand its true meaning.

75. Umar Khayyam (d. 1123?) classified algebraic equations up to the third degree and used geometrical methods for their solution. Cf. S. H. Nasr, *Science and Civilization in Islam* (Cambridge: Harvard University Press, 1968), pp. 160ff. According to Nasr, a thorough study of the mathematics of Umar Khayyam in Persian had been made by Gh. Musahab in his *Hakim Umar Khayyam bi unwan-i alim-i jabr,* Tehran, 1339 (A.H. solar).

76. The reference is to the meticulous discussions in the modern books of jurisprudences *Tawdih al-Masail*. Cf. Ayatullah Khomeini, *A Clarification of Questions*, tr. J. Borujerdi (Boulder: Westview Press, 1984); and Ayatullah Shariatmadari, *The Abridged Commandments of Islam*, tr. Syed Shamim-us-Sibtain Rizvi.

77. Many examples can be cited, but as one, regard the divine reward for recitation of a certain prayer. Every unit of that prayer is considered equivalent to the performance of a thousand *hajj* pilgrimages and a thousand *'umrah* minor pilgrimages, the freeing of a thousand slaves, and participating in *jihad* a thousand times in the companionship of the Prophet. For every step taken, a hundred *hajj* and a hundred *'umrah*, freeing a hundred slaves, having a hundred good deeds recorded and a hundred bad deeds erased from one's record! Cf. *Mafatih al-Jinan*, p. 505.

78. Traditionally, the eight doors to paradise are prayer, fasting, hajj, *zakat* (tithe), *khums* (tithe), *jihad*, enjoining the good and forbidding evil, and association with the righteous and disassociation from the unrighteous.

79. The quietistic potential of this hadith has also been recognized by the founder of the Egyptian Muslim Brotherhood, Hasan al-Banna. He goes so far as to suggest that this hadith is not reliable, although it is almost universally accepted. Hasan goes on to claim that even if the tradition were sound it would not warrant the abandonment of fighting while one's lands were invaded by colonialist powers. Hasan al-Banna, *Five Tracts of Hasan Al-Banna (1906-1949)*, tr. Charles Wendell, (Berkeley: University of California Press, 1978), pp. 155ff.

80. Uthman ibn Hunayf was Ali's appointed governor to the city of Basra.

81. In 627 Heraclius defeated the Persian army at Ninevah. Chosroes II Parvez ("the Victorious") (590-628) fled his residence near Baghdad, and as his despotism and indolence had roused opposition everywhere, his eldest son was proclaimed king, and he was murdered in his palace, according to some sources by his son. "Chosro" is the Persian term for *emperor*, and is philologically related in its Indo-European root to the Latin *"caesar"* (also *"tsar"* or *"czar"* in Russian and *"Kaisar"* in Gothic). Shari'ati may be referring to Yazdegerd III, the grandson of Chosroes II, whose army was defeated by the Muslims during the Caliphate of Umar. It is reported that at one point during his flight, Yazdegerd was overtaken in a crowd of mules and camels laden with honey, indicating the luxurious impediments of his entourage. Cf. Edward Gibbon, *The Decline and Fall of the Roman Empire* Vol. II, (Chicago: Encyclopaedia Britannica, 1952), p. 257.

82. After the death of the Prophet there was a meeting at Saqifah to discuss the problem of governance. At this meeting Abu Bakr was chosen as Caliph, although Ali had not been present.

83. *Shura*, consultation, is an important feature of Islamic government. Proponents of democracy in the Islamic world have used this concept to support the orthodoxy of their views. In the Qur'an, Muhammad is directed to consult with his followers in the governance of the community (3:159). In the only passage in which the word *"shura"* occurs, reward is promised for those "whose affairs are a matter of counsel." (42:38).

84. Cf. fn. 30.

85. Amr ibn al As was a famous Meccan who eventually became a Muslim and was a supporter of Mu awiyyah.

86. *Allāhu Akbar*, God is Great, is a frequently repeated expression of praise to God. *La ilaha illā Allāh*, there is no god but God, and *Muhammadun rasūl Allāh*, Muhammad is the messenger of God, together comprise the testimony of faith, *shahāda*, of Islam.

87. The Bani Hashim is the subgroup of the Quraysh in which the Prophet was born.

88. "Spend your wealth for the cause of Allah, and be not cast by your own hands to ruin; and do good. Lo! Allah loveth the beneficient." (2:195).

89. This is a ritual affirmation of one's presence before God which is repeated by those who make the *hajj*. "*Labbayka, Allahumma labbayka,*" I am here, God I am here. This phrase has great politico-religious significance for Shari'ati. In his *Hajj* (Bedford: FILINC, 1978), he writes, "Denying the dishonest, exploitative, and despotic super-powers of the world, the people shout: 'Labbaika, Allahomma Labbaika' ... " (p. 18).

90. For Abu Musa and Abu Darda cf. fn. 40. Shurayh was a judge of Damascus whom Ali tried to remove but was able to retain his office due to his popularity in Damascus which was under the Umayyad rule. He condemned Husayn by citing the *hadith:* "Anyone who rebels against his guardian *(wali),* his blood is wasted."

91. This is a portion of the poem "*Nadir ya Iskandar*" in the collection *Akher-e-Shāhnāmah* by the famous Iranian contemporary poet, Mehdi Akhavan Sales, known as M. Omid.

92. Cf. fn. 27.

93. Nimrod is not mentioned in the Qur'an, but in Muslim exegesis there is frequent reference to him. He is the king of Babylon whose power is challenged by Abraham, as reported in the Qur'an (2:258). When Abraham tells him, "My Lord is He who gives life and death," Nimrod replies, "I give life and death." See Mahmoud Ayoub, *The Qur'an and Its Interpreters* Vol. I, (Albany: State University of New York Press, 1984), pp. 257-259. Cf. Genesis 10:8-9.

94. Cf. fn. 25.

95. The tribe of Ad is mentioned in many places in the Qur'an, particularly at (26:123-140) and (46:21-26). They followed the Prophet Hud. According to Arabian tradition, they are descendents of Ad, a great-grandson of Noah. They occupied a large area of land, extending from the mouth of the Persian Gulf to the southern end of the Red Sea. They are known as great builders and its is reported that they irrigated much of their lands with canals. The rulers turned against monotheism and oppressed their people. Following a three year famine, strong winds destroyed them and their lands. A remnant to the tribe survived and was known as the Thamud, but they also were destroyed in a similar way. (Cf. Yasuf Ali, *The Holy Qur'an* (Washington, D.C.; The Islamic Center, 1978), p. 358, fn. 1040.

226 JIHAD AND SHAHADAT

96. Zaynab was a daughter of Ali and Fatimah.

97. The root of "'Āshūra" is *a sh r*, meaning "ten." Ashura is the tenth day of Muharram, on which day is commemorated the martyrdom of Husayn in 61 A.H., along with his seventy-two companions at Karbala.

98. This refers to Harun al-Rashid, the Abbasid caliph, who made it his custom to go on alternate years to *hajj* and to *jihād*.

99. There are four imams of Sunni jurisprudence: Abu Hanifah, Malik ibn Anas, Ahmad Ibn Hanbal, and al-Shafi'i. Although Shari'ati mentions only the first three, all of them suffered persecution under the Caliphs, or were active in the movement to overthrow the Caliphs. Muhammad ibn Idris al-Shafi'i (150/767-204/819) held an office in the Yaman where he became involved in Alid intrigues — he was secretly a follower of the Zaydi Imam Yahya ibn Abd Allah — and was brought prisoner with the other Alids to the Caliph Harun al-Rashid, who pardoned him. Cf. the entries under the names of these imams in H.A.R. Gibb and J.H. Kramer (eds.) *Shorter Encyclopedia of Islam* (Ithaca: Cornell, 1965).

100. Abu Bakr Muhammad ibn Sahl al-Sarakhsi was a man of letters, expert of jurisprudence, and judge. He died in 483/1090 in Fergana, Uzbek. His famous book, *Al-Mabsūt*, contains thirty volumes. He also wrote a commentary on imam Ahmad ibn Hanbal's *Al-Jami' al-Kabīr*.

101. Taqiy al Din ibn Taimiya (661/1263-728/1328) was a Hanbali scholar who spent much of his time in prison. A brilliant polemicist, his writings included attacks on Sufism, Shi'ism, and the legal innovations of the Sunni Jurists. Ibn Taimiya encountered continuous opposition in Syria and died imprisoned in Damascus. Nevertheless, Ibn Taymiya is famous for his support of established authority:

> God has imposed the duty of enjoining the good and forbidding the evil, and that is possible only with the authority of a chief ... It is thus that people say 'the Sultan is the Shadow of god on earth' and 'Sixty years with an unjust imam is better than one night of anarchy.' Ibn Taymiyya, *Siyasa Sharia* ('Le Traite de droit publique d'Ibn Taymiyya'), trans. H. Laoust (Beirut, 1948), p. 172. Cited in Malise Ruthven, *Islam in the World* (Oxford: Oxford University Press, 1984), p. 179.

102. Ibn Qayyim al-Jawziya al-Jawziya (d. 1350 C.E.) is the best known disciple of Ibn Taymiyah and a key figure in the history of the antirationalist reaction to theology, philosophy, and mysticism.

103. The issue of whether the Qur'an was created or not was one of the first important issues disputed by Muslim theologians. The Ahs'arites held that it was eternal while the Mu'tazilites said that it was created. The Abbasid Caliph Ma'mun (198/813-218/833) actually carried out an inquisition against the Ash'arite position. According to Tabataba'i, it is because the first issue of Muslim theology concerned the speech of God that theology became known as *'ilm al kalām*, the science of speech. Cf. al-'Allamah as-Sayyid Muhammad Husayn at-Tabataba'i, *Al-Mizān*, Vol. 4, Sayyid Saeed Akhtar Rizvi, tr., (Tehran: World Organization for Islamic Services, 1982), p. 149. Cf. also the extensive discussion of this issue in Wolfson (1976).

104. Shari'ati's doctoral dissertation was a translation with commentary of a part of *Faza'el-e-Balkh*. Contrary to widespread belief, Shari'ati's doctoral degree was not in sociology, but in medieval Iranian philology under Professor G. Lazard. Cf. Nikki R. Keddie, *Roots of Revolution* (New Haven: Yale University Press, 1981), p. 294. Also, Shahrough Akhavi, "Shariati's Social Thought" in *Religion and Politics in Iran* ed. Nikkie R. Keddie (New Haven: Yale University Press, 1983), p. 126.

105. The *"Ahl al-Bayt,"* are the people of the household of the Prophet, reverence of whom became a hallmark of Shi'ism.

106. *"Rawāfid"("rafīdi"* sing.) is a pejorative term applied to Shi'ites. The term stems from *"rafd,"* the *repudiation* of the legitimacy of the first three Caliphs.

107. *"Wisāyat"* is described by Shari'ati as "the prophet's appointing, by God's command, the most suitable and right people in his family, on the basis of knowledge, to leadership." Quoted in Shahrough Akhavi, *Religion and Politics in Contemporary Iran* (Albany: SUNY Press, 1980), p. 231.
   "Bay'at" is the oath of allegiance by which one becomes bound under the leadership of the Prophet, a caliph, an Imam, or a Sufi master.
   "Shūrā" is consultation; cf. fn. 81.
   "Ijima" is the consensus of the community. Sunni scholars of jurisprudence, *faqīhs,* hold that Muhammad said, "My community will never agree on an error," and thus allow *ijima'* as one of the ways by which legal decisions may be justified. For the Shi'ah, *ijma'* is not an independent source of legislation, rather it is a means for determining the *sunnah* of the Imams. Cf. Al-Muhaqqiq al-Karaki, "Tariq Istinbat al-Ahkam" in *Al-Tawhīd* (English) Vol. II, No. 3, 1985, pp. 42-55.

108. Cf. fn. 82.

109. Before he died, the Prophet designated Ali as his trustee and claimed that Ali would fight for the true interpretation of the Qur'an just as he, Muhammad, had fought for its revelation. When the Prophet ordered that ink and parchment be brought in order that he might leave a written testament, Umar judged him to be delirious, and would not allow the writing implements to be brought. These controversial claims are among the central elements of the Shi'ite case for the designation of Ali, and the disobedience of some of the Companions.

110. Cf. fn. 34.

111. Cf. (16:89-90); (57:25).

112. The term *"'itrat"* pertains to the family of the Prophet. There is a famous hadith which has been reported in two versions, one accepted by the Sunnis and one by the Shi'ites. The Prophet is reported to have said "I leave among you two heavy things, the book of God and my ..." Some reporters claim that the second thing is the *sunnah* of the Prophet (cf. fn. 52). Shi'ites claim that the second thing is the *'itrat.* For Shari'ati there was no contradiction between the two versions, since the family of the Prophet is the bearer of his *sunnah.*

113. "O ye who believe! Lo! many of the (Jewish) rabbis and the (Christian) monks devour the wealth of mankind wantonly and debar (men) from the way of Allah. they who hoard up gold and silver and spend it not in the way of Allah, unto them give tidings (O Muhammad) of a painful doom." (9:34). *Kanz* in Arabic and *Ganj* in Persian are etymologically related. Both mean "treasure" or "accumulation of abundant wealth," particularly, gold and silver.

114. This "first link" is a reference to Yazid, the first "Muslim ruler" to be a crowned prince and to inherit the throne of his father.

115. Cyrus had two sons: Cambyses and Bardiya. Cambyses succeeded Cyrus to the throne, and while he was on a campaign, a Majus named Gaumata rose in revolt in Persis on the eleventh of March, 522 B.C., claiming to be Bardiya. He was killed by Darius on September twenty-ninth, after which Darius became king. Some historians doubt this story, contending that it was an invention of Darius and his comrades to justify their disposal of Bardiya. Cf. J. M. Cook, *The Persian Empire* (New York: Schocken Books, 1983).

116. In Firdowsi's epic *Shāhnāmah,* Prince Siyavash and his seventy-two companions are killed by Afrasiyab. The number of the martyrs in the battle of *Badr* was seventy-two. To this day the celebration of Ashura (Cf. fn. 97) is called *Suvashun* in some parts of Iran. The number seventy-two also has mystical significance in Jewish as well as Muslim esoteric schools. More recently, there are said to have been seventy-two people martyred along with Ayatullah Beheshti when the Islamic Republic Party Headquarters was bombed in 1981.

117. "Kāfiristān" here, refers generally to the land of the infidels.

118. Suṃanat (or Somnath) was the largest Hindu temple taken by Mahmud of Ghaznah (998-1030 C.E.) who conducted a series of vast plundering expeditions on which he destroyed works of art (as idolatrous) and looted all accessible goods across the whole of northwestern India, in the name of *jihād* and the expansion of Islam. Cf. Hodgson (1974), Vol. II, pp. 39-41; also Clifford E. Bosworth, *The Ghaznavids* (Edinburgh: Edinburgh University Press, 1963).

119. Moses put his hand in his cloak and when he drew it out it was white, yet not leprous. This was a miracle by means of which the magicians of the Pharaoh were confounded. (7:108); (20:22); (27:12); (28:32).

120. Al-Husayn ibn Mansur al-Hallaj (858-922) was born in al-Bayda, a small town not far from the Persian Gulf. He is the foremost Sufi martyr. The official charge against him was his claim to be God, *"Ana al-Haqq"* ("I am the Truth"), and his claim to have the authority to free the pious of the ritual prescriptions of the Islamic law, although political sedition was a decisive factor in his final torture and execution. At one stage he identified himself with the Shi'ite cause. Louis Massignon, one of the most renowned French Orientalists, developed a Catholic appreciation of Hallaj in his monumental *La Passion d'al-Hallaj* of 1922, recently translated by Herbert Mason as *The Passion of al-Hallaj* (Princeton: Princeton University Press, 1982). Shari'ati was familiar with Massignon's work, and undoubtedly has it in mind here. For a criticism of Massignon's attitude toward Islam see Edward W. Said, *Orientalism* (New York: Vintage Books, 1979), pp. 264 ff.

121. There is an interesting defense of the traditional Shi'ite position on intercession in al-Allamah as-Sayyid Muhammad Husayn at-Tabataba'i's *Al-Mizan* Vol. 1 (Tehran: WOFIS, 1983), pp. 226 ff. The claim that the evil deeds of those who follow the true Imam will be changed into good deeds is partially supported by appeal to the *ayat* (25:70): " ... For God will change the evil of such persons into good ..."

122. Cf. fn. 70.

123. The battle of Uhud (3/625) took place near Mount Uhud some three miles north of Medina. The *munafiqun* led by ibn Ubay (cf. fn. 25) deserted. Although they were outnumbered, the Muslim forces were approaching victory when a party of them disobeyed orders so as to pursue their share of the booty. The Meccan forces started to gain the upper hand, and the Prophet was even wounded. According to Shi'ite accounts, it is the valor of Ali which saved the life of the Prophet and prevented a general rout. Nevertheless, many Companions were martyred that day.

124. The story of Ammar is typically given in support of the practice of *taqiya*. Cf. fn. 42.

125. Abu Jahl, "Father of Ignorance," was the nickname given by the Muslims to the leader of the opposition to Muhammad, 'Amr ibn Hisham, who was known to his supporters as Abu al-Hikam, "Father of Wisdom." He was killed at Badr (2/624).

126. Al-Hurr ibn Yazid al-Tamimi was the leader of the Kufan cavalry sent by Yazid's governor Ubayd Allah ibn Ziyad against Husayn. He joined Husayn and was martyred with him. He is thus a paradigm of sincere repentence. Cf. Taleqani's *"Jihad* and *Shahādat"* in this volume.

Dr. Ali Shari'ati   **6.**

A Discussion of Shahid

The term "martyr," derived from the (Latin) root *"mort,"* implies "death and dying,"[2] "Martyr" is a noun meaning "the one who dies for God and faith." Thus a martyr is, in any case, the one who dies. The only difference between his death and that of others is to be seen in the "cause." He dies for the cause of God, whereas the cause of the death of another may be cancer. Otherwise, the essence of the phenomenon in both cases, that is to say, death, is one and the same. As far as death is concerned it makes no difference whether the person is killed for God, for passion, or in an accident. In this sense, Christ and those killed for Christianity are "martyrs." In other words, they were "mortals," because, in Christendom, the term "martyr" refers to the person who has died [as such].

But a *shahīd* is always alive and present. He is not absent. Thus the two terms, *"shahīd"* and "martyr," are antonyms of each other. As it was said,[3] the meaning of **shahid** (pl. *shuhāda*) — whether national or religious — in Eastern religions or otherwise, embodies the connotation of sacredness. This is right. There is no doubt that in every religion, school of thought, and national or religious attitude, a *shahīd* is sacred. [This is true], even though the school of thought in question may not be religious, but materialistic. The attitude and feeling toward the *shahīd* embodies a metaphysical sacredness. In my opinion, the question from whence the sacredness of a *shahīd* comes needs hair-splitting scientific analysis. Even in religions and schools of thought in which there is no belief in sacredness and the sacred, there is however belief concerning the sanctity of a *shahīd.* This status originates in the particular relation of a *shahīd* to his school. In other words he develops a spring of value and sanctity. It is because, at any rate, the relationship of an individual with his belief is a sacred relationship. The same relation develops between a *shahīd* and his faith. In the same way, yet indirectly, the same relationship develops between an adherent to a belief and its *shuhāda*. Thus the origin of the sanctity of a *shahīd* is the feeling of sacredness that all people have toward their school of thought, nationality, and religion.

In existentialism, there are discussions which are very similar, in some parts, to our discussions concerning *wilāyat* and its effects. Man has a primary "essential" character and a secondary "shaping character." In respect to the former, every person is the same. Anyone who wears clothes exists! But in the true sense of the term, what makes one's character, that is to say, makes him distinct from other beings, are the spiritual attributes and dimensions, feelings, instincts, and particular qualities — the things that, once a person considers them, he senses (himself) as a particular "I." He realizes himself, saying, "*Sum*" (I am).

From whence do the particular characteristics of "I" come? "I," as a human being, after being born, developed characteristics, attributes, and positive and negative values. Gradually I developed a knowledge of myself. Where does this come from. Heidegger[4] says, "The sum of man's knowledge about his life's environment makes his character, that knowledge being the conscious relation of the existence of 'I' with an external 'thing', 'person', or 'thought.'" When I establish a mental and existential relationship with individuals, movements, phenomena, things, thoughts, etc., this relationship finds a reflection in me. This reflection becomes a part of my essence and shapes my character. Thus man's character is the sum of all his relations with other characters. Consequently my virtue and vice is relative to the virtues and vices of the sum of the individuals, characters, ideas ... which surround me and with which I have a relation.

This relation can be with a historical entity (if, for example, I read history). We have not had a [direct] relationship with Imam Husayn. But when we intellectually meet him through a book or words, he becomes a part of our knowledge, and then a part of our personal characteristics. In this sense, everyone exists relative to his knowledge and ideals.

Likewise, when we give a part of our existence for a cause, that part becomes a part of that cause. For example, in our mind, justice has sacredness. It is one of those values which has become a part of us thanks to our relationship and contact with it. If I donate a thousand dollars of my own money for the establishment of justice, that thousand dollars absorbs the sacredness of justice. As long as it was in my pokcet, it was merely one thousand dollars. When I negate it in the way of justice, it is affirmed in another form, because it transforms into the essence of justice. Or for example, we have some money and we feed a group of poor people. If feeding the poor has the attribute of sacredness, the amount of money which has come out of our pocket for the feeding develops a particular value. In other words, it develops a non-monetary value and adopts a spiritual value. If we had spent the same amount of money for promulgation of spiritual food, [for example, for] the writing, translating, of publishing of a book, the money finds a new value depending on how sacred the act in question is. In other words, the money negates its existence in a sense, but obtains a new existence and value. In fact, money is an external measure of energy and power. If it is spent on "partying," the energy develops a profane value or, as some may think, a sacred value! Money is like kerosene or gasoline, which can be used to move a machine or to light a lamp. Once it is spent and once it is burned, it turns into a spiritual energy, depending upon the purpose for which it has vanished. What is spent does not have an independent value. The value belongs to me who has spent it. That amount of money was a part of me. Thus the sanctity of the cause for which the money is spent reflects on me. Its value comes back to me. I earn it; because that amount of money was a portion of my existence. The hundred dollars that I have paid for the cause of justice transforms itself into "the sanctity of justice." The sanctity of justice is transformed into "the money," that is to say, something absolutely materialistic and economic. Likewise, if it is spent for feeding the poor, the value of such feeding transports its value to the money spent. But the same amount of money, once spent for filthy partying, does not adopt a value. It rather becomes less than its materialistic value. At this point, we reach a principle: "everything obtains a similar value to that for which it has been spent." As it is negated, it is affirmed. In other words, as its existence is negated, its value is affirmed. In self-annihilation, it reaches the permanence of the purpose, provided that the purpose is something permanent, such as an ideal, a value, freedom, justice, charity, thought, or knowledge. Money, once spent for the sake of knowledge, goes out of one's pocket and becomes zero; but at the same time it changes into the values of knowledge for which it is spent.

Just as money is a part of my existence, so my existence, my animal life, my instinct, and my time are parts of me. Suppose I spent an hour of my time to earn money. Because the earning of money has no value, the one hour cannot obtain any value, because I have sacrificed that hour for the sake of what does not have value or sanctity. But if I spent the same hour teaching someone something or guiding him without charging him anything, I have sacrificed that hour for a value. That hour takes on the value of the cause for which that hour was spent.

A *Shahīd* is the one who negates his whole existence for the sacred ideal in which we all believe. It is natural then that all the sacredness of that ideal and goal transports itself to his existence. True, that his existence has suddenly become non-existent, but he has absorbed the whole value of the idea for which he has negated himself. No wonder then, that he, in the mind of the people, becomes sacredness itself. In this way, man becomes absolute man, because he is no longer a person, an individual. He is "thought." He had been an individual who sacrificed himself for "thought." Now he is "thought" itself. For this reason, we do not recognize Husayn as a particular person who is the son of Ali. Husayn is a name for Islam, justice, *imāmat*, and divine unity. We do not praise him as an individual in order to evaluate him and rank him among *shuhāda*. This issue is not relevant. When we speak of Husayn, we do not mean Husayn as a person. Husayn was that individual who negated himself with absolute sincerity, with the ulmost magnificence within human power, for an absolute and sacred value. From him remains nothing but a name. His content is no longer an individual, but is a thought. He has transformed himself into the very school [for which he has negated himself].

An individual who becomes a *shahīd* for the sake of a nation, and thus obtains sacredness, earns this status. In the opinion of the ones who do not recognize a nation as the sum of individuals, but recognize it as a collective spirit[5] above the individuals, a *shahīd* is a spiritual crystalization of that collective spirit which they call "nation." Likewise, when an individual sacrifices himself for the sake of knowledge, he is no longer an individual. He becomes knowledge itself. He becomes the *shahīd* of knowledge. We praise liberty through an individual who has given himself to liberty; we do not praise "him" because he was a good person. This is not of course in contradiction with the fact that, from God's perspective, he is still an individual, and in the hereafter, he will have a separate destiny and account. But in the society, and by the criterion of our school, we do not praise him as an individual; we praise the thought, the sacred.

At this point, the meaning of the word *"shahīd"* is all the more clear. When the belief in a sacred school of thought is gradually eroding, is about to vanish or be forgotten in a new generation due to a conspiracy, suddenly an individual, by negating himself, re-establishes it. In other words, he calls it back again to the scene of the world. By sacrificing his existence, he affirms the [hitherto] vanishing existence of that ideal. For this reason, he is *shahīd* (witness, present) and *mashhud* (visible). He is always in front of us. The thought also obtains presence and permanence through him. It becomes revived and obtains a soul again.

We have two kinds of *shahīd*, one symbolized by Hamzah, the master of martyrs, and the other symbolized by Husayn.

There is much difference between Hamzah and Husayn. Hamzah is a *mujāhid* and a hero who goes (into battle) to achieve victory and defeat the enemy. Instead, he is defeated, is killed, and thus becomes a *shahīd*. But this represents an individual *shahādat*. His name is registered at the top of the list of those who died for the cause of their belief.

Husayn, on the other hand, is a different type. He does not go (into battle with the intention of) succeeding in killing the enemy and winning victory. Neither is he accidentally killed by a terroristic act of someone such as Wahshi.[7] This is not the case. Husayn, while he could stay at home and continue to live, rebels and consciously welcomes death. Precisely at this moment, he chooses self-negation.

He takes this dangerous route, placing himself in the battlefield, in front of the contemplators of the world and in front of time, so that [the consequence of] his act might be widely spread and the cause for which he gives his life might be realized sooner. Husayn chooses *shahadat* as an end or as a means for the affirmation of what is being negated and mutilated by the political apparatus.

Conversely, *shahādat* chooses Hamzah and the other *mujahidin* who go for victory. In the *shahādat* of Husayn, the goal is self-negation for the sanctity [of that ideal] which is being negated and gradually is vanishing. At this point, *jihād* and *shahādat* are completely separate from each other. Ali speaks of the two concepts in two different contexts with two [different] philosophies.

Al-Jihad 'izzun lil Islām ("*Jihad* is glory for Islam.") Jihad is an act, the philosophy of which is different from that of *shahādat*. Of course in *jihād*, there is *shahādat*, but the kind which Hamzah symbolizes, not the one Husayn symbolizes.

Al-Shahādat istizharan 'alal-mujahadat[8] ("*Shahādat* is exposing what is being covered up.") Yes, such is the goal of *shahādat,* and thus it is always different from *jihād*. It is discussed in a different chapter. *Jihād* is glory for Islam. But *shahādat* is exposing what is being covered up. This is how I understand the matter. Once upon a time a truth was an appealing precept. Everyone followed it and it was sacred. All powers surrounded it. But gradually in time, because that truth did not serve the interests of a minority and was dangerous for a group, it was conspired against in order to erase it from the minds and lives of the people. In order to fill its empty place, some other issue was supplanted. Gradually the original issue was completely lost and in its place other issues were discussed.

In this situation, the *shahīd,* in order to revive the original issue, sacrifices his own life, and thus brings the *demode* precept back into attention by repulsion of its sham substitute. This is the very goal.

At the time of Husayn, the main issue after the Prophet was that of leadership. The other issues were marginal. The main issue was: "Anyway, who is to rule and supervise the destiny of the Muslim nation?" As we know, during the entire reign of the Umayyads, this remained the issue. Uprisings, and thus the major crises of the Umayyads, all boiled down to this very issue. People would pour into the mosques at every event and would grab the neck of the caliph, asking him, "On the basis of which *āyah* or by what reason do you hold your position? Do you have the right or not?" Well, in the midst of such a situation, one cannot rule. No wonder then that the period of the Umayyads was no longer than a century.[9]

During their reign, the Abbasids,[10] who were more experienced (than the Umayyads), de-politicized the people; that is to say, they made the people less sensitive to the issue of *imāmat* (leadership) and the destiny of the society. By what means?! By clinging to the most sacred issues: worship, exegesis of the Qur'an, *kalām* (theology), philosophy, translation of foreign books, promulgation of knowledge, cultivation, expansion of civilization — so that Baghdad could be an heir to all great cities and civilizations of the world and so that Muslims could become the most advanced of peoples. [But to what real end?] So that one issue should become negated and no one talk about it.

For the purpose of reviving the very issue, the *shahīd* arises. Having nothing else to sacrifice, he sacrifices his own life. Because he sacrifices his life for that purpose, he transmits the sacredness of that cause to himself.

> To God belong both the East and the West. He guides
> whom He will to a straight path. Thus we have made you
> an *ummatan wasatan*[11] (middle community) so that you
> may be *shuhāda* (witnesses) over mankind, and the
> Apostle may be a *shahīd* (witness) over you. (2:142-143).

In this *āyah*, *shahādat* does not mean "to be killed." It implies that something has been covered and is about to leave the realm of memory, being gradually forgotten by people. The *shahīd* witnesses for this innocent, silent, and oppressed victim. We know that *shahīd* is a term of a different kind from others. The Apostle is a *shahīd* without being killed. without being killed, the Islamic community established by the Qur'an has the status and responsibility of a *shahīd*. God says, " ... so that you may be *shuhāda* over mankind ...", just as the Apostle is *shahīd* over you. Thus the role of *shahādat* is more general and more important than that of being murdered. Nevertheless the one who gives his life has performed the most sublime *shahādat*. Every Muslim should make a *shahīd* community for others, just as the Apostle is an *'uswah* (pattern) on the basis of which we make ourselves.[12] He is our *shahīd* and we are the *shuhāda* of humanity.

We have determined that *shahīd* connotes a "pattern, prototype, or example" on the basis of whom one rebuilds oneself. It means we should situate our Prophet in the midrealm of culture, faith, knowledge, thought, and society, and make all these to accord with him. Once you have done so, and thus have situated yourself in the midst of time and earth, all other nations and masses should rebuild themselves to accord with you. In this way you [as a nation] become their *shahīd*. In other words, the same role that the Apostle has played for you, you will play for others. You will play the role of the Prophet as a human and as a nation for them. It is in this sense that the locution *"'ummatan wasatan"* (a community justly balanced) appears quite relevant to the word *shahīd*. We usually think that *'ummatan wasatan* refers to a moderate society, that is to say, a society in which there is not extravagance or pettiness, which has not drowned itself in materialism at the expense of sacrificing its spirituality. It is a society in which there is both spirit and matter. It is "moderate"; whereas, considering the issue of the mission of this *'ummat,* this is not essentially the meaning of *wasatan* in this locution. Its meaning is far superior. It means that we, as an *'ummat,* we must be the *axis* of time; that is to say, we must not be a group cowering in a corner of the Middle East or turning around ourselves, rather than becoming involved in crucial and vital issues, which form everything and make the present day of humanity and tomorrow's history. We should not neglect this responsibility by engaging in self-indulgent repetition. We must be in the middle of the field.

We should not be a society which is *ghā'ib* (absent, the opposite of *shahīd),* isolated, and pseudo-Mutazilite[13], but we should be an *'ummat* in the middle of the East and the West, between Right and Left, between the two poles, and in short, in the middle of the field. The *shahīd* is such a person. He is present in all fields. An *ummatan wasatan* is a community that is in the midst of battles; it has a universal mission. It is not a self-isolated, closed, and distant community. It is a *shahīd* community.

The opinion I expressed last year concerning *shahādat* meant that, fundamentally in Islam, *shahādat* is an independent issue, as are prayer, fasting, and *jihād*. Whereas, in the common opinion, *shahādat* for a *mujāhid* of a religion is a state or destiny in which he is murdered by the enemy in *jihād*. Such is also correct. But what I have expressed as a principle adjacent to *jihād* — not as an extension of *jihād* and not as a degree that the *mujāhid* obtains in God's view or in relation to his destiny in the Hereafter — relates to a particular *shahādat*, symbolized by Husayn. We in Islam have great *shuhāda*, such as our Imams, the first and foremost of whom is Ali, who is the greatest Imam and the greatest man made by Islam. Even though Ali is a *shahīd*, we take Hamzah and Husayn as ideal manifestations of *shahādat*.

Hamzah is the greatest hero of Islam in the most crucial battle, Uhud (in 627). The Prophet of Islam never expressed so much sadness as he did for Hamzah, even when his own son, Abraham,[14] died, or when some of his greatest companions were martyred. In the battle of Uhud, Hamzah became a *shahīd* due to an inhuman conspiracy contrived by Hind (Abu Sufyan's wife and Muawiyah's mother) and carried out by her slave, Wahshi. The reaction of the Apostle was severe. The people of Medina praise Hamzah so much as a hero that the Saudis have accused them of worshipping him. It shows how much he is glorified, even though he was not from Medina. It was with his acceptance of Islam that Muslims straightened their stature. At the beginning of *bi'that*[15], Hamzah was recognized among the Quraysh as a heroic and epic personality. He was the youngest son of Abd al-Muttalib, a great hunter and warrior. After the episode in which the Quraysh insulted the Apostle and he defended the Apostle, Hamzah became inclined toward Islam. As he became Muslim, Muslims no longer remained a weak and persecuted group. Indeed, they manifested themselves as a group ready for a showdown. Afterwards, as long as there was the sword and personality of Hamzah, other personalities were eclipsed. Even the most sparkling epochal personality of Islam, that is to say, Ali, was under his influence. It is quite obvious that in the battle of Uhud, the spearhead was Hamzah, followed by Ali.

You know that when Hamzah was killed due to that filthy and womanly conspiracy, the Apostle became very angry and sad. When he attended the body of Hamzah, the ears, eyes, and nose of the latter had already been cut off. Hind had made frightening ornaments of these for herself. A man who had taken an oath to drink the blood of

Hamzah fulfilled his vow in Uhud. Muhammad, near the corpse of this great hero, this young and beloved son of Abdul Muttalib, and his own young uncle, spoke so angrily and vengefully that he immediatley felt sorry and God warned him. Muhammad vowed that at the first chance he would burn thirty of the enemy as a blood reprisal for Hamzah. But the heavens immediately shouted at him that no one except God, Who is the Lord of fire, has the right to burn a human being for a crime.[16] Thus the Apostle broke his vow. Since God took this sense of vengeance from him, he tried to console himself by reciting a eulogy for Hamzah.

On his return to Medina, the families were mourning their beloved ones; but no one was crying for Hamzah, because he had no relatives or home in Medina. He was a lonely immigrant. The Apostle, with such tender feelings, unexpected from a heroic man like him, waged a wailing complaint as to why no one cried for Hamzah, the son of Abdul Muttalib, "the hero of our family." And behold this tender feeling, that a Medinan family came to the Apostle and gave him condolences, saying, "We will cry for Hamzah's death and the Apostle will eulogize ours." And he thanked them.

At any rate, in the history of Islam, for the first time, Hamzah was given the title *Sayyid al-Shuhadā* (the Master of *Shuhadā*). The same title was later primarily applied to Husayn. Both are *Sayyid al-Shuhadā*, but there is a fundamental difference between their *shahādat*. They are of two different kinds which can hardly be compared. Hamzah is a *mujāhid* who is killed in the midst of *jihād*, but Husayn is a *shahīd* who attains *shahādat* before he is killed. He is a *shahīd*, not only at the place of his *shahādat*, but also in his own house. From the moment that Walid, the governor of Medina, asks him to swear allegiance [to Yazid] and he says, "NO!" — the negation by which he accepts his own death — Husayn is a *shahīd*, because *shahīd* in this sense is not necessarily the title of the one killed as such, but it is precisely the very witnessing aimed at negating an [innovative] affair. A *shahīd* is a person who, from the beginning of his decision, chooses his own *shahādat*, even though, between his decision-making and his death, months or even years may pass. If we want to explain the fundamental difference between the two kinds of *shahādat*, we must say that, in Hamzah's case, it is the death which chooses him. In other words, it is a kind of *shahādat* that chooses the *shahid*. In Husayn's case, it is quite the contrary. The *shahīd* chooses his own *shahādat*. Husayn has chosen *shahādat,* but Hamzah has been chosen by *shahādat.*

The philosophy of the rise of the *mujāhid* is not the same as that of the *shahīd.* The *mujāhid* is a sincere warrior who, for the sake of defending his belief and community or spreading and glorifying his faith and community, rises so that he may break, devastate, and conquer the enemy who blocks or endangers his path; thus the difference between attack and defense is *jihād.* He may be killed in this way. Since he dies in this way, we entitle him *"shahīd."* The kind of *shahādat* symbolized by Hamzah is a tragedy suffered by a *mujāhid* in his attempt to conquer and kill the enemy. Thus the type of *shahīd* symbolized by Hamzah refers to the one who gets killed as a man who had decided to kill the enemy. He is a *mujāhid.* The type of *shahīd* symbolized by Husayn is a man who arises for his own death. In the first case, *shahādat* is a negative incident. In the latter case, it is a decisive goal, chosen consciously. In the former, *shahādat* is an accident along the way; in the latter, it is the destination. There death is a tragedy; here death is an ideal. It is an ideology. There the *mujāhid,* who had decided to kill the enemy, gets killed. He is to wailed and eulogized. Here there is no grief, for *shahādat* is a sublime degree, a final stage of human evolution. It is reaching the absolute by one's own death. Death, in this case, is not a sinister event. It is a weapon in the hands of the friend who with it hits the head of the enemy. In the event that Husayn is completely powerless in defending the truth, he hits the head of the attacking enemy with his own death.

Shahādat has such a unique radiance; it creates light and heat in the world and in the cold and dark hearts. In the paralyzed wills and thought, immersed in stagnation and darkness, and in the memories which have forgotten all the truths and reminiscenses, it creates movement, vision, and hope and provides will, mission, and commitment. The thought, "Nothing can be done," changes into, "Something can be done," or even, "Something must be done." Such death brings about the death of the enemy at the hands of the ones who are educated by the blood of a *shahīd.* By shedding his own blood, the *shahīd* is not in the position to cause the fall of the enemy, [for he can't do so]. He wants to humiliate the enemy, and he does so. By his death, he does not choose to flee the hard and uncomfortable environment. He does not choose shame. Instead of a negative flight, he commits a positive attack. By his death, he condemns the oppressor and provides commitment for the oppressed. He exposes aggression and revives what has hitherto been negated. He reminds the people of what has already been forgotten. In the icy hearts of a people, he bestows the blood of life, resurrection, and movement. For those who have become accustomed to captivity and thus think of captivity as a permanent state, the blood of a *shahīd* is a rescue vessel. For the eyes which can no longer read the truth and cannot see the face of the truth in the darkness of despotism and *istihmār* (stupification), all they see being nothing but pollution, the blood of the *shahīd* is a candle light which gives vision and [serves as] the radiant light of guidance for the misguided who wander amidst the homeless caravan, on mountains, in deserts, along by-ways, and in ditches.[17]

NOTES

1. This piece consists of parts of two of Shari'ati's speeches, with some material added to the written versions by Shari'ati. We have no date for the speeches, but the written piece was only published after Shari'ati's death.

2. Shari'ati is mistaken with regard to the etymology of "martyr." The word "martyr," in French (in which Shari'ati was fluent) as well as in English, is derived from the Greek word, "martys," which, like the Arabic *"shahīd,"* means witness. The Greek word is never used in the Bible except in the sense of witness, with the possible exception of Revelation Ch. 11, in which reference is made to two witnesses, usually assumed to be Elijah and Moses, Peter and Paul, or simply two martyrs. This Biblical chapter seems to stand at the border where the word "martyr" became a technical term for witness unto death, or martyr. The parallel with the Qur'anic usage of the term *"shahīd"* is remarkable. (See the introduction to this volume.) *"Mort"* is derived from Latin and has no relation to the Greek *"martys."* Possibly, Shari'ati erred by seeking the root for "martyr" in the consonants, MRT, as one might do with Arabic.

3. This is a parallel to the opening paragraph of Mutahhari's *"Shahīd,"* in this volume.

4. Martin Heidegger (1884-1976) is a central existentialist philosopher. It is not clear what relation Shari'ati sees between the Shi'ite doctrine of *wilayāt* (guardianship), and the existentialist's thought, but perhaps the connection is along the following lines. In Shi'ite thought, no act of worship is acceptable to God without belief in Imamate and *wilayāt*. It is through the Imams that one may be lead toward God. For Heidegger, and authentic life is one which is guided by genuine understanding, through which one orients oneself toward existence.

5. This is a reference to both the philosopher Hegel and Durkheim, the founding father of functionalism in anthropology and sociology. Notice also, for both Shari'ati and Taleqani, "the cause of God" is almost synonymous with "the cause of the people."

6. Hamzah ibn Abd al-Mutallib, the uncle of the Prophet, was known as the "Lion of God." He participated in the battle of Badr (624) and was martyred at the battle of Uhud (627). See Mutahhari's *"Shahīd"* in this volume. For details of his martyrdom see Ibn Ishaq's *Sirat Rasūl Allāh*, pp. 371-387.

7. Wahshi was an Abyssinian slave of Jubayr ibn Mut'im who killed Hamzah with a javelin. See Ibn Ishaq's *Sirat Rasul Allah*, p. 371 ff.; particularly p. 376, where the story of Hamzah's martyrdom is related by Wahshi.

8. Cf. Shari'ati's *"Shahādat"* in this volume for a further discussion of this saying of Imam Ali.

9. The Umayyads reigned from 661 to 750 C.E.

10. The Abbasids reigned effectively from 750 to 945 C.E.

11. According to the *tafsīr* of Ibrahim al-Qummi (d. 328/939) the *'ummatan wasatan* is a community of the mean, which mediates between the Prophet and humanity. Al-Qummi took the true community of the middle path to consist exclusively of the Imams. See Mahmoud M. Ayoub, *The Qur'an and its Interpreters* (Albany: SUNY Press, 1984), p. 172.

12. Cf. (33:21): "Verily in the messenger of God you have a good example for those who look to God and the Last Day, and remember God often."

13. This refers to the Mu'tazalite school of thought (see Reynold A. Nicholson, *A Literary History of the Arabs,* second ed. (Cambridge: Cambridge University Press, 1930), pp. 222-224, but here Shari'ati also plays upon the literal meaning of the word *"mu'tazilite,"* which is "retirement, detachment, seclusion, retreat." The Mu'tazilite movement began with the detachment of Wasil ibn Ata ibn Ubayd from the circle of Hasan al-Basri.

14. The prophet's son Abraham, or Ibrahim died when he was about eighteen months old, in 9/631. His mother was an Egyptian slave, Mariya.

15. The beginning of the Prophet's propagation of his divine message is called the *"bi'that."*

16. According to most exegetes of the Qur'an (16:126), is related to the event of the martyrdom of Hamzah. The Prophet, furious over the death of his uncle, vowed to kill thirty of the enemy in retaliation. Muhammad then received the revelation, "If you punish, then punish in the way you were afflicted, but if you endure patiently, then truly it is better for those who are patient."

17. The Prophet is reported to have said: "Surely Husayn is the light of guidance and the boat of salvation."

Dr. Ali Shari'ati   **7.**

After Shahādat

Sisters and brothers! The *shuhāda* are now dead, and we — the dead — are alive. The *shuhāda* have conveyed their message and we — the deaf — are their audience. Those who were bold enough to choose death, when they could no longer live, have left; we — the shameless — have remained. We have remained for hundreds of years. It is quite appropriate for the whole world to laugh at us, because we, the symbols of abjection and humility, are weeping for Husayn and Zaynab, the manifestations of life and honor. This is another injustice of history: that we — the despicable — should be the mourners of these mighty ones. Today the *shuhāda* delivered their message with their blood and sat opposite us in order to invite the seated ones of history to rise.

In our culture, religion, and history — in Shi'ism — the most valuable jewels that mankind has created, and the most life-giving substances that bestow vitality, pulsation, and movement upon history and teach mankind the most divine lessons, elevating him as high as God, are concealed. The heritage of all these valuable divine treasures has fallen into our hands. We, the abject and humble, we are the heirs of the most beloved trusts, prepared by *jihād, shahādat* and great human values in the history of Islam. We are the heirs of all this. We have a responsibility to make ourselves a community which can be a model for humanity. "Thus we have made you a mediating community, that you may be *shuhāda* (witnesses, models) over the

nations, and the Apostle may be a *shahīd* (witness, model) over you."
(2:143). [This *āyah*] is addressed to us. We have a responsibility to
make — from the mighty and beloved heritage of our *shuhāda,*
warriors, imams, leaders, faith, and Book — a model community, in
order that we might be *shahīd* (martyrs) and *shahīd* (witnesses) for
the people of the world, as the Apostle should be the model and
shahīd for us.

Such a heavy responsibility, that of bestowing vitality and
movement to humanity, rests upon our shoulders, yet we are unable
to carry out our routine daily life.

God! What wisdom is there in this?

And we — drowned in the filthy swamp of our animalistic lives —
must be the mourners of such men, women, and children, who in
Karbala proved forever their *shahādat* and presence in history before
God and in the presence of freedom.

God! What oppression is this which is again committed against the
family of Husayn?

Now the *shuhāda* have completed their task. We declare its end by
mourning tonight. Behold that we — under the cloak of weeping for
and loving Husayn — are allied with Yazid, who wished this story to
end.

Now the *shuhāda* have completed their task and have left in
silence. All of them, one by one, have played their role well: the
teacher, the caller, the old, the young, men and women, master and
slave, and even a baby. Each of them, as representative, lesson, and
model to mankind, old and infant, man and woman ... chose such a
beautiful and live-giving death.

They carried out two tasks: from Husayn's baby to his brother,
from his slave to himself, from the reciter of the Qur'an to the teacher
of the children of Kufah, from the one who called out at the time of
prayer to others, both stranger and kin, from the one who was noble
and respectable to the one deprived of social honors — all stood as
brothers, face to face with *shahādat* men and women, the children,
the old and young of history in order to teach mankind how they
should live if they are able and how they should die if they are not.

This is the first task.

These *shuhāda* carried out another task as well. With their blood,
not with words, in the court of the history of mankind, each as a

representative of his social group, they witnessed that all human groups and human values are condemned in the one system ruling over the history of mankind, a system which employs politics, economy, religion, art, philosophy, thought, feeling, ethics, and in one word, humanity, as tools for sacrificing men to their own interests, which makes everything support the rule of oppression, aggression, and crime. There is one ruler over all history, one oppressor who rules history, and one executioner who martyrs. Throughout history, many children have been victims of this executioner. Many women have been silenced under the whips of this executioner who rules history. At the price of much blood, endless appetites have been appeased. Many cases of starvation, slavery, and massacres in history have been suffered by women and children, by men, heroes, slaves, and teachers, in all times and in all generations.

And now Husayn has come with all his existence to the court of history, so that he may witness on the banks of the Euphrates. He has come to witness for all the oppressed people of history, for all those condemned by the executioner ruling history, to witness how this merciless executioner, *Dahhak,*[2] continues to eat the brains of the youth throughout history. He has come to witness with his Ali Akbar.[3] He has come to witness how the heroes have died in the criminal regimes.

He has come to witness with himself. He has come to witness with his sister Zaynab that in the regimes ruling history, women must either choose slavery and thus remain in the harems or choose freedom and thus become *shuhāda*, thereby leading to the caravan of the captives and being heirs to the *shuhāda*.

He has come to bear witness with his nursing child, Ali Asghar, that in the regime of oppression, aggression, and crime, the executioner does not show mercy, not even to a nursing baby.

And Husayn, with all his existence, has come to bear witness in the criminal court of history for the benefit of those for whom there has never been a witness and thus have died defenselessly in silence.

Now the court has ended, and the witnessing of Husayn, all his dear ones, and all his existence, the best that anyone other than God is capable of, have completed their great divine mission.

Friends! In Shi'ism — which has presently taken this form we see, such that anyone who wishes to speak of genuine, dynamic, and awakening Shi'ism is victimized by his friends before the enemy has access to him — great lessons and messages, abandoned treasures, divine values, mighty capitals, and life-giving souls for the revival of society, nation, and history are hidden.

One of the best life-giving sources in the history of Shi'ism is *shahādat*.

As Jalal[4] has said, "Since the time that we have forgotten the tradition of *shahādat* and have become the guardians of the cemeteries of the *shuhāda*, we have submitted to the black death." Since the time that we, instead of being Shi'ites of Ali, Shi'ites of Husayn, and Shi'ites of Zaynab, that is to say, being followers of the *shuhāda*, our men and women have become mere mourners for the *shuhāda*, we have remained in eternal mourning. How intelligently the message of Husayn and his great, dear, and immortal friends has been metamorphosized — a message addressed to all mankind.

After he sees all his dear ones fallen on the battlefield, and when he has no audience except the vengeful and plundering enemy, Husayn cries, "Is there anyone to stand at my side?" Does he not know that there is no one to stand by his side? This is the question posed to future generations, to each one of us. This question revealed Husayn's expectations of those who love him. It is an invitation addressed to all those who respect and revere the *shuhāda*.

We belittled this invitation, this expectation, and this message by misreading its content. Instead of, "Husayn demands followers in every age and generation," we read, "Husayn demands only tears and weeping. He has no other message. He is dead and demands mourners. He is not a living *shahīd* in every time and place in search of followers." Thus we have been told.

For every revolution, there are two visages, the first is "blood" and the second is "message."

Shahīd means "present." The ones who personally choose the red death as a symbol of their love for a dying truth — as the only weapon of *jihād* for the sake of the great values which are being altered — are referred to as *shahīd*. They are alive, present, witnesses, and observers. They are not only so in the sight of God, but also in the sight of the masses in every age and every land.

Those who submit to any humiliation in order to remain alive are the silent, dirty, dead of history. Which ones are alive? Those who choose their own death and with selflessness have come with Husayn to be slaughtered, while hundreds of religious excuses permit them to remain alive, but who do not seek excuses and thus die; or those who left Husayn and thus submitted to abjection and obedience to Yazid — which ones are still alive?

Anyone who considers life as more than just an animate corpse sees and feels with his whole existence the life and presence of Husayn and the death of those who submitted to humiliation in order to remain alive.

In confronting oppression and aggression, the *shahīd* shows, teaches, and argues against those who think, "Inability means exemption from *jihād*," and those who say, "Triumph means victory over the enemy." The *shahīd* is the one who, in the age of inability to conquer, triumphs over the enemy by his own death, disgracing him if not defeating him.

A *shahīd* is the heart of history. The heart gives blood and life to the otherwise dead blood-vessels of the body. Like the heart, a *shahīd* sends his own blood into the half-dead body of the dying society, whose children have lost faith in themselves, which is slowly approaching death, which has accepted submission, which has forgotten its responsibility, which is alienated from humanity, and in which there is no life, movement, and creativity. The greatest miracle of *shahādat* is giving to a generation a renewed faith in itself.

A *shahīd* is ever-present and every-lasting.

Who is absent?

Husayn has taught us another lesson more important than his *shahādat*. Leaving *hajj* unfinished and proceeding to *shahādat*. He leaves half-finished the revival of the pilgrimage for which all his ancestors, his grand-father and father, struggled. From the half-finished *hajj*, he proceeds to *shahādat* in order to teach all pilgrims in history, all worshippers in history, and all the believers in the tradition of Abraham that if there is no imamate and leadership, if there is no goal, if there is no Husayn, and if instead there is Yazid, circumambulating the house of God is the same as circumambulating the idol houses. The ones who continue their circumambulation in the absence of Husayn are equal to those who moved around the Green Palace of Muahwiyah.[5] A *shahīd*, who is present in all the battlefields of truth and falsehood, reveals to all humanity: "If you are not in the battlefield of truth and falsehood, it makes no difference where you are. When you are not a witness in the battlefield of truth and falsehood of your time, be anywhere else you wish. Stand for prayer or sit down for wine. Both are the same."

Shahādat means presence in the battlefield of truth and falsehood of the eternity of history.

And absence?!

Those who left Husayn alone, and avoided presence, participation and witnessing, and thus were absent, are all the same. The three are one. Those who deserted Husayn and became Yazid's mercenaries, those who, longing for paradise, crept into the secure solitude of worship, left Husayn alone, escaped the conflict of truth and falsehood, and entertained themselves with prayers, and those who, fearing the ruling force, kept silent — are all one.

Where Husayn is present, and he is present in every century and every age, anyone who does not stand beside him, be they believers or non-believers, criminal or virtuous — are all equal. This is the meaning of the Shi'ite principle that the nature of each act depends upon imamate, leadership, and *wilāyat*.[6] Without it everything is meaningless and we see that it is meaningless. And now Husayn has declared his presence in all ages and for all generations, in all wars, struggles, and battlefields of any time and land. He has died in Karbala, so that he may be resurrected in all generations and ages.

You and I must weep over our own misery that we are not present.

Yes, for every revolution, there are two visages: *blood and the message.* Husayn and his companions undertook the first mission, that of blood. The second mission is to bear the message to the whole world, to be the eloquent tongue of this flowing blood and these resting bodies among the walking dead. The mission of conveying the message begins today. Its responsibility rests on the fine shoulders of Zaynab, a woman from whom mankind is to learn virtue. The mission of Zaynab is more difficult and heavier than that of her brother. Those who have the courage to choose their own death have simply made a great choice. But the responsibility of those who survive is heavy and difficult. Zaynab has survived. The caravan of the captives follows behind her. The ranks of the enemy, as far as the eye can see, are in front of her. The responsibility of conveying her brother's message rests solely upon her shoulders. Leaving behind a red garden of *shahādat* and the perfume of roses, spreading from her skirts, she enters the city of crime, the capital of power, the center of oppression and execution.

With peace and pride, she victoriously announces to the power and cruelty of the slave-agents and executioners, to the remnants of colonialism and dictatorship: "Thank God for all the generosity and glory which He has bestowed upon our family. The honor of prophethood and the honor of *shahādat*." Zaynab bears the responsibility of announcing the message of the alive but silent *shuhāda*. She has survived the *shuhāda* and it is she who must be the tongue for those whose tongue has been cut off by the sword of the executioner.

If blood does not have a message, it remains mute in history. If the message of blood does not reach all generations, it is as if the executioner has imprisoned the *shahīd* in the castle of one age and one time. If Zaynab does not convey the message of Karbala to history, Karbala remains as a mere historical event; and thus the ones who need this message will be deprived of it. Thus no one will be able to hear the message of those who spoke to the generations with their blood. It is for this reason that the mission of Zaynab is heavy and difficult. The mission of Zaynab is the conveying of a message to all humanity, to all those who weep for Husayn's death, to all those who bow down faithfully to Husayn, to all those who believe the message of Husayn that, "Life is nothing except belief and *jihād*." The message of Zaynab is as follows:

Oh, all of you who have a covenant with this family, who believe in the message of Muhammad, think and choose. In every age and generation, in whatever land you may be, you must learn to listen to the message of the *shuhāda* of Karbala who said, 'Those can live well who can die well.'

Oh you who believe in the message of monotheism and in the Qur'an, as well as in the way of Ali and his family, and you who will follow us, the message of our family to mankind is the art of living well and dying well. Everyone dies just as he lives.

The message of Husayn to mankind is this:

> If you are men of religion, then [live your] religion. If you
> do not follow a religion, then human freedom has placed
> a responsibility on your shoulders. As a religious person
> or a freedom-loving person, be the witness of your time
> and the *shahīd* of truth and falsehood in your age.

The eyes of the *shuhāda* are upon us. They are conscious, alive, and present. They are the paradigms, the witnesses of truth and falsehood, and the witnesses of the destiny of mankind.

And *shahīd* has all these meanings.

For every revolution, there are two visages: blood and message. Anyone who has accepted the responsibility of accepting the truth, and anyone who knows the meaning of the responsibility of being Shi'ite, of being a freedom-lover, knows he has to choose in the eternal battle of history, everywhere and in every land. All battlefields are Karbala, all months are Muharram, all days are Ashura? One has to choose either the blood or the message, to be either Husayn or Zaynab, either to die like him or survive like her, if he does not choose to be absent from the battlefield.

I apologize to you. It is too late, and there is no further opportunity. There is much to be said, but how can one sufficiently explain the miracle that Husayn has performed and Zaynab has completed. What I want to say is a long story, but I can summarize it as the mission of Zaynab after the *shahādat:* those who died committed a Husayn-like act. Those who survive must perform a Zaynab-like act. Otherwise, they are the followers of Yazid.

NOTES

1. This piece was originally delivered as a lecture the day after *"Shahadat,"* in 1970 in the Grand Mosque of Narmak in Tehran, the night after Ashura, 1970.

2. Dahhaak is a mythical Arab king who conquered Iran, also identified with Azhidehak of Media. In Firdowsi's epic *shahnamah,* he is said to have had two snakes which came out of his shoulders which had an insatiable appetite for the brains of young boys. Kavah, a blacksmith with seven sons, refused to give up the last of his sons, after having lost the other six to Dahhak. He mounted a rebellion against Dahhak and won popular support. The staff and apron of Kavah became symbols of Iranian nationalism.

3. Ali ibn al-Husayn al-Akbar was, according to some questionable reports, the son of Husayn and Shahzanan, the daughter of the Persian emperor Choesroe Yazdigard. He was the only son of Husayn to survive Karbala. He became the fourth Imam, Zayn al-Abidin (38/659-c.95/713). But usually in the Shi'ite literature, Ali Akbar refers to the second son of Husayn who was martyred on *'Ashura.*

4. Jalal Al-e Ahmad (1923-1969) was a social critic famous for his *Gharbzadegi (Westruckness),* tr. John Green and Ahmad Alizadeh (Lexington, Kentucky: Mazda Press, 1983?). The phrase Shari'ati quotes is from this work.

5. Cf. fn. 38 to *"Shahadat."*

6. For a discussion of the development of the concept of *wilayat* (guardianship) in twentieth century Shi'ite jurisprudence see Farhang Rajaee, *Islamic Values and World View* (Lanham: University Press of America, 1983), pp. 18-23. Also see Ruh Allah Khumayni, *Islam and Revolution,* Hamid Algar, tr. (Berkeley: Mizan Press, 1981).

7. This sentence is a famous slogan of Imam Ja'far al-Sadiq.

Dr. Ali Shari'ati   **8.**

Thār

Some terms cannot be translated because they are personal or cultural idioms. Uttered by a particular person or in a particular culture, they carry a load of meaning which cannot easily be conveyed to someone unfamiliar with that person or culture. What does the word "Florence" convey to a student of geography? A location on a map! Yet this is not the impression that the word would convey to someone like Picasso or Sartre. In his essay, *"Qu'est ce que la Poesie?"* Sartre expresses his feelings toward "Florence" as the word calls to mind a city, a flower, a lady, a flower-city, a lady-city, a lady-flower, and a melodious sound embodying the words *"fleuve"* (river) and *"or"* (gold). He feels the gentle and melodious movement of a river, the caressing tough of gold, as well as the endless and puzzling elasticity caused by the "e" with which the word ends. It is a familiar tune which slowly fades away, instead of ending suddenly. It is a fair lady whose gentle movement is as delicate as a poet's imagination ... It is a sensual young woman, chaste, married, and faithful to her husband, yet little understood by him. It is the name of an actress in the silent movies that Sartre watched as a little boy; and he loved her ...[2]

... So, in rich cultures, a word may have an important biography. For example, the Persian word, *"rend,"* with such depth and dimension as exhibited by Hafiz,[3] cannot be translated into any other language. Some have tried to translate it as (the French) *"clochard,"* which approximates "dervish," "beggar," or "carefree one"; while obviously none of these are adequate. Sometimes *"rend"* essentially denotes one of greater eminence than a learned or wise man — it is a peculiar word. Another such word is *"thawrah,"* which has a socio-historical biography which bestows upon it an extraordinary richness. In this regard, the meaning of this term extends far beyond its existential limitations. (From the same root) there is the word *"thar"* which finds mention in our prayers: *"Ya thar Allah wa ibna tharihi!"* ("Oh you *thar* of God and Son of His *thar*!) Such is our address to Husayn.[4]

Let us examine the significance of *"thar"* in the cultural sociology of the Arabs.

Before Islam, the (Arabian) social system is tribal. The greatest revolutionary task of Islam is to change this "tribal system" into a "societal system." The Apostle of Islam, over a few years — in one generation — accomplishes what cannot possibly be accomplished except over several centuries and provided that a deep change is made to gradually occur in the socio-economic infrastructure of the society. From the collection of tribes, which in itself comprises a particular social structure, he carries out an infra-structural revolutionary change. He changes the tribal system into a perfect societal system, an *ummat,* a *societe.* In the Arab tribal system, as in any other such system in the world, every tribe embodies one personality. There are no individuals. It is only the tribe itself which exists. An individual by himself is nothing; but at the same time, he is the whole tribe.

In some of [our] villages, distant villages which have not yet been contaminated by civilization, you have perhaps experienced this state. This spirit and so forth is still present. You, as a stranger, enter the village and everyone, upon your entrance, invites you to a certain house: "Please come to the house; rest here for a night!"; while the house does not belong to any of them. It belongs to none of them. Its owner is "on the farm," or perhaps he is not even present in the village! Why such [a strange invitation]? Because that "collective spirit," "collective originality," the "collectivity of the tribe" is showing itself there. You are a stranger; you enter; you are the guest. Whose guest? Somebody's guest — but that "somebody" is a member of this society, of this tribe. He is equivalent to his tribe. Therefore you are the guest of the tribe. Everyone thinks of himself as the owner of the house, your host. Because not everyone owns a house worthy of such a guest, the host invites you to a house worthy of you, even though the owner of the house may not be present. He is permitted to do this. It is apparent that private ownership, as it exists in a societal system in which every individual develops an independent character, has not come into existence, at least on the psychological level. Everything belongs to the tribe, including the character. If you are disrespectful to a person, the tribe does not perceive it as disrespect to an individual, but rather you have injured the feelings of the whole tribe. Everyone will feel humiliated and insulted, and everyone will try to show reaction. You must then apologize to the whole tribe.

In a society [like ours], if you insult a Frenchman or an American, you have insulted an individual only. Other citizens will not react. Likewise, if you insult a Tehrani or a Mashadi, the other citizens of Tehran or Mashhad will not feel insulted. Everyone has his personal account. In a tribal system, there is a "personality" representing the tribe. He may be the "chief," "totem," or "god" of the tribe, who is the crystallization of the "collective spirit." He (or it) is a spirit which has many bodies — perhaps 1000 or 2000 ... and this is the case in a legal context as well. "Tribal right" is "collective right." For example, if someone from the tribe of Bani Ghatfan kills someone from Bani-Zuhrah, the "murderer" is not the person who commits the murder; the "murdered" is not the person murdered. Everyone from Bani-Zuhrah thinks of himself as the "owner of the blood"; everyone from Bani-Ghatfan is perceived as the killer. As revenge, it is sufficient that one of the members of Bani-Zuhrah kills one of the members of Bani-Ghatfan, whomever it may be. As such, the blood is avenged, even though there may be no relation (as we understand it) between the actual murderer and the one who is later killed in retaliation. It is not even necessary for the avenger to have a detailed knowledge of the situation. Tribe 'X' owes tribe 'Y' a "blood." The "individual" in the tribal system does not have "individual right." Such is the infra-structure of the matter. Please pay attention, for here is where the matter becomes so beautiful and deep. A person from tribe 'A' kills one person from tribe 'B'. The tribe whose member is killed is "the owner of the blood." The one murdered is the *thār* of the latter tribe. Is this clear?

We are a *qabīlah*[5] (tribe); and one of the members of the enemy tribe has murdered one of our children. Neither the parents nor the son of the victim are "the owner of the blood." We are all the owners of the "blood." He is not the *thār* of his family; he is our *thār*. Well! What does this mean? Precisely that the enemy owes us a "blood." What does *ghayrat* (zeal) mean? It means "not to carry the weight of this *thār*." But this is not what the "zeal of the tribe" means. Anyone who forgives (the killer of) this *thār* or does not seek vengeance for his blood is like the one who is careless about his *nāmūs*.[6] For the one who "sells out" such blood, it is as if he sells his religion. He lacks "zeal." Every zealous tribe certainly avenges its *thār*.

Even though mythology is not true, there is nothing more truthful than the following myth in human history. How wonderful it is! They say, "When one from our tribe is murdered ... his body is gone, but his soul, like a bird, flies day and night around the tribe, screaming near the head of each person, inviting them to take vengeance. As long as the blood is not avenged, the bird does not settle." Is [the meaning of] this myth clear? Thus every tribe which has a *thār* has to avenge its blood. As long as one has not shed one "blood" in retaliation from the enemy, he feels himself to be cursed. The bird of *thār* constantly hangs over his head, day and night, whether he is at home, traveling, partying, eating, praying, or engaged in any other of his occupations. The bird hangs over his head and will not let him loose. If the member of the tribe is zealous, he hears the cry of invitation of that bird. Such is the traditional tribal relation pertaining to the issue of *thār*.

One of the cultural and intellectual revolutions that the Apostle of Islam has accomplished — and I have alluded to it elsewhere[7] — is that so often he has taken an element of traditional culture, even though it might have belonged to a period of savagery, and he has transformed its content into a scientific, revolutionary, and humanistic content. One example is *thār*. He has changed the tribal *thār* into an ideological and humanistic *thār*. He also changed the inter-tribal brotherly relationship into ideological brotherhood. Ideological relationship replaced blood relationship. Likewise the transformed the tribal *wilāyat*. Likewise he transformed the *bay'at* (allegiance) of an individual to the chief of his tribe into allegiance to *hajar al-aswad* (the black stone) in *hajj,* which symbolizes the right hand of God.[8]

We know that anyone who is under allegiance to a tribe or to its chief must follow the laws of that tribe. He is the follower of that chief. Once he gives his allegiance to another one, his former allegiances are nullified. The new allegiance has both a positive and a negative characteristic. It negates what was before it. It liberates the person (from former allegiances). thus all the individuals who have sworn allegiance with their tribe, but now swear allegiance to God, enter the tribe of God. They become *mawālī*[9] of God, and consequently, they become liberated from their tribal and savage relations of the past.

We can observe that these kinds of traditions exist in the society, but the Apostle transforms their decadent tribal content into the most supreme, modern, and revolutionary framework. He is not a superficial and ruthless revolutionary, who imposes fabricated and newly developed concepts on the people in order to puzzle them. He obtains his terminology from their life, reality, history, and culture, but gives them new meanings. One such term is *thār.* He takes a traditional and cultural concept, which has gone deep into their bones, blood, tradition, history, and culture, and he changed it into the ideological, historical, and humanistic *thār,* retaining all its other characteristics.

In a sense, he has changed the inter-tribal relationship into a bi-tribal one. The latter does not involve racial tribes, but intellectual ones. The two tribes are that of *taghūt*[10] and that of God. The two tribes recognize each other. In the Qur'an and in Islam, the invitation is on the basis of a new tribal system in the history of humanity. One tribe has sworn allegiance to God, and the other to *taghūt.* The two tribes still have the same *thār* relationship between them. The bird of *thār* screams constantly near the ears of one and invites them to take vengeance. The responsibility of avenging *thār* hangs on the neck of each member of the tribe of God. Anyone not lacking zeal constantly hears the cry of the bird. Such is the meaning of the concept *thār.*

Don't you think that the word *"thawrah"* is more meaningful than *"revolution"* or *"inqilāb"*? Don't the latter terms mean "the upheaval of the social system only"? Doesn't *"thawrah"* also embody the concept of *thār*? In this sense, *thawrah* is no longer a rebellion in a particular time, waged by a particular group against a particular system. *Thawrah* can be defined as the resurrection of the members of the tribe of God in every generation for revenge against the tribe of *taghūt*, from whom blood is owed.

In this respect, the word *"thawrah"* is connected with blood, with the chain of history, and with the constant responsibility of man within history. It is surprising that from the word *thār*, one can extract the whole Islamic philosophy of history from the point of view of the Shi'ite. If we conduct an attentive and fundamental examination, (we realize that) the philosophy of human history, from the perspective of Shi'ite Muslims, extends from Adam to *ākhir al-zamān* (the final age of the world). Such is the length of the philosophy of history that Islam manifests, interprets, and explains, in the Shi'ite world view.

It is strange that at the first stage of the history of humanity, there is a *thār*: Abel! First there is Adam, meaning "humanity, the human essence." He is everybody's father, the father of both tribes. After Adam, humanity divides into two tribes, the tribe of *taghūt* and the tribe of God, which division Islam has recognized. Without such duality, Islam cannot be understood. The chain of *imamat* cannot be understood. Fundamentally the school of Abraham cannot be understood. After Adam, the history of man begins. Adam is not a part of man's history. Adam is the truth of humanity. He is the whole humanity. It is after Adam that human society forms. Man, society, life, human relations, as we see them within a small limit, form. It is then that the bi-polarity of human society has begun. It begins with a *thār*. The tribe of Cain sheds a blood from the tribe of Abel, and thus *wirāthat* (the inheritance) begins.

There is a relationship between *wirathat* and *thār*. The two concepts comprise [the basis of] the philosophy of the history of man in Islam and interprets it. The word *wirāthat* is frequent in our prayers, particularly concerning Husayn. We have *ziyarat-i-wārith*, which is fundamentally based on inheritance terminology. They have given us these lessons [long ago]. These are not the kind of things that we have just realized or fabricated. These sort of things have always been clear in our school of thought. But the lack of consciousness has disconnected our relation with them. *Ziyārat* indicates to me that I see Husayn as one link in the long chain which begins with Adam and extends to the last days of the world. It is for the reason (of his permanent presence) that I speak to him and I stand in front of him and recognize him as such.

Thus in our philosophy of history, humanity begins with a *thār*. The tribe of Cain owes one blood to the tribe of Abel. The inheritance begins from there. Such inheritance in different forms and interpretations appears in the Qur'an, *ahādith* narrations, and in the Islamic culture and history in general. There is a tendency to connect the prophets, by means of a geneological tree or some other symbolic means, to each other and make them appear as one single movement in history, so that we would not regard each as an isolated historical event, each taking place in a different land and time.

In a traditional story, the prophet Joseph leaves an inheritance, including a staff. When the inheritance is being divided, Jethro says, "Please give me this staff as a memento." The others see that it is a piece of wood and not good for anything, so they give it to him. He keeps that piece of wood as a memento! Jethro establishes a garden and one day, while irrigating or planting a tree, he sticks the staff into the ground. When he returns to it, he sees it sprouting all over. He attempts to pull it out, but is unable. He realizes there must be a secret behind it. He leaves it as it is. Much later, Moses passes by the garden, and Jethro employs him. Among the trees, when Moses sees this staff/tree he recognizes the mystery. He sees it and he reads it. He pulls it out, as if pulling a hair out of some dough. He likes it, and he smoothens it and makes it his own staff. It is with the same staff that he deals with Pharaoh!

How wonderful it is! What deep lessons are there in these things. We see that the myth wants to connect the apostleship of Moses to that of Joseph — between whom, apparently, no historical connection can be established. The connection is an intellectual one. There are so many things like this. For example, in the carved gems in our culture, there is a great attempt to establish such connections.

Unfortunately, our world-view is so small that in our opinion the day of Ashura begins from Tasua and it ends at noon of the following day. After that nothing happens in history, until the day of Arbain, and then we eat *sholeh*, and that is the end of the story until the next year![12]

Ashura is not a one-and-a-half-day event. It is the issue of the eternity of history. Had I the time, I could compare this philosophical world-view of history with that of the most modern and scientific philosophy of history as all the intellectuals of the world understand it. Then one would be able to see the difference between this philosophy of history and that which is based on the dialectics of the means of production. The Islamic philosophy of history is based on self-realization and self-conscious responsibility of man. The other philosophy, that is to say, the Marxist historical determinism, is based on the material means of production, on the basis of which it evolves, at last — as destined — resulting in man's self-realization. In other words [according to the latter philosophy], man, his historical responsibility, and his self-realization, are the effects of the determinism of material production: economy. On the other hand, in the historical determinism of Islam, the foundation is the self-realization of man. It is the self-conscious man who is addressed. From the outset, it tells man, "You are the owner of blood. You must avenge it." When? From the beginning of man's history until its end. Your opportunity extends from the former to the latter.

The first *thār* which occurs is between the two tribes. The tribe of Abel is responsible vis-a-vis the tribe of Cain. On the basis of that inheritance, the "blood" is passed from one generation to another, just as the shedding of blood is inherited from one generation to another until the end of the world. Where is the end, according to the Shi'ite world-view, of the philosophy of the history of Islam? When does this history, as we know it, based on *thār* and vengeance, end? Again, with *thār*! Because [there will come] the world revolution, the human salvation, the establishment of justice, peace, and equality — all these — yes; but [more important] the title of the last savior of man in this relationship of *thār* and *thār* avenging, which comprises the whole of human history, is *Muntaqim* (the Avenger).[23] What will he avenge? Everyone says, "He will avenge the murders of the *Sayyid al-Shuhāda* (Master of *Shuhāda*), Husayn." Not at all! He will avenge the *thār* for which the tribe of Cain is responsible.

This *thār* develops a complex characteristic in every generation, being that in every generation — by the invitation of that soul-bird, which constantly hangs and screams over the heads of the members of the tribe, no matter what they do — the men of zeal and manliness will rise for revenge. In every rising for revenge for their *thār*, they donate another "blood." *Thār* adds to *thār*. Thus the responsibility of the next avenging generation increases. Now the tribe has to avenge two "bloods" from the enemy tribe of *taghūt*. Again and again ... We see in our philosophy of history that *thār* is increasing, *thār* over *thār*. In each generation, the cries [of that bird] become progressively louder. Were that zeal, manliness, and consciousness [among us, we would realize that] the whole atmosphere of our history is full of the cry and invitation to avenge *thārs*. The blood of our *thārs* — but no, they are not tribal *thārs*, but *thār Allah* — is to be avenged from the tribe of *taghūt*.

Now, where is fatalism? This history that places so much emphasis on blood revenge, mission, consciousness, and invitation must be based on our will. But at the same time, history, in accordance with its determinism, will end in comfort, triumph, victory, and pleasure of all the *thārs* of God, following the absolute and universal revenge of all their "bloods." This is unquestionably destined. We see that our historical determinism is based on the invitation of man to take vengeance.

We see that the two related concepts of *thār* and *wirāthat* interpret human history and its philosophy in the view of the Shi'ite Muslims. The history begins with *thār*, and as such continues and evolves until it reaches the point of explosion. Explosion is the vengeance taken upon the tribe of *taghūt*. It is then that the shoulder of the tribe of Able is relieved of the heavy burden of these "bloods" which it has inherited from one generation to another. It is then that man reaches peace, salvation, and justice. Until that time, the story of human life is that of struggle for vengeance. This is true from Adam to the end of the world. Husayn is one of these *warithūn* (heirs), who himself is a *thār*. So also are his son and his father. they are all *thārs* of God, fathers of *thārs* of God, and sons of *thārs* of God.

Behold what deep meaning the word *"thawrah"* finds. *Thawrah* means everything: struggle, rebellion, uprising. But to what end? The goal is vengeance from the tribe of Cain, whose hands are so stained with the blood of our *thārs*. It is acceptance of the invitation of those birds which are constantly hanging over the heads of our tribe, crying and inviting us to avenge.

Thawrah, thār, wirāthat — so begins history. The first *thār* is Abel; then there is *ākhir al-zamān,* that is to say, the universal vengeance. These concepts together interpret the Islamic philosophy of history in the Shi'ite view.

Ya Thār Allāh wa ibna Thārihī.

NOTES

1. This piece was transcribed from a tape of a lecture. Shari'ati delivered the lecture in Muharram, January of 1977, the last year of his life.

2. The first paragraph of the original lecture was not recorded. In its place the translator has inserted this paragraph from Shari'ati's *Collected Works*, Collection #25, pp. 397-398.

3. 'Hafiz' (c. 1320-1389) was the pen name of Shams al-Din Muhammad, a Persian poet.

4. The prayer from which this line is taken is called *"Ziyārat Wārith."* It is a prayer in which greetings are sent to Husayn as the heir of the prophets and previous Imams.

5. The word *"qabilah"* (tribe) has the same root, QBL, as *"qiblah"* (direction of prayer). The verb form, *qabila,* means to accept, and from this the idea of a group of people who accept one another is a tribe, and the accepted direction is the *qiblah.*

6. The word *"namus"* refers to the female members of one's family. *"Ghayrat"* is a kind of zeal or propriety concerning ones tribe and particularly the female members of one's family, which is common in Western Asian and Southern European societies.

7. See *Islam Shinasi.*

8. See Dr. Ali Shariati, *Hajj* (Bedford, Ohio: FILINC, 1978), pp. 30-32.

9. *"Mawāli"* refers to persons associated with Arab tribes otherwise than by birth; non-Arab converts to Islam. It is from the same root, WLY, as *"wilayat"* (guardianship).

10. Cf. fn. 3 to Taleqani's *"Jihad* and *Shahādat"* in this volume.

11. Both *"thawrah"* and *"inqilāb"* are Arabic words, however in Arabic the former means "revolution" while the latter means "turn around." In Persian, *"inqilāb"* has come to mean "revolution."

12. Ashura is the tenth day of Muharram, on which the martyrdom of Husayn is commemorated, Tasua is the ninth of Muharram. Arbain is the fortieth day after Ashura. Since it is customary to have a memorial on the fortieth day after someone dies, on Arbain Karbala is remembered again. It is a custom to eat *sholeh,* which is a type of soup, on Arbain.

13. The *Muntaqim* is the twelfth Imam, the Mahdi.

Bibliography

Abduh, Muhammad and Rashid Rida. *Tafsīr al-Qur'an al-Ḥakīm*, eleven vols. Cairo: 1325/1907-1353/1934.

Al-Saḥīfah Al Sajjādiyyah, Sayyid Ahmad Muhani, tr. Tehran: Islamic Propagation Orgainization, 1984.

Afrasiyabi, Buhram and Sa'id Dehqan, *Taleqāni va Tārīkh* (Taleqani and History), Tehran: Nilufar Publications, 1981.

Akhavān, Saless Mehdi. *Akhir-e-Shāhnāmah*, third ed. Tehran: Murvarid Publications, 1969.

Akhavi, Shahrough. *Religion and Politics in Contemporary Iran.* Albany: SUNY Press, 1980.

Akhtar, Wahid. Rev. of *Modern Islamic Political Thought* by Hamid Enayat. *Al-Tawhid*, Vol. II, No. 4, (1405/1985), pp. 165-189.

Al-e Ahmad, Jalal. *Gharbzadegi (Weststruckness).* Lexington: Mazda, 1983.

Algar, Hamid. *Religion and State in Iran: 1782-1906.* Berkeley, University of California, 1969.

Amini, Ibrahim. "Foreign Policy of an Islamic State in the Light of the Qur'an," *Al-Tawḥīd*, Vol. II, No. 4, 1405/1985, p. 78.

Arjomand, Said Amir. *The Shadow of God and the Hidden Imam.* Chicago: University of Chicago Press, 1961.

Asad, Muhammad. *The Principles of State and Government in Islam.* Berkeley: University of California Press, 1961.

Ayoub, Mahmoud M. *The Qur'an and its Interpreters.* Albany: SUNY Press, 1984.

Bainton, Roland H. *Christian Attitudes Toward War and Peace.* New York: Abingdon Press, 1960.

al-Banna, Hasan. *Five Tracts of Hasan Al-Banna (1906-1949),* Charles Wendell, tr., Berkeley: University of California Press, 1978.

Bosworth, Clifford E. *The Ghaznavids.* Edinburgh: Edinburgh University Press, 1963.

Boyce, Mary. *Zoroastrians: Their Religious Beliefs and Practices.* London: Routledge and Kegan Paul, 1979.

Brown, Michael. "Is There a Jewish Way to Fight?" *Judaism* Vol. 24 (1975), pp. 466-475.

Burton, John. *The Collection of the Qur'an.* London: Cambridge University Press, 1977.

Chittick, William C. *The Sufi Path of Love.* Albany: SUNY Press, 1983.

Cook, J. M. *The Persian Empire.* New York: Shocken Books, 1983.

Eliash, Joseph. "Misconceptions Regarding the Juridical Status of the Iranian Ulama," *International Journal of Middle East Studies* (Feb. 1979), pp. 9-25.

Enayat, Hamid. *Modern Islamic Political Thought.* Austin: University of Texas Press, 1982.

Fadl Allah, Ayatullah Muhammad Hussein, "Islam and Violence in Political Reality," *Middle East Insight* Vol. 4, Nos. 4 and 5, 1986, pp. 4-13.

Fadl Allah, Ayatullah Muhammad Hussein and George Nader, "Interview with Sheikh Muhammad Hussein Fadl Allah," in *Middle East Insight* Vol. 4, No. 2, 1985, pp. 12-19.

Fakhry, Majid. *A History of Islamic Philosophy.* New York: Columbia University Press, 1983.

Firdowsi, Abu al-Qasim, *Shahnamah,* third ed., eight vols. Tehran: Jibi, 1974.

————. *The Shahnama of Firdausi.* A. G. and E. Warner, tr., nine vols. London: Kegan Paul, 1905-25.

Fischer, M. J. *Iran: From Religious Dispute to Revolution.* Cambridge: Harvard University Press, 1980.

Hamidullah, Muhammad. *Muslim Conduct of State,* seventh ed. Lahore: Sh. Muhammad Ashraf, 1977.

al-Hilli, al-Muhaqqiq, *Sharayi 'al-Islam,* four vols. Najaf: Adab, 1389/1969.

al-Hindi, al-Fadil. *Kashf al-Litham,* two vols. Isfahan: n.p., n.d.

Hiro, Dilip. *Iran Under the Ayatollahs.* London: Routledge and Kegan Paul, 1985.

al-Hurr al Amili, Muhammad ibn al-Hasan. *Wasa'il al-Shi'ah,* twenty vols. Beirut: Dar Ihya al-Turas al-Arabi, n.d.

Hodgson, Marshall G. S. *The Venture of Islam,* three vols. Chicago: University of Chicago Press, 1974.

Ibn Ishaq. *The Life of Muhammad.* Oxford: Oxford University Press, 1980.

Ibn Khaldun, Abd al-Rahman. *The Muqaddimah,* tr. Franz Rosenthal, abridged and edited by N. J. Dawood, Princeton: Princeton University Press, 1981.

Ikhwan al-Safa, Basra. *The Case of the Animals versus Man Before the King of the Jinn.* Lenn Evan Goodman, tr., Boston: Twayne, 1978.

al-Isfahani, Raghib. *Mufradat al-Qur'an.* Al-Takhadum al-Arabi, 1392/1972.

Jafri, S. H. M. *The Origins and Early Development of Shi'a Islam.* London: Longman, 1979.

Jannati, Aḥmad. "Defence and Jihad in the Qur'an," *Al-Tawḥid,* Vol. 1, No. 3 (1404/1984), pp. 39-54.

————. "Legislation in an Islamic State," *Al-Tawhid,* Vol. II, No. 3 (1405/1985), pp. 56-70.

Jansen, G. H. *Militant Islam.* New York: Harper and Row, 1979.

Jeffery, Arthur. *The Foreign Vocabulary of the Qur'an.* Baroda: Oriental Institute, 1938.

Johnson, James Turner. *Ideology, Reason, and the Limitation of War.* Princeton: Princeton University Press, 1975.

————. *Just War Tradition and the Restraint of War.* Princeton: Princeton University Press, 1981.

al-Karaki, al-Muhaqqiq, "*Tariq Istinbat al-Ahkām,*" *Al-Tawhid* (English) Vol. II, No. 3, (1985), pp. 42-55.

Kassis, Hanna E. *A Concordance of the Qur'an.* Berkeley: University of California Press, 1983.

Keddie, N. R., ed. *Scholars, Saints and Sufis.* Berkeley: University of California, 1972.

————. ed. *Religion and Politics in Iran.* New Haven: Yale University Press, 1983.

Khadduri, Majid. *War and Peace in the Law of Islam.* Baltimore: Johns Hopkin Press, 1955.

————. *The Islamic Law of Nations.* Baltimore: Johns Hopkins Press, 1966.

————. *The Islamic Conception of Justice.* Baltimore: Johns Hopkins Press, 1984.

Khumayni, Ruh Allāh. *Kashf Asrār.* Qumm: 1944.

————. *Islam and Revolution,* Hamid Algar, tr., Berkeley: Mizan Press, 1981.

————. Extracts from *Taḥrir al-Wasīlah, Resaleh Novin* Vol. 4, Abdulkarim Biazar Shirazi, tr., ed., Day: Anjam-e-Ketab, 1360/1981.

————. *A Clarification of Questions,* J. Borujerdi, tr. Boulder: Westview Press, 1984.

Kohlberg, E. "The development of the Imami Shi'i Doctrine of *Jihād,*" *Zeitschrift der Deutschen Morgenlandishen Gesellschaft* 126, (1976), pp. 64-86.

Kulayni, Muhammad ibn Ya'qub ibn Ishaq. *Al-Kāfi,* eight vols. Tehran: Dar al-Kutub al-Islamiyah, 1388/1968.

Lambton, Ann K. S. "A Nineteenth Century View of Jihad," *Studia Islamica* Vol. XXXII, (1969-70), pp. 181-192.

Lerner, Ralph and Muhsin Mahdi, eds., *Medieval Political Philosophy.* Ithaca: Cornell University Press, 1978.

Louis, F. *Al-Munjid.* Beirut: Dar al-Mashriq, 1973.

Massignon, Louis. *Salman Pak et les Primices Espirituelles del'Islam Iranien.* Paris: Societe des etudes Iraniennes, 1933.

————. *The Passion of al-Hallaj,* Herbert Mason, tr. Princeton: Princeton University Press, 1982.

Maududi, S. Abul a'la. *Jihad in Islam.* Lahore: Islamic Publications, 1980.

al-Mufid, Shaykh. *Kitab al-Irshad,* I. K. A. Howard, tr., London: Muhammadi Trust, 1981.

Mutahhari, Murtada. *Khadamat-e-Mutaqabil-e-Islam va Iran.* Tehran: Sherkat-e-Enteshar, 1970.

———— *The Mutual Services of Islam and Iran,* Mehdi Abedi, tr. Houston, IRIS, forthcoming.

————. *Ilal-e-Girayish be Maddigari.* Mashhad: Tus, 1971.

Ibn al-Nadim. *The Fihrist of al-Nadim,* two vols. Bayard Dodge, ed. and tr., New York: Columbia University Press, 1970.

Najafabadi, Ni'matullah Salihi. *Shahid-e-Javid.* Qum: 1968.

Nasr, S. H. *Science and Civilization in Islam.* Cambridge: Harvard University Press, 1968.

Nicholson, Reynold A. *A Literary History of the Arabs,* second ed. Cambridge: Cambridge University Press, 1930.

————. *The Mystics of Islam.* New York: Schoken Books, 1975.

Paskins, Barrie and Michael Dockrill. *The Ethics of War.* Minneapolis: University of Minnesota Press, 1979.

Peters, F. E. *Children of Abraham.* Princeton: Princeton University Press, 1984.

Peters, Rudolf. *Jihad in Mediaeval and Modern Islam.* Leiden: E. J. Brill, 1977.

————. *Islam and Colonialism: The Doctrine of Jihad in Modern History.* The Hague: Moauton, 1979.

Phillips, Robert L. *War and Justice.* Norman: University of Oklahoma Press, 1984.

al-Qummi, al-Saduq. *Al-Khisal.* Tehran: 1322.

Qummi, Shaykh 'Abbas. *Mafaith al-Jinan.* Tehran: Khazar, n.d.

Qutb, Sayyid. *Milestones.* Cedar Rapids: Unity Publishing Co., 1981.

Rahman, Fazlur. *Islam,* second ed. Chicago: University of Chicago Press, 1979.

Rajaee, Farhang. *Islamic Values and World View: Khomeyni on Man, the State and International Politics.* Lanham: University Press of America, 1983.

Rizvi, Seyyid Saeed Akhtar. *Islam.* Tehran: A Group of Muslim Brothers, 1977/1397.

Russell, Frederick H. *The Just War in the Middle Ages.* Cambridge: Cambridge University Press, 1975.

Ruthven, Malise. *Islam in the World.* Oxford: Oxford University Press, 1984.

Sachedina, Abdulaziz. *Islamic Messianism: The Idea of the Mahdi in Twelver Islam.* Albany: SUNY Press, 1981.

Said, Edward W. *Orientalism,* New York: Vintage Books, 1979.

Schleifer, Abdullah. "Understanding JIHĀD: Definition and Methodology," *Islamic Quarterly* Vol. XXVII, No. 3, (1983), pp. 117-131.

─────── . "Jihad and Traditional Islamic Consciousness," *The Islamic Quarterly,* Vol. XXVIII, No. 1, (1984), pp. 173-203.

─────── . "Jihad: Modernist Apologists, Modern Apologetics," *The Islamic Quarterly,* Vol. XXVIII, No. 1, (1984), pp. 25-46.

Shari'ati, Ali. *Kavīr.* Mashhad: Tus, 1970.

─────── . *Ensān-e-Bikhud.* Tehran: Qalam, 1972. tr. Mehd: Abed: in *Reflections of Humanity.* Houston: IRIS, 1986.

─────── . *Vizhegihā-ye-Qurūn-e-Jadīd.* Tehran: Chapakhsh, 1972.

─────── . *Islam Shināsī,* three vols. Tehran: Qalam, 1973.

─────── . *Hajj.* Bedford, Ohio: FILINC, 1978.

─────── . *On the Sociology of Islam,* Hamid Algar, tr., Berkeley: Mizan Press, 1979.

Shari'atī, Muhammad Taqī, *Tafsīr-e-Novīn.* Tehran: Intishar, n.d.

Shaw, Stanford and William Polk, eds. *Studies on the Civilization of Islam.* Boston: Beacon Press, 1962.

Suyutī, Jalāl al-Dīn Abd al-Rahmān. *Al-Itqān fī 'Ulūm al-Qur'ān.* second ed. Lahore: Suhayl Academy of Lahore, 1400/1980.

al-Tabari, Muhammad ibn Jarīr. *Ta'rīkh al-Rusul wa al-Mulūk.* M. J. de Geoje, ed. fourteen vols. Leiden: Brill, 1879-90.

Tabaṭabai, Seyyed Muhammad Ḥusayn: *Al-Mizān fi Tafsīr al-Qur'ān,* twenty vols. Beirut: Muassisah al-Alami li-al-Matbu'at, 1393/1973.

─────── . *Al-Mizān: An Exegesis of the Qur'an.* Sayyid Saeed Akhtar Rizvi, tr. Tehran: World Organization for Islamic Services, 1403/1983.

————— . *Shi'ite Islam*. Houston: FILINC, 1979.

Ṭaleqānī, Ayatullah Sayyid Mahmūd. *Islam va Mālikiyyat*. Tehran: Intishar, 1344/1972.

————— . *Islam and Ownership*. Ahmad Jabbari and Farhang Rajaee, tr. Lexington: Mazda, 1983.

————— . *Society and Economics in Islam*, R. Cambell, tr. Berkeley: Mizan Press 1982.

Taqīzādeh, Sayyid Hasan. *Mānī va Dīn-e-Ū*. Tehran: Majlis Dar Tehran, 1917.

Walters, LeRoy. "The Just War and the Crusade: Antithesis or Analogies?" *The Monist,* October 1973, pp. 584-94.

Watt, W. M. *Islamic Philosophy and Theology*. Edinburgh: Edinburgh University Press, 1979.

Williams, John Alden, ed. *Themes of Islamic Civilization*. Berkeley: University of California Press, 1982.

Wolfson, Harry Austryn. *The Philosophy of the Kalam*. Cambridge: Harvard University Press, 1976.

Yazdī, Ibrāhīm. *Yād Nameh Shahīd-e Javīd: Dr. Shari'ati*. U.S.A.: Nehzat Āzādī, 1977.

Zaehner, R. C. *The Dawn and Twilight of Zoroastrianism*. London: Weidenfeld and Nicolson, 1961.

Index